THE
REDISCOVERED
COUNTRY

The WORKS of STEWART EDWARD WHITE

*A collection presented by
Wolfe Publishing Co., Inc.*

Limited Edition '1 of 1000'

THE BIGGEST OF THE FOUR LIONS
SEE PAGE 183

Amazon
July 2017

THE
REDISCOVERED
COUNTRY

BY

STEWART EDWARD WHITE, F. R. G. S.

ILLUSTRATED
FROM
PHOTOGRAPHS

Wolfe Publishing Co., Inc.
6471 Airpark Drive
Prescott, Arizona 86301

Originally published in 1914 by Outing Publishing Company

Manufactured in the United States of America
Reprinted April 1987

ISBN: 0-935632-51-4

1987
Wolfe Publishing Co., Inc.
Prescott, Arizona

ILLUSTRATIONS

v

THE
REDISCOVERED
COUNTRY

THE REDISCOVERED COUNTRY

CHAPTER I

INTRODUCTORY

IN 1910-11 Mrs. White, R. J. Cuninghame, and myself, with a small safari of forty men, took the usual route via the Kedong valley, Mount Suswa, Agate's Drift to Vandeweyer's *boma* on the Naróssara River. At this point we diverged from the usual route and pushed for some distance south into the Naróssara Mountains. We found ourselves eventually confronted by a barrier range which we could not then cross, owing to lack of time, lack of men, and lack of provisions. Inquiries among the Masai elicited very vague descriptions of high mountain ranges succeeded by open country. When we had returned to civilization we discovered, to our surprise, that we could find out little or nothing of what lay beyond those mountains. They ran in a general northwesterly direction approximately along the Anglo-German border, so that their hinterland would naturally fall within the German protectorate. But whether the large triangle was plains, hill, or dale; whether it was watered or arid; whether

3

it was inhabited or desert; whether it was a good or bad game country, we were unable to find out. No Englishman or American had been in there, and as far as we could find out only the German military reconnoissances of many years previous possessed even the slightest knowledge of what the country might be like. This intrigued our curiosity. We resolved to go in.

In the meantime both Cuninghame and myself tried every possible source of knowledge, but in vain. As far as we could find out no sportsman or traveller had ever traversed this territory save the two or three officials mentioned. The net results of the latter's efforts—for the outside world—were in two maps, which we procured. They were of great assistance, and were in the main quite accurate for the line of route actually trodden by their makers. Outside of that they were to be trusted only in general. To all intents and purposes we were the first to explore the possibilities of this virgin country. If not its discoverers, we were at least its rediscoverers.

I think this was the very last virgin game field—of any great size—remaining to be discovered and opened up to sportsmen. There are now no more odd corners to be looked into.

That at this late stage of the world's history such a place still remained to be disclosed is a very curious fact. The natural question that must arise in every one's mind, and that must first of all be answered, is

IN THE COAST BELT

M'GANGA—MY HEAD MAN ON TWO TRIPS. HE WAS A VERY ABLE
EXECUTIVE AND SPOKE MANY NATIVE LANGUAGES

how this happens, for the prevalent belief is that English sportsmen have pretty well run over all the larger possibilities. This is a legitimate question and a legitimate wonder that should be answered and satisfied before full credence can be placed in so important a discovery. That unknown to sportsmen there still remained in the beginning of the year 1913 a country as big as the celebrated hunting grounds of British East Africa and even better stocked with game is due, briefly, to three causes:

In the first place, the district in question has escaped the knowledge of English sportsmen because it is situated in a very out of the way corner of a German protectorate. The Englishman is not at home in German territory, and, as long as he can get sport elsewhere—as he has been able to do—is not inclined to enter it. In the second place, the German himself, being mainly interested in administrative and scientific matters, is rarely in the technical sense a sportsman. The usual Teuton official or settler does not care for shooting and exploration, and the occasional hunter is quite content with the game to be found near at home. He does not like to go far afield unless he is forced to do so. In the third place, this new country is protected on all sides by natural barriers. Along the northern limits, whence the English sportsman* might venture, extend high,

---

*The sportsmen of other nationalities, including the Germans, are inclined to hunt in British territory for the simple reason that the sporting facilities are there perfected.

rough ranges of mountains through which are no
known tracks. On all other sides are arid and nearly
gameless wastes. Until we entered the country there
had been no especial reason to believe these wastes were
not continuous.

Thus the people naturally given to adventure were
discouraged from taking a go-look-see by a combination
of natural barriers, racial diffidence, and political and
official red tape. Beside which the English had not
yet come to an end of their own possibilities in British
East Africa; and the race in possession simply did not
care enough about sport to go so far merely to see more
animals than they would see nearer home. In other
words, from the German side this patch on the map
was much too far; from the British side it was practically
inaccessible.

With this brief but necessary explanation accomplished, we can go on. It must be remembered that
when Cuninghame and I first began to consider this
matter there was no suspicion of the existence of any
large, unexplored hunting fields. South Africa is finished; Nyassaland offers good sport, but is unhealthy,
and the species to be obtained are limited in number;
small open areas in the Congo, Uganda, the Sudan,
offer miscellaneous shooting, but are isolated and remote;
Rhodesia and British East Africa are the great game
countries par excellence, and these, while wonderful,
are well known. There is no lack of game in these

countries—indeed, it would be difficult even to convey a faint idea of its abundance to one who had never seen it—but in a rough way they are well known, they have all been more or less hunted, and conditions have been to a greater or lesser degree modified by the white man and his rifle.

Now I think you will all bear me out that from earliest boyhood the one regret that oftenest visits every true sportsman is that he has lived so late, that he has not been able to see with his own eyes the great game fields as we read about them in the days of their abundance. It is an academic regret, of course. Such things are not for him. Trappers' tales of when the deer used to be abundant on Burnt Creek; old men's stories of shooting game where the city hall now stands; the pages of days gone by in the book of years—we listen and read and sigh a little regretfully.

At least that is what I had always thought. Then in 1910 I undertook a rather long journey into the game fields of British East Africa. There I found the reports not at all exaggerated. The game was present in its hundreds, its thousands. If I had done what most people do—hunted for a few months and gone away— I should have felt the fullness of complete satisfaction; should have carried home with me the realization, the wondering realization, that after all I had lived not too late for the old conditions. But I stayed. I became acquainted with old-timers; I pushed out into odd corners of the known country. And by degrees I came to see that most of British East Africa is a beaten track. Shooters are sent by the outfitting firms around one or the other of several well-known circles. The day's marches are planned in advance; the night's camps. There is plenty of game, and the country is wild; but the sportsman is in no essentially different conditions here than when with his guide he shoots his elk in Jackson's Hole or his deer in the Adirondacks.

And again I heard the tales of the old-timers, varying little from those at home—"in the old days before the Sotik was overrun, the lions would stand for you"— "I remember the elephants used to migrate every two years from Kenia across the Abedares"—"before Nairobi was built the buffalo used to feed right in the open until nine o'clock." In short, spite of the abundance of the game, spite of the excitement and danger still to be enjoyed with some of its more truculent varieties, the same wistful regret sooner or later was sure to come to the surface of thought—I wish I could have been here then, could have seen it all when the country was new.

And then unexpectedly came just this experience. We found that after all there still exists a land where the sound of a rifle is unknown; as great in extent as the big game fields of British East Africa; swarming with untouched game; healthy, and, now that the route and method have been worked out, easily accessible to a

man who is willing to go light and work. Furthermore, I must repeat, this is the last new game field of
real extent. All the rest of the continent is well
enough known. Therefore we have the real pleasure
not only in opening a new and rich country to the
knowledge of sportsmen, but the added satisfaction of
knowing that we are the last who will ever behold such
a country for the first time.

When we started we had no very high anticipations.
There is plenty of waste desert land in Africa. The
country between Natron and Kilimanjaro—to the
east—is arid and unproductive of much of anything but
thornbush; there was no real reason why the corresponding country between Natron and Victoria Nyanza
—to the west—should be any different. Only that
the former was useless was a well-known fact; while of
the latter the uselessness was only supposition. Cuninghame and I resolved to take a chance. We might
find nothing, absolutely nothing, for our pains; but even
that would be knowledge.

As far as we could see, our difficulties could be
divided into several classes. In the first place, we
must get permission to cross the boundary between the
English and German protectorates at a point where
there is no custom house. This was a real difficulty, as
those who know the usual immutability of German
officialdom will realize. It took us a year to get this
permission; and in the process many personages, in-

cluding Colonel Roosevelt, the German Ambassador, and high officials in Berlin, were more or less worried. Once the matter was carried through, however, we received the most courteous treatment and especial facilities from the German Government.*

Our second important difficulty was our lack of knowledge as to where the water was to be found. We resolved never to move any but light scouting parties until we were certain as to where next we were to drink. In order to be able to make reconnoissances we had built three pairs of bags made from double canvas, with tin spouts, and arrangements for slinging them on donkeys. The latter animals can go two full days without water. Therefore we counted on a scouting radius of a day and a half before it would be necessary to return to the main camp. If we found more water within that period we would naturally be able to extend this radius. As a matter of fact we were never reduced to straits for water. The country is in many places very dry, and waterholes few and small; but one accustomed to arid regions who knows where to look should never, *with reasonable precaution*, get into difficulties.

Our third great difficulty was to feed our men. In

---

* We arranged with the German consul at Mombasa to meet a German customs official at a designated point near Lake Natron on August 8th. Evidently when the authorities came to a realization of what a long, dry, unknown journey that unfortunate official would have to take in order to keep this rendezvous, they changed their minds. At any rate, we were later—as will be seen—met by native runners with dispatches absolving us from this agreement.

an explored country, or in a country known to be inhabited, this is a simple matter; one merely purchases from the natives as one goes along. In an unknown or uninhabited region, however, the situation is different. Each porter must receive, in addition to meat, a pound and a half of grain food a day to keep him strong and in good health. That is forty-five pounds per month per man. One must know where that can be found.

As a porter can carry sixty pounds only, it can readily be seen that supplies must be renewed at least every month. To overcome this difficulty we resolved to use donkeys for the purpose of carrying grain food— or *potio*—for the men; and to cut down the numbers of the men to the lowest possible point. We did not feel justified in depending on donkeys for our whole transport for the reason that, in this land of strange diseases, we could by no means feel certain of their living; and we could not take a chance of finding ourselves stranded. Each donkey would carry two loads, and would not require feeding.

For these twenty beasts Cuninghame had built pack-saddles after the American "saw buck" pattern, the first, as far as I am aware, to be so used in Central Africa.* The usual native saddle is a flat pad, across which the bags, fastened loosely together, are laid. On the level this works well enough, but up or down hill

---

* One other American hunter had experimented with them near Nairobi, but reported against them. This was, I think, because he did not take the time, trouble, and patience personally to train his men.

the loads are constantly slipping off. Then the donkey must be caught, held, and the loads hoisted aboard. It takes a man for every four donkeys, and the pace, as can be imagined, is very slow. We hoped to be able to train natives to pack American style; and trusted that by means of the special saddles the usual objection to donkey transport—viz.: its extreme slowness and uncertainty—would be overcome.

Our personal outfit we reduced to a minimum, departing radically from the conventional and accepted customs of African travel. Thus our tents were small and light, made, floorcloth and all, of one piece, after a pattern invented by Cuninghame. We used chop boxes as tables. Our personal effects, instruments, surgical and medical material, and repair kits of all sorts, we compressed to the compass of three tin boxes. All the usual extra paraphernalia of African travel we cut out completely. By way of provisions we took merely the staple groceries: beans, rice, coffee, tea, sugar, flour, oatmeal, and dehydrated fruit. Two luxuries only did we allow: golden syrup and a light folding camp-chair apiece. Nothing rests one more than the latter article of furniture. Indeed, for this sort of a hard trip I should *almost* be inclined to look on it as a necessity rather than a luxury! Our light tents, beds, seven boxes of provisions, trade goods, river ropes, ammunition, and the three tin boxes made something like twenty full loads. We decided to take thirty

KONGONI, MEMBA SASA, SANGUIKA

DOLO, SULIMANI, THE TOTO—OUR DONKEY FORCE

DONKEY FULLY PACKED

porters,* three donkey men, and seven others, including gunbearers, camp men, cook, and head boy. Beside these burden bearers were twenty donkeys equipped with pack-saddles, and twenty-five other donkeys rigged in the native fashion, hired to take their loads of grain *potio* over the mountains, there to leave them, and then immediately to return.

We started out with two riding mules, but after about twenty-five or thirty miles of riding we had to pack them. They died; and we walked afoot the rest of the seventeen hundred miles.

Our men we picked very carefully. Some of them, notably M'ganga, Memba Sasa, Kongoni, and Abba Ali, had been with me on former expeditions. All were personally known either to Cuninghame or myself.

As will appear in the course of the journals, we encountered many difficulties.

I would impress it on my readers as emphatically as I am able that this is not a soft man's country. The "adventurer" who wants to go out with a big caravan and all the luxuries should go to British East Africa. The man too old or fat or soft to stand walking under a tropical sun should stay away, for, owing to prevalence of tsetse, riding animals are impossible. The sport will not like it; but the sportsman will. This country is too dry for agriculture; the tsetse will prohibit cattle grazing; the hard work will discourage the fellow who

---

*Extra men to make up for sickness and accident are absolutely necessary.

likes his shooting brought to his bedside. But the real out-of-doors man who believes that he buys fairly his privilege to shoot only when he has paid a certain price of manhood, skill, and determination, who is interested in seeing and studying game, who loves exploring, who wants extra good trophies that have never been picked over, in whose heart thrills a responsive chord at the thought of being *first*, such a man should by all means go, and go soon, within the next five years. It is a big country, and much remains to be done. He can keep healthy, he can help open the game fields for the future brother sportsmen, and he can for the last time in the world's history be one of the small band that will see the real thing!

Nevertheless, it is fully appreciated that, to the average man with limited time, even a virgin game district is of no great general value unless it can be got at. The average sportsman cannot afford to make great expenditures of time, money, or energy on an ordinary shooting trip. The accessibility as well as the abundance of British East Africa game is what has made that country so famous and so frequented. It would be little worth your while as practical sportsmen to spend a great deal of time over descriptions of a game field so remote as to remain forever impossible except to the serious explorer, nor would in that case the value of discovering an unshot country possess other than academic interest.

If future safaris had to retrace our footsteps in this expedition, the game would hardly be worth the candle. It would take too long to get there; it would involve too much hard work; it would involve also the necessity of doing just what we did in regard to food; viz.: carrying it in on expensive beasts that would surely be fly-struck and die soon after crossing the mountain barrier. But fortunately this is not necessary. We suffered only the inconveniences inseparable from the first penetration of a new country. We paid for mistakes in route that need only be paid once. The problems of food, transport, and water still remain; but we have worked out a solution of them that makes the country practicable to the ordinary sportsman. In the appendix details are given.

I am convinced that these are the hunting fields of the future, that they will be as extensively visited in years to come as British East Africa is at present. British East Africa is still a wonderful hunting field; but it is passing its prime. The shooting by sportsmen would never much diminish the game; but the settler is occupying the country, and game and settlers cannot live together. I can see a great difference even in three years. In time the game will be killed or driven far back—game in great numbers—and even now, abundant as the animals still are, it is difficult to get really fine heads. They have been well picked over.

This particular part of the German country, on the

other hand, as said before, will probably never be occupied. It is not fitted for agriculture, the rainfall is slight,
water is scarce;. it is not adapted to grazing, for tsetse is
everywhere. The game has it all, and will continue to
have it all. Indiscriminate shooting during a great
many years and by a great many people would hardly
affect this marvellous abundance over so extensive an
area; but, of course, indiscriminate shooting in these
modern days of game laws is impossible. The supply
is practically unlimited, and is at present threatened
with no influence likely to diminish it.

For the next five or ten years this country will, in
addition, possess for the really enterprising sportsman
the interest of exploration. Our brief expedition determined merely the existence of the game country,
and, roughly, its east-to-west extent. We were too
busily engaged in getting on, and in finding our way,
to do as thorough a job as would have been desirable.
Even along the route we followed months could be
spent finding and mapping waterholes, determining the
habitat of the animals, searching out the little patches
where extremely local beasts might dwell, casting out
on either side one, two, three days' marches to fill in
gaps of knowledge.

To the south of us lay a great area we had no opportunity even of approaching, and concerning which we heard
fascinating accounts—for example, the Serengetti,* a

* Not to be confused with the Serengetti near Tsavo.

grass plain many days' journey across, with a lake in the middle, swarming with game and lions; the Ssalé, a series of bench plateaus said to be stocked with black-maned lions beside the other game; some big volcanoes (some of which we spied forty miles away) with forests and meadows and elephants in the craters; and so on. All this remains to be looked over and reported on. As the waterholes are found, the possibilities of reaching out farther will be extended. We have really only made the roughest of rough sketches. The many sportsmen who will follow us must fill in the picture.

CHAPTER II

JULY 7.—Worked all the morning at N. T. & Co.'s store fitting saddles to donkeys—our safari kit was all made ready yesterday. At 12:45 the men set out; and at 2:25 we got off with the beasts. Started out over the hills past Government House, over a new piece of road on which some hundreds of Kikuyus were working strictly by hand, and so out to a rolling wooded green country of glades and openings, tiny streams, and speckled sunlight. Little forest paths led off in all directions. Natives were singing and chanting near and far. There were many birds. Toward evening we passed a long safari of native women, each bent forward under a load of firewood that weighed sixty to eighty pounds. Even the littlest little girls carried their share. They seemed cheerful, and were taking the really hard work as a tremendous joke. We passed them strung out singly or in groups, for upward of half an hour; then their road turned off from ours; and still they had not ceased. Camped after nine miles near the mountain of N'gong. Vanderweyer's farm is near here; and there are staying the guides he promised us to take us across the dry country to his trading *boma* on the Naróssara River. M'ganga went over to see them.

July 8.—Up at five, with breakfast in the dark. Then we sat ourselves down to wait for the guides who had promised to be over early. They drifted in at 8:10, and we set out. After we had been going some little time they blandly informed us that the track we had been advised to take was without water for three days. That they told us at all was entirely accidental. We immediately called a halt and after some *shauri*,* we headed at right angles for Kedong. It was a park country all day, with forests, groves, open meadows, side hill *shambas*,† and beautiful intimate prospects through trees. Kikuyus were everywhere.

At about ten o'clock we came to a little boggy stream, insignificant to look at, and unimportant to porters, but terrible to donkeys. We built a sort of causeway of branches, rushes, earth, etc., and then set in to get our faithful friends to use it. Then and there we discovered that when a donkey gets discouraged over anything, he simply lies down, and has to be lifted bodily to a pair of very limber legs before he will go on. Luckily these were small donkeys; we lifted most of them.

After a time we topped a ridge and came out on rolling grass hills, with lakes of grass in valleys, and cattle feeding, and a distant uplift that marked the limit of the Likipia escarpment. At two o'clock we

*Confab, pow-wow.
†Native clearings.

made camp in the high grass atop one of these swells. All afternoon we worked busily remedying defects in our saddlery, riveting, sewing, and cutting. That night we heard again our old friends the fever owls.

Four and three-quarter hours; $11\frac{1}{2}$ miles; elevation, 6,900; ther., 5:00 A. M., 52; 2:00 P. M., 78; 8:30, 58.

July 9.—Daylight showed us a beautiful spectacle of lakes of fog in the shallow valleys below us, and trailing mists along the hills, and ghostlike trees through thin fog. We stumbled for a time over lava débris under the long grass. At the end of an hour or so the sun had burned the fog—and dried our legs. We came to the edge of the escarpment and looked at the Kedong a half mile directly below. Atop the bench we saw our first game: a herd of impalla and twelve zebra.

Then we went down 2,400 feet, nearly straight. We did not do it all at once—not any! Not until nearly sundown. The men went all right, but the donkeys were new to the work,* the saddlery not yet adjusted, and we ignorant of how to work this sort of *cazi*. We had to adjust packs every few minutes, sometimes to re-pack. About noon some of the beasts lay down and refused to get up. We unpacked them, took off their saddles. They stretched out absolutely flat and

---

* These African donkeys have for generations lived their lives on the plains. They are quite unaccustomed to hills, and have no idea of how to handle themselves in difficult country. In this they differ markedly from our own western burros.

TYPICAL CAMP—TENTS IN A CIRCLE, GOODS AND DONKEYS IN THE CENTRE

PORTER'S CAMP

looked moribund. We thought three of them dying. Not a bit. After half an hour they arose refreshed. In all we left eight loads of *potio* by the trail and drove the donkeys on light. The going was very steep and stony, and the sun fierce. Our little force of white men, two donkey men, and three gunbearers certainly worked hard.

At four o'clock, all but four being off the hill, I rode ahead across the flat to camp and sent back fifteen men with lanterns to bring in loads. On the plains I saw many Grant's gazelles, one oryx, some kongoni, zebra, and ostrich. Our camp was by the Kedong "River," a little stream a few feet wide. About us were lava beds and benches. The high sheer escarpment lay on one side, and the lofty cone of Mount Suswa on the other. It was perhaps twenty miles to the south from my camp of 1910.

At six o'clock all the animals were in; but some of the men who went after loads were out all night. It was amusing to see how the donkeys sidled up to one, insistently, begging plainly to have their loads taken off.

Eleven and one half hours; 9 miles; elevation, 4,500; ther., 5:00 A. M., 50; noon (?); 8:30, 68.

July 10.—A warm night. It was agreed that I was to push on with the men to the next water, while Cuninghame rested and grazed the donkeys, and awaited the men who had been out all night. Climbed successively several low lava benches to a plateau, and

then marched across a broken volcanic plain south of
Suswa.   Memba Sasa stayed to help with the donkeys,
and Kongoni accompanied me in advance to pick up
meat.   We were here in the game reserve and were not
supposed to do any shooting, but in view of the terribly
hard work the men were performing Cuninghame's
judgment was in favour of shooting a really necessary
beast or so.   Later we would report the fact to the
Game Department and obtain official absolution.

Kongoni's conversation was most engaging as he told
me all about a number of safaris he had been on since
last we met.

"Now," said he in conclusion, "when you were here
before, you shot well.   See that you shoot well now,"
with which admonition he fell silent and dropped behind.

Heard a lion up near Suswa, and saw many fresh
tracks.   The sky was thinly overcast.   Saw a good deal
of game of the following species: Roberts' gazelle, impalla, zebra, eland, kongoni, steinbuck, ostrich, guinea
fowl, and spurfowl.   The grass is very long.   When
near the next water I fired my first shot this trip at a
gazelle at about 200 yards.   It was a miss, but shortly
I killed one at 155 yards.   This settled our own meat.
Next, for the men, I hit a zebra at 260 and brought him
down by a good long one at 377.   The last was very
lucky, but it pleased Kongoni immensely.   He clapped
me on the back.   The safari came along, picked up the

meat, and we marched off the rocky plateau into a deep gorge where were rock pockets of water. The gorge is one running out from Suswa. Indeed, we are only barely off the slope. Here we made camp by some extraordinarily vivid green bushes.

Cuninghame waited four hours before starting, in order to graze the donkeys. He got in about two o'clock, reporting a quick easy trip with everything going nobly.

Three and a half hours; 9¾ miles; elevation, 4,500; ther., 5:00 A. M., 58; noon, 83; 8:30 P. M., 68.

July 11.—Porter preparing my box for the march. To him M'ganga:

"If you put that meat on that box, it will smell; and the *bwana* will say something, and he'll say it to *me*."

Off at 6:40. The early mornings are most strenuous times for Cuninghame and me. Our usual dispositions are as follows: At once on reaching camp the loads are removed from the donkeys, and they are allowed to graze about a while with their saddles on until their backs have had time to cool a bit. Then off-saddle and the Toto takes them grazing until dusk. At dark they are driven into the circle formed by our tents. There two heavy ropes have been stretched along the ground between pegs. At intervals rawhide thongs have been attached to these ropes, and by the thongs the donkeys are made fast by the foreleg. No American animal would stand for this treatment, but these beasts are quite peaceable. In the morning Memba

Sasa, Kongoni, Sanguiki, Sulimani, and Dolo have the task of saddling up. Cuninghame and I circulate rapidly, keeping track of things. It is astonishing how many wrong ways there are of saddling a donkey; but most of the boys are bright, and are learning rapidly all the little kinks. When the job is finished we make a final inspection, seeing that the breeching, breasting, and cinches are all right, that the saddle is well back from the withers—an absolute necessity with donkeys —that the pads are well loosened along the backbone, etc. All being in order, the men come up in pairs, lifting the loads aboard. We cinch them in place, and are off.

During the day our chief concern is to keep those blessed donkeys on their feet. Once one lies down, for any reason whatever, it takes three men to get him up again—one to urge, the other two to ease him of his loads. Often he must be unpacked before he will rise. As a general thing they toddle along well enough the first part of the day, but toward ten o'clock they begin to flop down in almost any likely place. A patch of sand or dust seems irresistible. When such is encountered, everybody begins to yell and shout and rush to and fro trying to hustle them across. And if one lies down, many others are apt to follow his example. It is dusty, hot aggravating work; but it has to be done if we are to get into the unknown country at all.

Travelled all morning through an Arizona-like coun-

try of buttes, cliffs, and wide grassy sweeps. Against
Mount Suswa we saw many steam blowholes like camp-
fire smokes. Footing bad. At first cool; then a very
powerful sun. Saw considerable game in streaks—
kongoni, a few zebra, many Robertsi, a herd of eland,
a few Tommy, and ostrich. About noon we entered the
hills through a gateway and almost immediately came
to a dry stream bed in lava rocks, well up in the hills.
The sun here was reflected with fearful strength. Everybody pretty well done. We had the men sit down, and
started out to search for water. A mile or so up we
discovered a rock "tank" with gravel beach containing
a sort of green liquid. It was atrociously bad, but by
digging holes in the gravel, nearly enough filtered
through to supply man and beast with a *passable* beve-
rage. Sun very fierce among these rocky hills.

Out making observations with the prismatic, saw a
klip-springer, and was followed by my old friend the
kalele plover.

On my return Cuninghame and I crawled up the
stream bed until we found a natural bower where the
bushes overarched, and there we ate and sat until the
heat of the day had passed. One of the boys, out looking for better water, found a fresh lion lair. As I have
said, we always pitch the tents in a circle, and tether
the donkeys in the middle at night, but have intended
to make no attempt to keep up fires. Sulimani was
once an *askari*, however, and he has taken it on himself

to keep a night fire. To this end he sleeps in the open alongside his blaze. Periodically he arises, buckles on a cartridge belt, seizes his gun, puts a stick on the fire, lays down the gun, takes off the cartridge belt, and stretches himself out to sleep. Great is habit! It is very amusing.

Five hours; 14 miles; elevation, 4,500; 5:00 A. M., 60; noon, 84; 8:30 P. M., 65.

July 12.—Start at 6:40 through a rocky volcanic pass out on to a long scrub slope, miles and miles wide, at the foot of which was the N'gouramani River* and the Mau escarpment. Beyond and above the latter we could see the Naróssara Mountains.

The men knew this was to be a long, hard march, and they were all improvising songs the burden of which was "*Campi m'bale, campi m'bale sana.*" ("Camp is far, camp is very far.")

We saw little game until within four or five miles of the river. Then appeared Robertsi, zebra, kongoni, one herd oryx, ostrich, many warthog, and six giraffe. Brilliant bul-buls, horn-bills, mori, and many grouse represented the bird family. Near the river were hundreds of parrots.

The river which we reached at last about two o'clock proved to be in flood and running fast. A rotten old rope spanned it. Four Kikuyus were drowned here

---

*Otherwise the Southern Gwaso Nyero. I prefer the other name to distinguish it from the Northern Gwaso Nyero, from which it is separated by some hundreds of miles.

last week. By means of the rope we crossed several men who pulled over our own sound rope and strung it between two trees. I crossed—up to my armpits, and holding very fast—and took charge of the farther end. The moment I entered the water the men set up a weird minor chant to the effect:

"The *bwana* is entering the water; the *bwana* is in the water; the *bwana* is nearly across; the *bwana* is out of the water."

They tightened the rope by song also:

Headman (sings): "Ka-lam-bay! *Men* Huh!"

Headman: "Ka-lam-bay! *Men* Huh!"

Headman: "Kalambay oo chak a la fa! *Men* Hu-a-a-y!"

The pull comes only at the hu-a-a-y, but it is a good one. On the cable we strung a snatch block and a light line, and thus pulled all the loads across. This took us all afternoon so the donkeys we left until to-morrow. To cross seventy loads one at a time is some *cazi*, for each has to be slung separately. At dark we changed our wet clothes and enjoyed dinner!

Seven hours; 19 miles; elevation, 4,100; 5:00 A. M., 58; noon (?); 8:30 P. M., 60.

July 13.—Leaving Cuninghame to rig the tackle, I took a three-hour jaunt downstream to get meat. The little strip between the escarpment and the river is only a few hundred yards to half a mile wide, but is diversified with brush, trees, and grass country. Saw three waterbuck, fifteen kongoni, twelve zebra, one dik-dik, and some impalla, and heard lion and hyena. Game birds, however, were in swarms. At every step I flushed grouse, quail, guinea fowl, or pigeons. Killed a kongoni with ones hot off hand at 247 yards, and returned to find Cuninghame ready for business.

We then tackled the donkey question. Our method was as follows: Cuninghame and half a dozen huskies hitched a donkey to the end of a long rope the other end of which I, across the river, held. Then they lifted that reluctant donkey bodily and launched him in. I tried to guide him to the only possible landing-place fifty yards or so downstream. This was easy enough with the two mules; I merely held tight, let them swim, and the current swung them around. Not so the donkeys! They naturally swim very low, the least thing puts them under, then they get panicky, they try to turn back, they try to swim upstream; in short, they do everything they should not do. Result: about 25 per cent. went across by schedule, the rest had to be pulled, hauled, slacked off, grabbed, and yanked out bodily. Some just plain sank, and them we pulled in hand over hand as fast as we could haul them under water—in the hope of getting them over before they drowned. Succeeded, but some were pretty groggy. One came revolving like a spinner, over and over. Each animal required individual treatment at the line, and after two experiments with the best of the men we

CROSSING THE SOUTHERN GWASO NYERO—OR N'GOURAMANI—RIVER. GETTING
THE FIRST LIGHT LINE OVER

SEE PAGE 27

CROSSING THE SOUTHERN GWASO NYERO. GETTING THE LINE OVER

SEE PAGE 27

SLINGING LOADS, BY MEANS OF A SNATCH BLOCK, ACROSS THE SOUTHERN
GWASO NYERO RIVER

SEE PAGE 29

THE SOUTHERN GWASO NYERO RIVER

decided I'd better keep that job. Talk about your tuna fishing! I landed twenty big donkeys in two hours!

Then we had lunch; and to us, out of the blue, came Vanderweyer's man, Dowdi, saying that his master's donkeys and loads of sugar had been camped a mile or so back for the past twenty-two days waiting for the river to go down so they could cross, and would we cross them? Now, beside doing Vanderweyer a good turn, we had counted on hiring some of these same donkeys for a short time to help us on with our *potio;* which obviously we could not do if the beasts were on the wrong side of the river. Dowdi told us there were twenty-five. So we took on the job.

The men crossed the loads by cable while Cuninghame and I went to submarine donkey fishing again. Muscularly it was hard work, but actually it was rather fun, with a dash of uncertainty and no two alike. After we had worked an hour or so and were just getting down to the last of the bunch, more donkeys appeared. Instead of twenty-five there proved to be forty-seven. Wily Dowdi had lured us on! We got quite expert. The moment the line was hauled back by means of a cord, Cuninghame clapped on the hitch, the donkey was unceremoniously dumped in, and I hauled him across any side up he happened to be. We had long since got over being tender of their feelings. My men received him, yanked him to his feet, and left him blowing and dripping to take care of himself. We crossed twenty-one in the last hour! In all sixty-seven and two mules. Remained only to reclaim our tackle, and we are ready for to-morrow's march. But we are dead dogs to-night!

Five o'clock, 49; noon (?); night, 63.

CHAPTER III

JULY 14.—At our usual 6:40 we were off to climb the first step of the escarpment. Struck a Masai track and so went up rather easily. The donkeys travel much better uphill than down. Met four Masai runners, their spears bound in red indicating that they were bearers of messages.

At the top which was a matter of some fifteen hundred feet, at a guess, we journeyed through a steppe of thin scrub and grassy openings, with occasional little hills. On this same steppe two years ago, but much farther to the south, I killed two lions. Passed some Masai villages, with the fair ones seated outside polishing their ornaments while the naked children and the dogs played around them. Here I shot a marabout, but his tail proved not worth saving. Shortly after saw some Robertsi far down the valley to the left, and got lured away after them. In the course of my stalk I passed thirteen giraffe, very tame, that looked on me with mild curiosity. Got within 200 yards of my herd, and hit my buck, but only in the ribs. Then began one of those long, stern chases that take so much time and work. The buck was "unreasonably suspicious," and there was no cover in which to approach him.   I sometimes had great difficulty in keeping tabs on him at all through the heat haze.   After great difficulty got within 250 yards—and missed.   A mile farther took another chance at somewhere beween 200 and 300 yards and hit high in the flank.   Missed again, as he made off.   A mile farther killed him with a square shoulder shot at 277 yards.

Much relieved, we took the meat and trophy, found the trail of the safari, and set out to follow it.   This led us across the plains, through a low pass and into a pocket of the hills just like some of the little hot valleys in our coast range.   A dry wash ran through it, but some holes contained enough water for our purposes. The mountains round about were covered with chaparral.

In this, rather to our surprise, we saw zebra.   In fact later (these notes are being written August 8th) we found a great deal of plains game in the brush hills, driven from the plains by the increase of Masai cattle. Cuninghame is inclined to think that the future of the plains game in British East Africa is just this, and not extermination.   If so, good-bye the millionaire safari! To hunt game, no matter how abundant, on these hills and in this brush would require altogether too much work and skill for those "softlings."

Incidentally, the zebra, so conspicuous on the plains, is very hard to make out, even near-to, in the brush. This is in thin brush where the concealing quality of the cover, *per se*, is very slight.   The direction of the light has little to do with it.   They are quite invisible where the neutral-coloured kongoni are plainly seen. Even the natives often overlook them at less than 100 yards!

At three o'clock Cuninghame and I sauntered up into the hills to pick up men's meat, if possible, and to see what we could.   We found ourselves in a broken, hilly, brushy country, semi-mountainous, again like California coast ranges.   A few Roberts' gazelles in an opening atop a round hill and two giraffe were about the size of it until late, when we made out a herd of zebra on the mountain opposite.   I sneaked over, stalked within range, and missed through the brush.   The herd clattered away up the side hill, dodging in and out the brush.   Catching a glimpse of a darker object, I took a quick sight and had the luck to bring it down dead at 310 yards.   It proved to be a fine old bull wildebeeste that had strayed off with the zebra!   Think of a wilde-beeste far within the mountains, in thick cover, and miles from the nearest plains!

Leaving the men to take in the meat, we went home along the top of a very high ridge, or mountain range, enjoying the cool sunset and the view far abroad over the land.   On this extreme summit we found impalla and kongoni in numbers!   Three years ago I should certainly have considered country of this nature as probably quite barren of game.   Change of habitat under stress is a very curious thing, and should be more taken into consideration.

This evening the camp, which has been rather silent of late, burst into many little fires and the chanting of songs. Meat once more was roasting and frying and broiling, and everybody was happy! Though the temperature in the shade has been low, the sun was very strong.

Eight miles; 5½ hours; elevation, 6,600; 5:00 A.M., 50; noon, 72; night, 62.

July 15.—Start 6:30. Clambered through a rocky brushy pass, out of the hills, to the high, rolling grass hills below the Naróssara. Saw a great many zebra, but no other game until we caught sight of a lone wildebeeste to the left. I made a long and careful stalk in good cover to leeward, but he was wary and was frightened away by the birds. However, by careful work I managed at last to get within 240 yards, when I hit him low in the shoulder. He ran some 300 yards, but then went down.

While we were preparing this trophy, M'ganga came with reports of eland in the next valley. Leaving men with the wildebeeste, Cuninghame and I at once set off. If the report proved true, we considered ourselves in luck. One of our desiderata was a female eland; and if we could get it before leaving Vanderweyer's we would save ourselves carrying farther a very heavy trophy. We found a lone cow lying under a tree and guarded by several hundred zebra. To get within range we had to slip down the side hill, practically no cover, taking care to be seen neither by her *nor* the zebra. We took much time and got as near as we could. She was lying down, facing away from us, and to get her I had to hit about ten inches of spine. It would be impossible to get any nearer, so I rested up from the crawling and tried the shot. Had luck, and hit the exact spot. She got to her feet, staggered ten yards, and went down—263 yards. Fine female to go with my big bull.

Got in to Vanderweyer's about one o'clock, and camped in our old place by the Naróssara River.* Vanderweyer has shaved off his beard. He still trades with the Masai, and tames chickens to sit on his shoulder. We had a talk, got some trade goods of him, and had him to dine.

With him we talked over our next step, for from his *boma* we started three years ago when we got our little taste of the new country to the south.* He advised our going on to the village of old Naiokatoku,* otherwise known as Sendeu, promising that that chief would supply us with guides. Remembering the old fellow's friendly attitude in 1911, we agreed. Furthermore, we made an arrangement with Vanderweyer for the hire of twenty-five of his donkeys, together with six men to run them, to carry *potio* for us until we had crossed the mountain barrier to the south. Then they

---

* See "African Camp Fires."

were to return.   The hire was Rs 12 ($4) per diem for the lot.

Vanderweyer's dog has a litter of puppies down an old warthog hole and refuses to bring them up.

Note: The steeper the hill the louder the porters sing. Where do they get the breath?

Four and three-quarter hours; 9½ miles; elevation, 6,300; 5:00 A. M., 50; noon, 79; night, 68.

July 16.—Start 7:00. Sky overcast and cool. Marched ahead of the safari through the forest pass of the Naróssara Mountains to the Fourth Bench, as in 1911.* Saw many Masai, and a few kongonis, zebra, and Robertsi.   Passed the Sacred Tree stuffed full of stones, bunches of grass, and charms.   Memba Sasa looked a little ashamed—but he contributed.   Donkeys scrambled up the hill well.

Vanderweyer has sent, in addition to the twenty-five donkeys we hired of him, a dozen of his own laden with trade goods as a sort of flyer.   They are equipped with the native *soga*.   This is a padded gunnysacking strapped about the animal's body.   Two loads of *potio* are sewn together and thrown across this pad.   There is no fastening; they ride by their own weight and balance.   Even in level country they are apt to get out of balance and occasionally to fall off; but on hills they are hopeless.   It takes one man to hold a donkey and two to lift on the load.   The little beasts get quite

---

* See "African Camp Fires."

MASAI GIRL AND MARRIED WOMAN
SEE PAGE 37

MASAI MARRIED WOMAN

expert, not at deliberately dumping their burdens, perhaps, but at least in assisting the forces of gravity. Vanderweyer's head man is a little wrinkle-faced, baboon-like Swahili, named Dowdi, and his second man a very airy and nonchalant Wakamba. The whole six certainly earned their wages. Driving, yelling, lifting loads, they seem to be indulging in a sort of stationary riot, but somehow the whole mess does move forward. For an ordinary five hours' march they take from eight to nine hours, however. Now that our own beasts are getting accustomed to the work, they come in very close after the porters; so we are very well pleased with our American pack-saddle rig.

Climbed the beautiful forest trail, and out to the bench. Made camp just where in 1911 we turned off to our Topi Camp.* Thousands of brilliant butterflies fluttering just over a waterhole made a pretty sight. Many Masai, men and women, visited us. I had a wonderful success with simple coin tricks, a sword cane George Bachelder had presented and which Ali proudly carries as a safari stick, an old opera hat Newland gave us, and the image in the Graflex. Tried in vain to buy spears, but was offered a girl of fifteen—who seemed pleased—for three rupees. This by a man who had seen me—and Mrs. White—in 1911. Said he gravely:

"You did not bring *any of your women* with you this time."

* See "African Camp Fires."

Elevation, 7,200; 5:00 A. M., 58; noon, 70; night, 50.

July 17.—Clear before dawn, but at sunrise a heavy fog descended. Very heavy dew. The long grass immediately wet us to the waist.

We went on our old trail of 1911 as far as the first camp on the side hill; then instead of keeping ahead crossed directly to the right over the swamp. I looked for signs of our old camp, but the two years had absolutely obliterated every trace. While waiting for Cuninghame and the donkeys to go around the swamp, I had a long chat with two old Masai. They were quite in awe of the keenness and temper of the sword stick, told me of a lion, etc. When Cuninghame arrived we proceeded on down the side of the swamp, and reached our old friend Sendeu's permanent *manyatta*. It was located on an elevation above the swamp, among forest trees, with high wooded hills at its back, and a magnificent prospect of great forests a mile or so across the way. It differed from the usual Masai temporary village in that it was strongly stockaded, with large houses. Another similar enclosure fairly adjoined it, and several nearby ordinary *manyattas* completed the entourage of so great a chief.

We marched directly through, and made camp in the woods. The surroundings and outlook were beautiful; great trees and vines, and vistas out through them of valleys and green marshes and great wooded mountains all around. Our camp farthest south in 1911 was opposite and about two miles away.   I could make out the site through my glasses.

Many very gorgeous warriors in full panoply visited us. They said the chief was sleeping. More likely drunk, said we, remembering him of old. Of course we could not disturb his majesty, so had to wait patiently.

As he had not showed up by two o'clock, I agreed to climb the high hills at the back (to the west) and get a look abroad over the to us unknown country through which we must go. An hour's hard climb and I gazed out over a tumble of lower hills ending in a sheer rampart of great mountains about fifteen miles away. At first glance it took my breath away and looked absolutely hopeless: below me was a labyrinth and against me was a wall. Then I sat down with my glasses, prismatic compass, and notebook and carefully took stock. There seemed to be two *possible* passes, and I noted them and marked them by landmarks. I congratulated myself that we did not have to work through that on our own! Of course the Masai must have a track down through, and I remembered old Sendeu's cordial friendliness and promises of 1911. He would, naturally, supply us with guides, and we would go down sailing! We counted on getting through in about five days!

Saw many impalla, zebra, and kongoni in the brush on the mountainside, like so many California deer, a most remarkable habitat. Shot a zebra up the mountain at 237 yards, and a buck and doe impalla at close range in bush, first missing a doe.

Returned to camp to find Sendeu and his court just arrived. Drink has made him very flabby and puffy since we saw him last. I greeted him with cordiality, but to my surprise found him surly, taciturn, and unfriendly. To our questions as to trails, guides, etc., he replied that there was no trail, he had no guides. He said barefacedly that he did not remember us; he had no milk, no sheep. Between whiles he stared at the ground. His beautiful warriors were plainly uneasy.

"Very well," I said at last, "the *bwana m'kubwa* has many presents for those that help him. He is sorry you cannot help him. But he is generous, nevertheless; take this knife. Good-bye."

They filed out sullenly. Later we tried through some of our men to get information from underlings, but without success, except that we learned that two Masai from the German side were at that moment in another *manyatta* and about to return! Why this change of front we could not at that time make out.*

The situation was rather a facer, for we had relied absolutely on Sendeu to get through this difficult

---

*On our return to Nairobi we were told by Vanderweyer that a certain Englishman and an Italian baron had procured guides from Sendeu. These sportsmen procured lion, elephant, and buffalo within two weeks and came out; but as they alleged some cause of complaint against the guides they

jumble of country.   However, we agreed to tackle it.
In former years I had done a good deal of pioneer
mountain travel with animals, and believed I could get
through by observation of formations.   Cuninghame
was willing to try.

Heard lions to-night.

Five hours; 11 miles; elevation, 7,000; morning, 40;
noon, 70; night, 58.

---

refused to pay the stipulated wages.   Hence Sendeu's hostility to ourselves.
If this is as reported it is a remarkably good example of how not to handle
natives.   The sportsmen had been guided, had procured what they went
after, and had returned in a short time.   Therefore they owed the wages.
If they had any cause for complaint they should have taken the matter up
with Sendeu, *after payment.*   The wages go to Sendeu, not to the guides;
and Sendeu had done his part of the bargain.   As it was they made it very
difficult for the next white men—ourselves.   As will be seen, we not only
had to nose a way through very difficult country at great expense of time
and energy, but we early got into tsetse fly that could have been avoided.

CHAPTER IV

JULY 18.—Started very early over the high hill on which I hunted the day before, and down the other side into the welter of smaller hills. When we were halfway down two Masai with arms passed us on a run without deigning us a greeting. Subsequent experience made us certain that these were at once spies on us to see which way we would go and messengers to warn other *manyattas* to give us no information. At the bottom of the hill we sent Sanguiki to a village to try to find out something. He returned to tell us that the Masai were *kali sana** and would tell nothing. Therefore we struck along the top of a likely grass ridge that took our general direction, found a Masai trail that went our way, and jogged on. The ridge, after six or seven miles, ran down into a broad grass ravine that led to a small river flowing along the base of the high mountain wall.

We were amused by a small herd of zebra that kept just ahead of us, and seemed vastly indignant at being repeatedly driven forward. In the grass swale I jumped seven big eland at about fifty yards—a fine sight.

*Very fierce.

42

We soon discovered that the banks of the stream were too swampy to permit us to cross, so we went down a mile or so and camped. After lunch Cuninghame and I with four men set out to scout a way. I had located as a landmark a small green patch on the mountainside below the possible pass, and toward this we bent our energies. We found a ford—after being scared by a crashing old rhino at close quarters—and ascended the mountain toward the green patch. The way proved feasible until we reached a round elevated valley below the final rise of the escarpment. At this point we found a spring of water and marked it on our sketch map. A herd of zebra and kongoni were here. I killed one of the former, after one miss, with a heart shot at 270 yards. Leaving the men to attend to him, Cuninghame and I toiled directly up the precipitous side hill to the summit. Here we got an extensive view of a wild tumble of hills that looked impracticable, but could see plainly below us and to the the west a feasible pass to a stream on the other side of the ridge. Also across the way another water, with a great concourse of baboons sitting around it. Quite satisfied for the moment, we named it *Gilbert Pass* in honour of my brother's birthday.

The long tramp brought us back to camp at dusk. Wonderful moon, and very chilly night.

M'ganga back from another Masai village with no news except that the runners had been there warning them to give no information. Sendeu's animosity seems complete.

Safari, three hours; 8 miles. We in addition, five hours; 10 to 12 miles; elevation, 6,300; morning, 48; noon, 72; night, 48.

July 19.—Over Gilbert Pass to the stream, and then downstream for some distance over an old Masai trail in a narrow valley between mighty mountains. A honey bird followed us for over an hour beseeching us to turn aside, and then flew away in disgust at our stupidity. Saw duiker, reedbuck, kongoni, zebra, eland, warthog, and mongoose. The trail ended in a small round valley and a salt lick. Shot a Chanler's reedbuck standing by the lick at 94 yards.

The situation here is wonderful, great frowning peaks and mountains over the way; narrow cañons and valleys, forest caps and groves here and there on the steeps, all very austere and grand.

After lunch Cuninghame and I took up our regular job of scouting. The river here entered a deep narrow rock gorge, so we spent much toil in ascending the hill to the left of it, whence we looked out over so tumbled and broken a country that we immediately gave up going south and returned for a cast to westward. River here quite big, and we forded up to our waists. For some time we had no luck in getting through the westward hills on account of dense forest, but finally discovered a game trail that led us through the woods and up over a low pass to look abroad on so beautiful a wide shallow grass valley dotted with groves that we named it Pleasant Valley.   Here we saw a few head of game, including some eland.   Cuninghame climbed the south ridge of Pleasant Valley and reported precipices.   Therefore our only possible course must be down the valley.   We must take our luck at the lower end.   Got in at sundown.

At midnight two rhinos from the salt lick blundered into the edge of camp.   Great excitement and row, and we had to turn out to scare them off.

Safari, five hours; $11\frac{1}{2}$ miles.   We did in addition four hours; about 9 miles; elevation, 6,200; morning, 38; noon, 72; night, 58.   Coldest morning I have ever seen in Africa.

July 20.—Marched up through our forest pass and on to lower end of Pleasant Valley.   There we squatted the safari, and Cuninghame and I each went in for a long hunt for a way out of the cup.   Each found a feasible route.   Surmounted the ridge that hemmed in the valley and looked out upon another very big oval valley filled with thorn scrub.   It was completely surrounded by another high rampart, with only an apparent narrow break where a river went through about six miles distant and at the lower end.

Headed for that.   Hard travel over rough country in high grass and thorns that tore at us eagerly.   At the lower end of the valley we marched high above a cañon for a couple of miles, then camped below two enormous peaks, one of which we named Mount Bellfield in honour of the present governor of British East Africa. We are now in the heart of the range, and accept with thankfulness each mile vouchsafed us. A narrow forest bordered a stream of beautiful clear water. Never have I seen so marvellous a display of curtain vines and gorgeous flowering trees.

Six hours; 13 miles; elevation, 5,800; morning, 49; noon, 84; night, 58.

July 21.—The outlook was now so very uncertain that Cuninghame and I scouted ahead before breaking camp at all. Enormous rugged mountains compassed us about, and we feared the river would end in an impassable gorge. We took a rhino track that speedily led us into a cañon bed with a wonderful forest of great trees, looped snaky vines, lacy underbrush, tree ferns, and flowering bushes. There were many baboons and monkeys swinging about. The sun rarely penetrated. Great rock cliffs towered at either hand, and the clear stream dashed down cataracts and waterfalls among the boulders.

The rhino track led true for some distance, then petered out to a monkey trail and ended in a gorge. There was evidently no further way down the stream bed. If we were to win through, it must be by way of the steeps on either hand. Therefore I tackled the slope to the right, while Cuninghame took the other.

By dint of crawling, climbing straight up, and worming my way, I gained the top of a ridge and most unexpectedly found it to be a spur, or "hogsback" between our stream and another flowing into it some distance below. Followed the ridge until I found it did not "jump off" at the end, then returned and shouted for Cuninghame. He scrambled up, and together we set to find a practicable back way down to the level of our stream. Found a blessed—but disused—rhino trail.

Cuninghame returned for men. When they arrived, he and I each took charge of a squad with axes and *pangas** and slowly we hewed out a good path. We landed finally at a grove of trees near the junction of the two streams and sent the men back to get camp. Sufficient unto the moment was the progress thereof. We were farther along, but apparently not much better off, for our river here plunged into another gorge flanked with high cliffs. A wide valley led to a mountain range to the left. Evidently we were in for another climb somewhere, the only question was as to which made the best climb. Cuninghame agreed to tackle the range near the gorge, while I explored the valley.

Went up about three miles to where I could see that it ended in a cul-de-sac. Returning, turned aside to stalk a bull eland—absolutely the only game seen for two days—and found a concealed narrow tributary valley that led to a possible pass. Very hot.

---

* Panga—a sort of universal tool something like a machete.

At camp found that Cuninghame had hit on my same route from above. The cliffs opposite are hung with trailing rope-like cactus, and inhabited by many baboons.

Made only 4 miles, but walked nine and a half hours; elevation, 5,400; morning, 50; noon, 88; night, 57.

July 22.—Started the day with a terrific climb, almost straight up to the summit of the ridge. The footing was very bad and it made very sweaty hard work for men and beasts. Got there finally. Very fine view back over the way we have come. Wondered how we ever got through. From above it looks absolutely hopeless. This looks like the top.

From here south the ranges get smaller, so that we can look out over lesser and lesser systems until far away we could guess at the brown of plains. Men fairly cheered at the sight of the latter. But it looked like a puzzler to get down there. Our river has hopelessly plunged somewhere off to the right, leaving us marooned in the high country, and the ridges and cañons seemed to be heavily grown with a kind of chaparral and to have no order or system or open passes. Far away to the south we dimly made out two enormous craters that must be upward of 12,000 feet high.

However, across the shallow cañon head that ran up from the profundities of the river, and in the next transverse ridge, was a notch opposite, so we made for that. From its saddle we saw another small valley, and beyond that another notch. We descended into the valley. Very hot. As we had no idea how far back the donkeys might be, Cuninghame took a twist to the right, and shortly whistled us down to him. At the foot of the valley stood a single shady tree, with big smooth trunk, great buttressed roots, broad leaves, and a small fruit. It was big limbed and broad, and just beyond it was a waterhole of mud and little pools forty or fifty feet broad. This was enclosed with a low thorn *boma*, and at a dozen openings left for the purpose tall saplings had been planted and bent over by means of well-made native sisal rope. Buried loops were to be sprung by the animals that entered. What they could be we could not imagine as there were no signs of game—probably stray reedbuck. However, it was encouraging to find this first sign of life in the new country. It must be inhabited by somebody, even though they might be only wild Wanderobo hunters. In the tree was a beehive made of a section of a hollow log bound all round with faggot-like sticks. Why the latter we were unable to find out. They seemed to subserve no useful purpose, but may have been of religious significance.

We sprung all the snares, and made camp beneath the tree. In the afternoon Cuninghame and I made a very high, hot climb through the second notch; found it led nowhere; cast about; and finally came on a long hogsback that led gently down two miles to end abruptly.

We looked straight down on another scrub-grown valley
with some queer rounded rock outcrops a hundred feet
or so in height. The descent was sheer, but it was
the only way to a lower elevation so we figured out
zigzags. Over opposite lay another big black range,
but around its lower end our river broke through a
notch. We figured we would either go through the
notch or climb the range as the case might be; and so
returned to camp pretty tired. Cheered by the sight
of a dozen kongoni and three Chanler's reedbuck atop
the hogsback. Missed a shot at one of the latter as
he flew.

Five hours' march, four hours' scout; 6½ miles; elevation, 5,900; morning, 48; noon, 78; night, 54.

July 23.—Start at 6:40. We got down the length
of the hogsback all right, but the descent of the zigzags
proved to be a terror for men, and especially for donkeys. The last of Dowdi's did not get in until 6:00 P. M.!
Once down, we crossed the elevated little valley by the
rocks, and found ourselves in face of another lesser
drop. Thornbush very bad, so that we moved a
hundred feet at a time and our clothes and skin suffered.
For a long time it seemed that we were "bushed," but
at last I found a rhino trail down. It was very thorny
and overgrown. The men dropped their packs and
set to work with *pangas* and axes and finally cleared a
trail.

Cuninghame and I then pushed ahead. We de-

scended the hill, crossed a ravine, and soon found ourselves on the banks of a fine river. A shady thicket
and great trees ran alongside, elephant grass reached
ten feet above our heads. We followed the rhino trails
downstream, and after some search discovered a ford.
Here we sat down and took a rest.

After consultation Cuninghame remained to place
camp and cross the animals while I pushed ahead as
rapidly as possible to scout out a way through the scrub
to the end of the range, and to find out whether we could
follow the river or would have to make another climb.

I soon discovered difficulties: in the first place, to get
a feasible path through the terrific jungle of thorn and
scrub, and, in the second place, to dodge rhinos. The
valley was about five miles by three, grown ten feet
high by a thorny jungle, and literally infested by the
beasts. Their broad, well-beaten trails went everywhere. These were a help, but there was always a
doubt as to whether their rightful owners might not
want to use them. I went along singing at the top of my
voice all the songs I knew, in spite of the fact that the
close heat of the thicket and the powerful sun were not
conducive to vocals. After about a mile of this a huge
bulk reared itself not over fifteen yards ahead, snorted,
and rushed down the trail toward me. I literally could
not force myself a foot into the wall of thorns, so brought
the Springfield into action and fired at its head. The
beast stopped five yards from me, and turned square

across the trail. In perhaps ten seconds he showed signs of swinging back. I, who was much on the alert for any move, gave him one in the shoulder. This decided him. He turned away around and disappeared.

After a decent interval I followed him. At last I reached the point where the range met the river. A cliff only twenty feet across reaching down to deep water seemed to bar the route, though the approach on both sides was good. It was impossible to ford.

Rested ten minutes, and returned to camp, blazing a way with my hunting knife as I went. Saw one bushbuck, the only game. Got in at sundown, and drank one quart of tea all at once. Quite weary. Last February I broke my leg badly, and the hard work is beginning to bother it.

During the evening two rhinos tried to enter camp, but we scared them off with our Colt's and firebrands.

March six hours; 8 miles; scout, five hours; elevation, 4,200; morning, 48; noon, 86; night, 68.

July 24.—Marched by my blazes to bend of river. Here to our delight we found a monkey trail leading up the face of the cliff and around a sort of concealed ledge. A half hour's work widened it so we could lead the animals one at a time around the forty feet of cliffs.

On the other side we found ourselves in a wide cañon hemmed in by low and diminishing hills, and thickly grown in the bottoms with dense thorn scrub. The river wound from side to side leaving a flat, first to right, then to left.   This meant finding a ford every mile or so, and getting the donkeys through it—no small task, as they remembered their former experience and did not care for water at all, at all!   We were alternately wet to the waist and baked by the furnace heat.   When we had had enough we camped in the scrub.

Five hours thirty-five minutes; 6 miles; elevation, 3,800; morning, 50; noon, 90; night, 58.

July 25.—Resumed the struggle without the slightest idea of how much longer we were to keep at it.   There were no especial indications that the character of the country would change.   We kept bucking thornbush across the flats until we were forced by the bend of the stream to ford; then we repeated the performance on the other side.   This kept up for four hours.   Then at one of the bends, instead of the usual fordable shallow rapids, we found a crude dam made of woven saplings and earth.   First signs of settled human habitation on this side of the mountains.

A friendly native—the first human being in the New Country—appeared on the opposite side and shouted at us.   Since he seemed to know of no way of crossing to his side, I struck off to the left, soon found a rhino trail along the hills, and signalled the men to come on. Across the river I saw from my elevation bananas and other signs of cultivation.   Without waiting for the safari, I pushed on ahead, blazing a way.   It was hard, exasperating, hot work. About two miles down I struggled through a particularly dense thicket—and came out plop! on an old bean field and easy walking! The mountains had let go of us at last!

It certainly felt good to stride out upright and unimpeded by thorns or hills or both. We went down the old bean field, crossed the river again, and struck across another bean field. High up on the side of the mountain we finally made out a native village; its scattered roofs so much like the gray rocks about them that for a long time none of us distinguished them. Here an old man met us, and signalled us to follow him. He turned at right angles through the field out onto a broad path, led us past a second dam, and up to a little open patch among the scrub. Here were some trees. He seemed to think that a good place for us to camp. We agreed with him; in the first place, because we were tired, and, in the second place, because we wanted to get into communication with his people.

A half hour's work cleared us a shady room in the thicket, surrounded by a thorn *boma*. By this time a dozen savages were in camp. They call themselves the Wasonzi and are unacquainted with whites. They resemble the Kikuyus somewhat, only they are better built, wear a negligent skin around the shoulder, and are armed exclusively with bows and arrows and short swords. Their expression is alert and intelligent, and they are most eager to be friendly and answer all our

CURTAIN VINES IN THE CAÑON NEAR MT. BELLFIELD
SEE PAGE 46

THE WASONZI VILLAGE NEAR OL-SAMBU. AT A VERY SHORT DISTANCE
THE HUTS RESEMBLE BOULDERS
SEE PAGE 54

WASONZI HUT WITH FORTIFIED DOORWAY

GUIDES FROM THE WASONZI

questions. Their ear ornaments are cylinders of red clay, polished, in which have been imbedded scraps of bright wire. The whole is moulded around the lower periphery of the stretched lobe, and so can never be removed without breaking. The bows are short and powerful, the arrows broadly headed, and with the poison smeared in *back* of the head. They told us they approached game by feeding flocks of sheep and goats toward the quarry, accompanying the flocks on all fours. Their dams they use for irrigation; and later we found an elaborate system of checks and ditches with wicker and earth gates. In their fields they raise rape, beans, and tobacco beside a sort of sweet potato and a vegetable somewhat like squash. In times past they have been victims of slave raiders from Tabora and Ikoma, and have been much attacked by the Masai; hence they build high up the mountain whence they descend to their fields, and whither every drop of water is carried in gourds!

We told them slave days were over and the Masai moved away; why did not they build now in a more convenient place? They shook their heads. After all, what is ten years of peace after two hundred of war?

There is another village three days to the south; and one four hours to the west; that is the whole remnant of the tribe.

We engaged two to guide us to Lake Natron at an

equivalent of two rupees (66 cents) each (about ten days in all).

Also we sent a present of a blanket to the chief with a request that he call to see us. All this through M'ganga who talks their tongue.

We did a little trading with beads and snuff for vegetables. Gillette blades don't go here.* As we wanted meat badly, our guides then took us a long hike over the hills to a long slope of grass and scattered bush where we saw one lonesome little herd of kongoni, one of zebra, and a single duiker. These beasts departed the very instant they caught sight of us at 300 or 400 yards, and never even turned back to look. So we are still meatless.

M'ganga and two of the men have fever; the first fever of the trip.

Five hours twenty minutes; $4\frac{1}{2}$ miles; morning, 53; noon, 92; night, 68.

---

*Old Gillette razor blades are in some places greatly in demand. They are inserted in cleft sticks and used for shaving the head. This is not to be wondered at when one considers that a common implement for that purpose is a bit of broken glass!

CHAPTER V

JULY 26.—We here left all the donkeys, our own and Vanderweyer's (together with our surplus effects), in *boma* until our return from Natron, and started off with men only. The guides were on time at 6:oo, and before we had gone a mile three others had joined us. One beautiful little savage had in our honour donned a horrible greasy old patched khaki suit eight sizes too large for him. He had been once to Moschi, he proudly explained. He certainly looked like a scarecrow. The other three, they told us, would not expect wages but would go along for meat.

We rode our mules for two hours then sent them back. This, although we did not know it, was our last ride on those unfortunate animals. In all we have used the mules only about twenty-five miles. The rest of the time the country has been too rough, or we have had to scout afoot.

Marched along the base of high mountains, to the left, on a plateau of high grass and thin scrub. Far to the south, over the edge of the world, we could see immense craters. They were forty or fifty miles away and glittered as though with snow, each rising by itself from the plain.

At the end of ten miles we approached the edge of the escarpment, and the last water before the plunge. Therefore, I turned off to see if it were possible to land any meat. It had been in the dark ages past since either we or the men had 'ad any, and one cannot work long, even under the equator, for ten or twelve hours a day without meat and plenty of it.

All the game here was very wild. It saw us a long way off and immediately ran without waiting to stare for an instant as does even the wildest game anywhere else. We finally hit on the reason: The Wasonzi are great on snares for small stuff, and probably every head of large game in the district has at one time or another been caught and had to kick out of one of these snares. That was no great job, of course, but it made them very distrustful.

At last I took a desperate chance at a zebra just topping a ridge 450 to 500 yards away and hit him! Lost him for the time being, but on returning from a search got, by chance, the herd so fixed that they had to run past, between me and a rocky butte 100 yards away. How they did run, like runaway horses! I saw my wounded beast and hit him again. He slowed, so turned my attention from him and landed a second zebra in the ribs. Had to aim ahead twice the length of the animals. Followed them up and killed both with four more shots, of which one was a miss. Just then blundered on a kongoni that had not expected me and quickly downed him with a shoulder shot at 160 yards before he made off. Left a savage at each carcass hunted up camp, and sent out men for the meat. No one can imagine what a godsend those three beasts were to us at that time. We had plenty of *potio* and plain groceries, of course, but had been almost completely out of meat for some time. Under the hard work we were beginning to feel it. Also we wanted desperately to make our reputation as good providers with the savages. For some time we have had a very silent, not to say glum, camp in the evenings. To-night racks are up drying meat, spits are up roasting it, pots bubble, bright little fires gleam, and a continuous chanting arises.

This happy *kalele*, which I had not the heart to stop, and the hot night, kept me awake for an hour. Suddenly I heard a scurrying outside and agonized calls for "Ali! Ali!"

"*Nini*," says Ali.

"Call the *bwana*, a rhinoceros is very near and coming into camp!"

Get the point? Even a rhino attack was not enough to get them to overstep etiquette and call the *bwana* themselves! I hopped out with a Colt's. Once beyond the dazzle of the fire I could make out the great black mass advancing steadily and about twenty-five yards away. I fired over its head. The flash and noise turned it. Another shot sent it crashing away.

Elevation, 4,250; four hours thirty minutes; 10¼ miles; morning, 59; noon, 80; night, 70.

July 27.—An hour took us to the edge of the escarpment, and we looked almost straight down 2,300 feet to the broad lower expanse in which lay Natron. It extended farther than we could see to the south. Its upper end was guarded by two great lava mountains (about eight miles apart) with faces that ran almost sheer for more than 4,000 feet. The upper flats for miles and miles shimmered white with soda. A green line marked the meanderings of the N'gouramani, and the nearer flats were covered with scrub. The distance melted into illimitable plains. To our right was a deep-riven cañon to the edge of which our guides led us for a look.

After admiring the grandeurs and blue distances of this very impressive scenery we commenced the descent. It was by way of a very steep little spur jutting from the main escarpment, and went almost straight down by a series of zigzags. Two rhinos across a ravine stared at us and we at them. We were each safe from the other. Hard descent for men. Everybody happy, however, because carrying meat. The guides, Cuninghame, myself, and gunbearers pushed ahead. I have, to the great delight of everybody, introduced the expedient of blazing trails, in order to keep various divisions in touch. They knew nothing of it before.

Sweltering hot, and sun very strong. In the lower

scrub it was fearful. We debouched on the flat at ten o'clock. Very glad to ease our knees. Marched an hour longer and came at eleven o'clock to an ordinary mudpuddle in an opening of the scrub. The guide said it was the only water in that part of the country. Many zebra, wildebeeste, and impalla, and hundreds of game and other birds were here gathered. Since we must either camp here or push on to the N'gouramani, Cuninghame and I crawled under the shade of a bush to await the safari.

One sort of small brown bird with a very long tail were so abundant that when they flew they roared like the wind, and the aggregate weight of them actually bent over a fair-sized sapling. This is literal.

When the safari arrived we tackled the mudpuddle. First, we dug a ditch and drained off all the foul water. Then we extended the hole. This accomplished, Memba Sasa planted a staff in the middle tied peculiarly with wisps of grass—a sort of magic, in which, apparently, everybody firmly believed. In a little while the hole began to fill again. Overjoyed with this indication that it was a real spring and not merely a rain puddle, we pitched camp.

After lunch and a rest Cuninghame and I scouted in different directions. I wounded an impalla which got away; the second beast to escape. Saw many impalla, zebra, wildebeeste, waterbuck, Grant's gazelle, dik-dik, and game birds. Also an ostrich nest with two eggs.

Wandered widely, always in the thorn scrub, and toward evening came out on coarse grass savannahs near
the head of the lake; and there enjoyed some marvellous
mirage effects on game, on the flat, and on distant
mountains.   Here fed a herd of zebra one of which I
killed at 256 yards to the huge delight of the natives.
They use every scrap of a beast, even to the sinews for
bowstrings, and were much chagrined that I would not
shoot another before the herd got out of range.   They
are a cheerful, friendly lot.   In camp, Cuninghame
reported that he had gone out on the flat, and had there
found buffalo tracks.   We decided to cross the head
of the lake to where the N'gouramani empties into it
in the hopes of one of the beasts.

This evening the little fires down the length of our
tiny glade, the light reflected from the leaves, were very
fine.

Five hours; $9\frac{1}{2}$ miles; elevation, 1,950; morning, 63;
noon, 93; night, 83.

July 28.—Up at daylight.   Leaving the bulk of our
goods and some of the men, we marched across the soda
flats at the head of the lake.   The whole surface looked
like a map of the moon, mountains, craters, queer knife-
edged peaks, all in a miniature of four inches high.
When we stepped on them they collapsed with a loud
crackling.   Distances were very deceitful.   An object
might be a mile away or ten yards, and you could not
tell what it was.   A herd of zebra looked like an orange

grove until we came close. But the most wonderful sight—one of the most wonderful I have ever seen—was that furnished by a huge flock of flamingoes. There must have been thousands upon thousands of them. When we first saw them, they were far in the distance and flying. We took them for a rosy sunrise cloud. They looked just like that: one of those cotton-wool clouds—the cotton-wool that comes in jewellers' boxes. We did not find out our mistake for some few minutes. Then the cloud miraculously dropped to the edge of the water, and the shore turned pink for miles.

This is *not* an argument for protective coloration. There is a lot more in that theory than its sternest critics seem ready to admit; but much less than its most violent partisans claim. Any feeder on flamingoes (what does feed on flamingoes, by the way?) in our position might, as we did, *temporarily* mistake them for a pink cloud. But any carnivore or raptore at a closer range could not possibly do so; nor could he long continue to do so even from where we stood. And a carnivore or raptore that did not stir around enough to discover in a very short time what that pink cloud was composed of would deserve to starve. It is inconceivable nonsense to believe that several hundred thousand large birds, in an open country, could long remain undiscovered, whatever their coloration. I have seen it stated in support of the extreme theory of protective coloration that flamingoes are night feeders. That

may or may not be true of the species in general.   But
I personally know of some hundreds of thousands that
do their feeding daytimes!

In identically the same way a pure white cloud hang-
ing in the sky proved to be snow geese.   Another was
of white pelicans.

By and by we came to a papyrus marsh in the water
along the edge of which were countless hordes of geese,
ducks, waders, and many sorts of ibis, plover, egrets,
etc.   Never have I seen so many and so varied water-
fowl.   They were quite tame and did not take wing
until we were less than forty yards away.   Over them
wheeled a cloud of insect-catching birds.   And still
higher soared grandly the hawks and eagles and carrion
eaters.

A great deal of game comes here for salt—wildebeeste,
ostrich, zebra, and many giraffe.   We saw considerable;
but were especially impressed by the abundance of
spoor.

We wanted to get over to an island around which the
N'gouramani divided, and we slopped about for an
hour trying to find a ford.   The river had here over-
flowed for a quarter of a mile, and the channel was
discoverable only when one fell into it.   Finally we
made passage a little over waist deep and camped on
our island.   This was a barren piece of land about
four miles long by a half mile wide.   No shelter.   Put
our blankets over the tents for additional shade.

EUPHORBIA FOREST NEAR N'DIGADIGU

THE BIG TREE NEAR N'DIGADIGU

CURIOUS EXAMPLE OF A STRANGLING VINE

About three went scouting for buffalo. Cuninghame took one side of the island and I the other. After about a mile I jumped a bull in the edge of the papyrus and gave him both barrels at twenty yards. He fell with a mighty splash. Hunted up Cuninghame and we waded after him. Very weird, in water nearly to our waists, surrounded by papyrus that completely shut in everything but the sky immediately overhead, water-birds all about, indignant hippos booming to right and left, very much on the alert. Followed very bloody spoor for twenty yards, and found the buffalo had toppled into the swift current of the main river and been swept away. Great disappointment, as he was very dead.

In evening mosquitoes out by millions. The air was full of them. We could hardly eat. Some of the boys built platforms in the leafless trees and slept aloft. Others dug holes.

Four hours; 6½ miles; elevation, 1,900; morning, 68; noon, 95; night, 83.

July 29.—Up and out before daybreak. Saw three buffs on edge of swamp across the river, and slopped after them. We got close but could not see them on account of high reeds. This would be a good place to hunt buffalo in drier season, but now that the river is in flood it is hopeless. It was interesting to see the water-fowl, however, and our rosy cloud of flamingoes was again in the sky. Heard many lions.

Decided this was no good, so packed up for return.

On the flat I made two very long shots and killed two wildebeeste of the new species described by Heller and Roosevelt, one at 343 yards (shoulder, dead in tracks), and the other alongside of him (343). This last moved off very slowly, and I knocked her down, after one miss, with a shoulder shot at 421 yards.

The safari headed directly back for our waterhole, but I made a circuit through the scrub in the course of which I missed an impalla at 90 yards.

In the afternoon I went out a half mile and killed some guinea fowl. To-night the boys all slept up trees on account of mosquitoes. In the night one fell out of bed! Three more Wasonzi showed up in hope of meat.

Morning, 61; noon, 91; night, 69.

July 30.—We now decided to put in our time before the German customs official should show up on August 8th by going up river a distance in search of buffalo. Accordingly we took a light outfit and put in a very hard day's march through stifling scrub and all up-hill. Very thorny and we had difficulty at times in picking a way. We thought it *hot*, but I overheard one porter saying to another, "Fine weather; just like Mombasa." Saw a number of rhinos and baboons. Just before the day's end, when everybody was feeling pretty tired and subdued, men ahead began to jump aside, dropping loads. Thought it was a rhino, but immediately saw a small animal tearing directly down the middle of the trail toward me. I had just time to leap aside. So close did it pass to me that it caught my rifle sling and broke it! Memba Sasa, who had not seen the thing, was hit square in his tummy and knocked flying, falling heavily. The beast was a bushbuck doe, frantic with terror, apparently running with both eyes shut!

At last we arrived at a village of the N'gouramani. These dwell under the escarpment, keep goats, and live in separate *bomas*. They resemble the Wasonzi, but are poor and few in numbers, probably the last remnant of a tribe. We camped thankfully under a wide tree completely overgrown by a thick vine so dense it was like an umbrella.

At supper time came in the hunter of the village. After a long parley we agreed with him that if we got a buffalo we would pay him one blanket and five rupees. He was a very old and skinny man, and we soon discovered that, outside the fact that he knew where the buffalo were, he was beyond his usefulness as a hunter. I could not help but be sorry for the poor old thing, and speculate on his latter end; and was glad he made something of us.

Nine and a half hours' hard uphill march; 20½ miles; elevation, 3,400; morning, 60; noon, 99; night, 65.

July 31.—Our rather scattered dispositions are now as follows: two men at waterhole living in *banda* guarding supplies, eight men on the road to the donkey *boma* to bring up *potio*, one man sick and three donkey men at the *boma* near the village, the rest with us. Consequently we are travelling with only bare necessities.

Our old N'gouramani was promptly on hand, so we were off at sunrise. He led us by a rocky trail down a series of steps and over a 600-foot escarpment back to the river level. On the way flushed hundreds grouse. The cliffs were occupied by hordes of baboons that came out and barked at us.

We are now so used to heat that our morning temperature of sixty degrees seems chilly! Saw some fresh tracks of greater kudu; and in a tree a huge structure five feet high by three broad, pear-shaped, with a wide hole at the top. I thought it was some sort of a hunter's blind, but Memba Sasa says it is the nest of the crested ibis!

Camped among thin thorn trees. Stony underfoot, and brown, but alongside is a crystal clear stream flowing over rocks. In the afternoon our old guide led us an hour through the thorn to the border of a long wet marsh surrounded by higher ground. He sneaked along the edge of this looking for buffalo. Finally he had us lie down in a thicket until near dusk. The idea was to wait until the buffalo came out in the marsh to feed, but there would have to be a thousand thousand of them or else mighty good luck to bring them out at exactly our spot!

On his way across a little wet arm he stooped over,

without bending his knees, and drank; which shows he was a limber old gentleman after all!

We lay in the thicket for an hour. A rhino came and sniffed at us ten yards away, but decided to depart. I had sufficient amusement watching the various birds. Of course nothing happened. On the way home, as we needed meat badly, I killed an impalla buck at 210 yards with the .465—a good deal like taking a club to a butterfly.

Two hours twenty minutes; $5\frac{1}{2}$ miles; elevation, 2,000; morning, 60; noon, 86; night, 66.

August 1.—Having no faith whatever in the old gentleman's system, we resolved to hunt buffalo our own way, viz.: search for fresh spoor and then follow it until something happened. Accordingly we returned to the swamp, waded it, and begun to cast about on the other side. By 7:30 we had found tracks of a bull, and for two hours we puzzled along them. The ground was hard and confused with all sorts of other tracks new and old. The men were often at fault, and by 9:30 we had followed the brute only about half a mile. The spoor led across a small opening, through a fringe of sparse brush, and apparently to a distant thicket. Eleven giraffe ambled across in front of us in single file. The spoor finally led past a dark ant heap under an isolated small tree in high grass. When only thirty yards from the ant heap, I saw it heave slightly and suddenly recognized it as the curve of the buffalo's back. I promptly planted a .465 where the shoulder ought to be. The beast leaped to his feet and rushed in our direction. My second barrel in the chest turned him. Cuninghame gave him both barrels in the side, and he came down within fifty yards. Another in the spine finished him. He was a good big one, five feet two inches at shoulder, and eight feet eleven inches in straight line, as he lay, from nose to rump. We ordered the old savage to rustle to camp after men, but he told us earnestly that he was very old and very tired. This was true; we had not realized that he had been doing pretty strenuous work for so aged a man. Therefore we left him to sit by the buffalo, sent Sanguiki to camp for men, and went on.

Hunted hard for eight hours more, always on fresh spoor, stooping double in hot thickets, crawling, scratched by thorns, and generally working hard. Had lunch under a shady bush where a whole lot of little monkeys scouted us thoroughly. On the way home I killed another impalla with the .465 (carry only heavy guns after buff) at 90 yards.

In camp we found everybody with heads freshly shaved in the most marvellous designs. Collected some of the most fantastic for a picture. M'ganga's tent accidently burned up. He is most heartily ashamed! *Potio* men back, accompanied by nine more Wasonzi after meat. Our fame as providers is spreading. Every one promptly departed for the buffalo, where they made fires and stayed all night.

Ten hours' hunting; morning, 66; noon, 95; night, 74.

August 2.—Spoored buffalo all day without result, except to trail them into impossible places. By noon we had reached the N'gouramani River, here a big wide rushing stream with a forest strip. It was very cool and pleasant under the trees. Thousands of game birds everywhere on this grassy thornbrush flat. Jumped a giraffe at close range, and was much amused at the rear view. He held his tail stiffly at an affected and rakish angle to one side for about a dozen steps, then *swish!* he flopped it over to the other side for about the same length of time.

On the way home I dropped a young Robertsi buck at 120 yards, and a doe for the head (and meat) at 167. Saw two leopards together, but did not get a shot. Sun very powerful.

In camp we found the third mediocre batch of bread in four days. Had up the cook and cut his wages in half. Have not had a bad lot since (this is written August 23rd.).

Morning, 67; noon, 95; night, 78.

August 3.—Having scouted this country fairly well, and the time drawing near when we were to meet the German customs officials, we started back for the waterhole along the base of the escarpment, intending to camp about halfway and look over the country.

For some distance we had really fine marching, which was quite a novelty and relief, over low rolling swells, with wide grass openings, and long parklike swales in which fed considerable game. Saw a great many cow eland (no bulls), Robertsi, zebra, kongoni, one wildebeeste, a serval cat, and many dik-dik. After a time we came to a long dry soda arm of the lake, which we crossed; plunged into scrub; climbed over a hill; and dropped down into one of the loveliest spots I have seen in Africa. A crystal stream running over pebbles; a flat terrace; then a single row of enormous, wide-spreading trees as though planted; and from beneath their low-flung branches sight of a verdant hill, and distant tiny blue glimpses of a miniature landscape far away.

"This is going to be the pleasantest camp we have ever had," said we, and sat down to eat lunch before the safari should come.

But with the safari came two lovely naked savages with a letter in a cleft stick. Said letter proved to be from the German governor. It absolved us from meeting a customs officer August 8th, and requested us to send a list of dutiable articles. This was very good of him; also it saved his officer a hard march into an unknown country. However, it altered the situation. No need to hang around this country until August 8th. We resolved to hike back as soon as we could to the Wasonzi village, pick up our donkeys, and pro-

THE PLEASANT CAMP—AT WHICH WE DID NOT STOP

SEE PAGE 72

HOW WE SENT OUT OUR FIRST LETTERS—IN THE SPLIT STICK. THE MEN ARE CARRYING THE BLANKETS
WE PAID THEM FOR PERFORMING THIS SERVICE

SEE PAGE 72

ceed eastward into our Unknown Land. By continuing on to the waterhole, the long march would save us a day. Accordingly, after a rest we abandoned our beautiful camp and went on.

A half-hour out ran across giraffe. Colburn wants one, for which he pays special license, and this was the very last chance before entering German territory. There were in the herd a dozen smaller ones and one large one, apparently bull and cows. Sent Memba Sasa sneaking about for a point of vantage, and he reported the big one a male. At this moment they became aware of us and started to run. It was now or never, so I opened fire. Hit, high shoulder, running at 200 yards with the Springfield. It went thirty yards and fell dead. It proved to be a very large cow! There were no bulls at all, and Memba Sasa's zeal had outrun his judgment. We were all very sorry for this, but took the trophy—and left a dozen or so delighted Wasonzi.

At the waterhole we found our boys had been living high on guinea fowl they had snared.

Eight hours; 16 miles; morning, 66; noon, 100; night, 83.

CHAPTER VI

AUGUST 4.—Out and off before daylight to get the 2,300 feet of straight-up escarpment behind us before it should get too hot. Hard climb, and we sure perspired some! Every Wasonzi was draped with spoils. Don't suppose they have ever before struck, or ever will again strike, such luck—meat, hides, sinews, fat! They could hardly navigate.

Made our rhino camp at the top in four and one half hours. The afternoon Cuninghame and I spent in preparing our papers for the Government *in re* customs, and in constructing a surveyor's protractor. We made an excellent one which we have used successfully since. In its construction we employed a mica from the candle lantern, a pair of scissors (as compasses), a darning needle, an envelope, the thermometer slide, steel tape, and a pocket compass. The air seems cool and grateful at this altitude.

Morning, 73; noon, 80; night, 66.

August 5.—Started on a cool day for a fine march back to the Wasonzi. A mile or so from camp I killed two kongonis, by a right and left off-hand at 237 yards, dead in their tracks. The Wasonzi took charge, as these were intended as a final gift. A little farther on we heard a movement in a small patch of brush next a spring. Suspecting buffalo I ran around the other side just in time to meet a sleek black rhino that came out about twenty yards away.

Everything was lovely and happy, but we were destined to a setback. Two hours out we met Sulimani in full regalia, musket, bandolier, and all, accompanied by a Wasonzi guide. He had started out to hunt us up, if it took a week, and was delighted that his errand was cut so short.

He reported that two of the donkeys had died, "and all the rest are sick."

This was a facer. Much perturbed, we hurried on. Arrived at the base camp we found one donkey dead, two on the point of expiring, and five more of ours and six of Vanderweyer's evidently out of sorts. Both mules had symptoms of fly.*

We called in from pasture all survivors, packed them, and hastily dispatched them off across the hills to N'digadigu, the next Wasonzi village, hoping thus to get them out of the fly belt. Then I put bullets through the brains of the two.

In the afternoon Cuninghame and I paid a visit to the village on the hill. There was a long, well-made

---

* To determine if a beast is fly struck, take a fold of its neck skin between your thumb and finger. If it smooths out immediately on being released, the beast is all right. If, however, it stands out in a ridge, without elasticity, and only slowly subsides, your animal is a goner. He may last six days or six months, but eventually he is doomed. He will die next time he gets wet or chilled.

trail up the hill between flowering aloes, euphorbia, and dense briars and thorn. First it climbed a steep rocky escarpment, then it ran perfectly straight and open for three quarters of a mile. Because of the thorny thicket no enemy could have progressed an inch except on this road, which was visible and open for its whole length. Next we came to a little round stockade of heavy timbers, built square across the road, perhaps ten feet in diameter. It had doorways leading in both directions, but timbers lay at hand by which these openings could be closed. Then after another interval we began to come to the houses, perched all over the side hill. Even near at hand their resemblance to the big gray boulders was most deceiving, and at 180 yards Cuninghame and I had to guess which was which. They proved to be circular, thatched with gray grass in rounded roofs. Each entrance was fortified in miniature just like the gate.

We bent double and entered the first one. It was very dark and warm, but after our eyes had become accustomed to the dimness we found we were calling on a young lady, stark naked except for ornaments, squatted before a tiny glow of coals over which she was drying tobacco. Beds of skins were suspended at right and left. New skin garments hung in the apex, together with bundles of provisions, skins of beasts, gourds, and such treasures. She seemed not at all disturbed, and we nodded cheerfully and said $\bar{a}$-$\bar{a}$-$\bar{a}$-$\bar{a}$

THE SULTAN OF THE WASONZI—"THE OLDEST MAN I EVER SAW"
SEE PAGE 73

FORTIFIED GATE BELOW THE WASONZI VILLAGE
SEE PAGE 76

THE PRIME MINISTER OF THE WASONZI
SEE PAGE 77

in friendly fashion.   Then we crawled out and continued our tour.

Some of the wealthier houses had little *bomas* about
them.   All had pear-shaped jet-black masses of some
substance that looked like asphalt drying in the sun;
these we ascertained to be manufactured tobacco.   Met
and grinned at many gaudily painted warriors and
old men.   Coveys of naked children scrambled like
goats up the mountainside ahead of us, and perched
on crags to gaze down at us.   Everybody was most
friendly.

Finally we inquired for the chief and were led down
to a naked old fellow sitting on a piece of skin.   He was
the most ancient piece of humanity I have ever beheld,
a mere skeleton, his joints twice the size of his limbs,
his skin a wrinkled parchment, his eyes bleared.   We
stood and stared at him, but he never looked up.

"Nothing to do here," said Cuninghame, but had
Sanguiki address him in Masai.

The skeleton rattled and a slow, deliberate, powerful voice issued from it.

"I am chief not only of this village," Sanguiki
translated, "but of another village far away there, and
another great village, nearer, there. I am a great
chief."

By this time three younger old men, evidently prime
ministers, came up, accompanied by a half-dozen warriors.   One had a delightfully quizzical humorous

face, and all had a look of great intelligence. With them we chatted for some time. We motioned to Sanguiki to give the old chief a paper of snuff we had brought as a present. The old fellow mistook us, and helped himself to an enormous pinch.

"It is yours, *all* yours," we told him.

As soon as he understood this, he hastily returned to the packet the large pinch and took for immediate use only a very little one.

"He must be Scotch," laughed Cuninghame.

We left him, carrying away the impression of a very old man sitting in the sun.

On our way down the trail we met the water safari, a long string of women and children carrying innumerable gourds, by means of which the whole village is supplied from the stream, a toilsome mile away. Also we met one of our guides returning laden with spoils from the two kongonis I had killed. He had with him an old man with a spear, a young warrior, and a *toto*. We passed the time of day, and asked him if the *toto* was his.

He laid his hand on the warrior's shoulder. "This is my *toto*," said he, "the little one is his." We were about to move on when the old man seized my hand and placed it on the guide's arm, at the same time pointing to his own breast. Thus four generations were returning laden with the white man's bounty. The Wasonzi are a friendly, pleasant, *human* people.

M'ganga to his joy discovers that the *askari* who
brought us the letter is his brother-in-law. Ramadan
begins, and all our good Moslems must abstain food
and drink from sunrise to sunset.

August 6.—Started off at 6:30 over a high rocky pass
with good trail through the hills to southwest. Shortly
we looked out over a tumbled valley of hills with another high rampart five or six miles away. Made out
through our glasses the village of N'digadigu perched
high, like the other. It was five or six times the size of
Olsambu, and the fertile valley was cultivated far and
wide. On the slope I killed a kongoni for meat with
two shots at 210 and 260. Crossed a flowing stream
and came to a fine upsloping grass and cultivated land
with water singing down innumerable winding ditches,
and the finest single big trees, spaced here and there,
I have ever seen. They are very green, with wide
leaves, thick great branches spreading far, spacious
domes, and thick, grateful shade. Flowering aloes were
all about, and groves of strange twisted or stately
euphorbias about some of which python-like vines
were doing their choking best. Paths ran in all directions. We made several false starts, once landing
at the fortified gate of the village, but at last found our
donkeys camped near the *askari* post. This had been
constructed under one of the aforementioned big trees,
with a heavy twisted outside *boma*, a ditch and palisades. Two Monumwezi *askaris* occupied it. We

found the ground under another big tree swept clean and bare, and three grass bandas ready for us. We pitched our tents, the men theirs, the donkeys were already *bomaed*—and we utilized only half the space under that great tree! It was 64 feet in circumference, and its branches extended 120 yards.

We sent back men to the last camp with instructions to lie there to-night, and to-morrow to bring some *potio* loads we had to leave there. About 8:30, to our surprise, they returned with the loads, having made thirty-one miles in all, over mountains, and over twenty miles of it loaded!

We had swarms of visitors, with the most important of whom we exchanged courtesies. The German *askaris*, very trim in their uniforms, reported formally, saluted, and returned to their fort. Found another donkey dead.

This night the village held a grand *n'goma*—fortunately at a distance—in honour of the advent of the first white men since the Germans established the post in '96. The *askaris* are changed every two months, and apparently are never inspected. The Mohammedan month of Ramadan, the month of fasting, is now on. The good Moslem is supposed to eat between sunset and sunrise. As we have about fifty per cent. of that faith in our safari, we called up Ali, and asked him how about it—whether men like porters working hard had to keep it.

CROSSING THE SWAMPS ABOVE LAKE NATRON

SODA INCRUSTATIONS AT THE HEAD OF LAKE NATRON

HEAD SHAVING BY THE PORTERS
SEE PAGE 70

"Ramadan can be postponed," he told us, "so that it can be kept any other month."

"How do you do that?"

"By killing a camel," says Ali.

"Are all the men keeping Ramadan?" we asked.

"Only me."

We haven't noted any defunct camels, so don't know how they work it. Perhaps they consider their credit good for one camel; or perhaps, like white men, they leave their religion outside a wild country.

Four hours; $10\frac{1}{4}$ miles; elevation, 3,900; morning, 68; noon, 74; night, 68.

August 7.—About two o'clock last night a tremendous burst of talking broke out. This was strictly against all discipline. When the light in *bwana's* tent goes out all conversation is supposed to cease. This is a necessary regulation, as otherwise somebody would be talking all night long. It would not be the same somebody; he would have finished and gone to sleep. But by that time another fellow, who had been peacefully slumbering, would wake up, feel sociable, punch the fire and his dearest chum, and start in for a good comfortable *shauri*. The native has no regular hours for eating and sleeping as we have. He goes on the dog's system.

Therefore, at breakfast, we started an inquiry. M'ganga was very apologetic and deprecatory.

"I am very sorry," said M'ganga apologetically.

"I hope the *bwana* will excuse me.   A sick donkey fell through my tent upon my head."

We forgave him!   The sick donkey died.

After a long *shauri* we found two men who knew the Masai route through the mountains and engaged them to pilot Vanderweyer's men and donkeys back to the *boma*.   With them we sent all our trophies, our riding saddles, and the syce.   We went over Vanderweyer's beasts very thoroughly for symptoms of fly, and kept with us six that seemed likely to die anyway.* Dowdi left us without many regrets, I think.

The men spent the day trading with the savages. Each brought out an unexpected little store of beads and entered into bargains for milk, vegetables, fruit, etc.   They have also started the fashion of unravelling the sleeves of their jerseys, and with the yarn weaving lanyards.   Gave Ali some beads and snuff, and with them he bought us enough yams, green beans, and a sort of squash to last us a fortnight.   Amused myself wandering around and listening to the bargaining.   Overheard this, delivered in a voice of scorn:

"You might sell that to the white men, but not to me!"

Then he turned and discovered me at his shoulder!

Some of them have caught quite a lot of fish which they are drying on sticks.   Memba Sasa started a

---

*All six died; and when we returned to Nairobi we found that of those we sent back, nineteen were lost.   Old Sendeu's hostility had cost us dear.

new lace-work cap. I explained how the Memsahib had made the others into sewing baskets and he was much interested. Poked around and took pictures. Slept three and a half hours. Wrote in log. A high cold wind came up in afternoon.

Morning, 64; noon, 74; night, 66.

August 8.—Our plan is now to strike westward until we reach Victoria Nyanza, going out at Shirati, near the Anglo-German boundary. The first task is to pass the high barrier of north-and-south mountains directly before us. Fortunately our Wasonzi friends know a way through them to a high plateau. This joins the regular route to Ikoma eventually. Beyond the edge of the plateau they know nothing. It keeps going on, indefinitely, "to where the sun sets," they say; and they want none of it. They are perfectly willing to take us as far as they know, however, and we engaged three guides. When we came to pack up, however, a dozen reported; and one of the German *askaris*, in full regalia, came along, too. He says he is given seven cartridges a month for meat. After I had looked his blunderbuss over, I did not wonder he took every chance to supplement his supply. They all say there is lots of game up there; and we have assured them in return that we will feed them all well.

As it is exceedingly difficult, as well as wasteful of time, to try to keep our different units together on this sort of a march, we divided into three sections: First, myself, guide, gunbearers as a sort of reconnoissance party to spy out—and blaze—best routes, hunt for water, etc. Second, the carriers, with guide, to take their own gait with the outfit. Third, Cuninghame, the donkey men, and guide, to get up as best and as far as they were able. For two miles we followed down the valley close to the hills. Little naked children perched on dizzy crags far above us to watch us go. At every little crossroad squatted a group of women who arose at our approach and waved and screamed us into the proper path. We met many people going to their fields, each carrying a gourd, a leaf packet of provisions, and a smouldering brand with which to start his fire. They all shouted and screamed at us in their own language.

Then we turned into a rocky cañon with a stream, at the head of which we accomplished a terrific straight-up climb of 1,100 feet. Very hot, bad footing, steep; a regular heart-breaker. Up at last, this brought us to rolling mountain tops and low summits a few miles away to which we rose slowly; and then a wooded shady pass through the main crest with a beautiful high still forest and monkeys and trailing vines and still cool shadows and breathless leafy glimpses and bright birds; next slowly opening out to grassy openings and tree clumps; and so over an edge to find not a drop on the other side, but yellow plains undulating away before us as far as we could see with single dim blue hills sailing hull down below the horizon.

Just here we began to see game, and I dropped two kongoni, at 180 yards—after one miss—and at 282. Also saw a Bohur reedbuck running hard through tall grass. As my only specimen had been burned up in Colburn's fire I tried him, but missed.

Camped near a spring under a lone tree, a mountain range rising abruptly at our back and the plains before us. The men came in an hour later, but Cuninghame did not show up. I thought of that fearful 1,100 foot climb!

After a short rest I went out to get more meat* from some of the game herds feeding in plain sight. The wind was blowing hard which as always made the game very wild. This is invariable, and I have tested the theory perfectly; having been within 50 yards of *the same game* on a still day that would not let me get within 400 yards in a wind. After considerable stalking I managed to hit a kongoni at 238 yards. He ran slowly for 300 yards, when I sneaked up and finished him.

Well satisfied, I returned to camp. About 5:30 Cuninghame came in alone, nearly tired out. He reported a fearful time getting to the top with the donkeys, and left them encamped at the top of the rise all in. He was pretty much all in himself.

---

* We had temporarily a good many men to feed.

Distant grass fires were wonderfully beautiful after dark, throwing a glare into the heavens, and running forward in long wavering lines of flame. Some of it had crept to the top of the other side of the very distant hills, where first it showed like a star, and then burst forth into a beacon. The high wind continued all night.

Six hours; 12½ miles; elevation, 6,250; morning, 60; noon, 69; night, 60.

August 9.—Since we sent back the syce and our saddles, we are packing the mules. Sent out a relief expedition to help Dolo and carry donkey loads if necessary.

Then Cuninghame and I started off together to explore. For an hour and a half we skirted the base of the mountain, then crossed a small stream called the Dorodedi where in some rocks we saw hyrax. From this point Cuninghame headed straight west across the plain toward the single lone kopje to scout for water for the next camp, and I swung down to the left to look over the game. Stacks of game—Tommy, Robertsi, kongoni, zebra, ostrich, small antelope, and several black compact herds of wildebeeste like ink spots in the distance. A strong fresh wind blew from the east and everything was wild and suspicious. Very hard to shoot as the wind was strong enough to swing the gun, and most of it had to be offhand, on account of the long grass. Missed a Tommy twice at 120 yards. Then after an interval missed a first shot at a Robertsi at 180, but downed him with the second. Farther on attempted in vain to stalk wildebeeste, and tried Colby's *lucky* bullet at 300 yards, but could not hold on. Later one came toward me as I lay concealed and I dropped him, after a miss, at 315 yards. Leaving a busy little group at each carcass, I dipped back toward the river where I saw many guinea fowl, and a big herd of mixed game going along single file, among which I distinguished two topi.* In the smoke of a nearby fire made out dimly the darting forms of savages with firebrands running along and setting fire to the grass. They disappeared when we came near them. Air full of smoke and the crackling of flames. Got out of there. Just as we topped the hill came upon a herd of kongoni. Put Baxter's lucky bullet low in the shoulder at 110 yards, and followed it with two others before he left his feet, though he did not move twenty yards. This finished the desired quota for ourselves and Wasonzi, so I returned to camp after seven and a half hours.

All afternoon the Wasonzi drifted in from N'digadigu until twenty had arrived. Each was escorted to my tent by the one who talked Swahili with the statement:

"I have arrived."

"Make it so," I replied, like the captain of a warship.

Then the newcomer joined his friends in the big leafy bower. After tea I went over and had quite a chat with them. At sundown some eland appeared and

---

* This seemed to be the easterly range of these animals.

looked at camp.   I went down in my mosquito boots to get one, but they skipped out.   Came on a kongoni at 110 yards, and shot him for our friends, who leave us to-morrow.

The Wasonzi tell me it was they who set fire to the grass.

"Thus the rhino are driven off," they say, "and if there are no rhino the Wanderobo stay away."

At sundown, the men, carrying the donkey loads and driving the donkeys, came slowly in.   The donkeys and one of the mules died at the top of the hill.   Shortly after Cuninghame came in after a thirty-mile tramp. Under the little kopje after long search he found a puddle of water "as big as his hat," and by digging proved it to be a spring.

So that determines the direction and distance of our next move.   This evening the fire has crept up the other side of a lone mountain peak ten miles away, and has appeared at the top, so it is like a volcano.

Morning, 50; noon, 66; night, 60.

August 10.—This is a rest day for the donkeys—and for Cuninghame!   They have both had as much as they need.   Again high gale and cold.   Walked with Memba Sasa to the Dorodedi, with shotgun, and shot four rock hyraxes, a steinbuck, and some guinea fowl.   Out four and a half hours.   Loafed, wrote log, etc.   Wasonzi departed for home.

Morning, 52; noon, 64; night, 62.

CHAPTER VII

AUGUST 11.—Another donkey died, and our transportation problems have begun in good earnest. We have now more loads than we can handle, and we do not yet feel like abandoning anything. Therefore we leave here twelve loads in charge of two sick men, together with two more sick donkeys. They are to camp here until we send for them. This, by our plan, will not be from the next camp. We shall push forward until we find a good country.

Marched across rolling open grass plains to the end of a hill. Not much game in the middle of the plain, but ran into it again near Cuninghame's spring and thereabouts. Still blowing hard, and game almost impossible to approach. Near the hill I branched off to the left after desired meat, while Cuninghame and the men went on to make camp. Missed a Robertsi at about 200 yards; impossible to hold on in this gale, and have to snap for it when the sights touch. Then after a long stalk hit a wildebeeste, too far back at 300 yards. Sat down to watch him. He stopped about a mile away and lay down. Stalked him carefully and tried again. Tried sitting down, against a tree, over a limb to get a decent sight; but brace myself as I might, the wind swung the sights across him and ten feet either side. Snapped at him and gave him a surface wound. He went two miles and lay down again. Broke down his foreshoulder at 310 yards. Sent Sanguiki back for porters and with Memba Sasa took a long circle to the right. Missed a Tommy at 140 yards. At last got a game herd outside some small thorn, through which I crawled on my face until I got a shot at a wildebeeste at 280 yards. Facing me. Hit him well, and raked him twice as he ran, at (about) 300 yards and (exactly) 340.

While Memba Sasa took care of the meat and went for men, I continued on to the top of the swell westward, and took compass bearings of the hills so as to know how to cut a river called the Bololedi, reported to us by the savages. From this present camp we cut loose from all native tracks and all native knowledge, and enter absolutely virgin country.

On the way to camp I picked up a fresh ostrich egg. It made a huge omelette.

Nine hours. Pretty tired. Safari, 16½ miles; I, about 25; elevation, 6,300; morning, 51; noon (?); night, 64.

August 12.—Struck directly across country by compass by the bearings I took yesterday, and after some hours' march came to the edge of low mountains, or high hills, with easy slopes, sparsely grown with small trees, and valleys between. It had been recently burned; and

TOPI

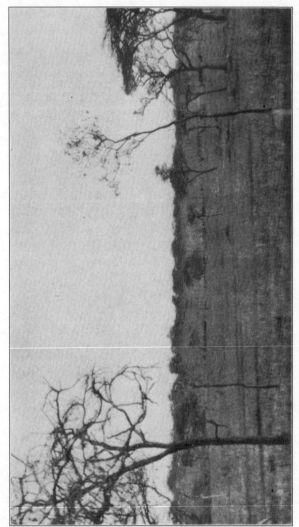

BIG HERDS OF MIXED GAME IN TYPICAL HUNTING COUNTRY

indeed for the next ten days or so we were never out of fine charcoal footing which arose in clouds and which grimed up everything. We were always very dirty, but it was a good, clean, healthful antiseptic sort of dirt, and the absence of high grass made shooting easier.

But here we ran into multitudes of game, game that had never heard a rifle shot; had probably never seen a man save possibly a stray Wanderobo. It stood about in groups and singly, and stared at us in stupefied astonishment while we went by, never taking the trouble even to move unless it happened to be to leeward of us. Never will anybody again get into virgin game fields like these, for they are the last bit unexplored and we dropped into the abundance of them so suddenly! Wildebeeste, even, stood at 100 yards and let us pass, and topi and kongoni, zebra, Tommy, eland, Robertsi, steinbuck, dik-dik merely trotted a few steps, and stared, and trotted a few steps more, and stared again. I expected some of them to come up and beg for peanuts. It was a wonderful sight.

By and by we passed a bold outcrop of rocks, wherein were klip-springers and reedbuck bounding around, and began a long gentle downward slope that led to the river. We arrived at hot noon—to find it a dry wash!

However, we soon discovered a pool in the rocks, and made camp on a little patch of clean grass that had escaped burning. A donkey died on the road.

In the afternoon Cuninghame and I took a little stroll up the wash to see if there was more water above. A short distance out I downed a Bohur reedbuck at 80 yards (my only specimen was burned). A little farther on we heard a chorus of zebra barkings, a regular *kalele*, persistent, shrill, and numerous. Of course we went to investigate the cause, supposing that they must at least be harried by wild dogs. We found it to be sheer exuberance! From a big water-hole, up through the scrub, came a mighty procession of all sorts of animals, seemingly endless, back for feed after their four o'clock watering. They were biting, and racing, and plodding soberly along, and kicking playfully, and all lifting up their voices in sheer joy and thankfulness. We stood behind a little tree and watched them through our glasses with the keenest pleasure until they had all passed on. Then we moved forward to look at the waterhole.

This little piece of country is like the Garden of the Gods—we wind our way on firm level earth between domes and monoliths. The water lay deep and cool in a hollow with tall green reeds all about. And in the reeds we saw a fine bull eland!

My first shot raked him at 277 yards. I followed it immediately with three others as he turned, all in the shoulder. It was now near dark, and we had no men with us. Cuninghame hiked to camp for men, and I first built a protection fire and then set about skinning.

The entire safari turned out, and we had that excellent meat and trophy in a jiffy.

Saw a steinbuck that thought itself hidden, crouched flat to the ground, with its ears *folded* neatly *forward* like those of a spaniel dog! That is a new one on me! One of the porters (wandering idly from the camp in the afternoon) reported to us that he had come across four roan. We do not know whether or not this is true, but if so, this country is being pretty good to us!

Six hours' march; morning, 54; noon, 78; night, 64.

August 13.—Out early after roan as reported by the porter. I put in Harry Ross's lucky bullet, as this beast ranks after the greater kudu, and with the sable, as the finest trophy of African antelope, and the most difficult to get. My only one burned. Sent M'ganga and Soli to scout forward for water.

About half-hour out saw a wild dog, and a little later three roan bounded across our front and disappeared before we could get a shot. While looking after them I heard Memba Sasa snap his fingers and looked to see a fourth, behind us, stopped and staring. I could just see a piece of his forequarters between two trees, and the rising sun was square behind him. However, Harry's bullet was indeed lucky, and I hit in his fore-shoulder. This was probably enough, but I took no chances, and landed another quartering from behind as he staggered forward. This brought him down, but I gave him a third in the shoulder to hold him. Great triumph!

Spent the rest of the morning quartering the thin woods below the hill looking for more. Saw quantities of the very tame game, and several steinbuck that thought themselves hidden, and which we passed within a few yards. At camp found another donkey dead. Two more died in the course of the afternoon. This makes thirteen, and one mule. Big thunder storm far to the north, in the mountains.

Morning, 54; noon, 90; night, 68. Men call this Campi ya Korongo (Roan Camp).

August 14.—Fine Japanese effect of flat acacias against the glow of the morning sky. Unfavourable reports from M'ganga as to water ahead, so cut back in the hills to the north, between a big round mountain and high rock outcrop. Passes low, and travelling open and very easy. *Loads* of game. This led us to a wide interior valley sweeping upward to the north between two low ranges, across which we angled toward the upper end where our glasses had disclosed a green spot that looked like water. About noon we found this to be a trickling little clear cold stream, with big trees. The trickle soon ran underground, leaving the country dry and parched, but it made us a shady, pleasant camp in which we resolved to stop for some days.

While waiting for the safari, Memba Sasa and I went on to find the source, and got a very fine sight of a magnificent black-maned lion. The wind was wrong, and he bounded into the thicket, but he was a beautiful creature.

Our camp was made in a shady grove. The donkeys came in very late and tired.

In the afternoon Cuninghame and I went upstream to the pass whence we looked down the length of another narrow valley, widening between the hills. It headed against ours, but on the other side of the low transverse range. Here at 120 yards I hit a Bohur doe low in the shoulder, and brought her down by a second, running, shot at 80. Then we made a high climb up the mountain to our left, and found at last a rounded grassy summit on which were many Chanler's reedbuck. These graceful, and generally shy, creatures, bounded all about us, stopping within a few yards, and uttering their high shrill whistles. East, north, and south were spread before us fine big tumbled hills and mountains, through the smoke of many grass fires. West extended a boundless plain, undulating and black with brush and fire. The sun struck in bars through the smoke, and the distance was lost in haze.

Got back to camp at dark to find it well stung by bees. An enterprising porter had found a bee tree too near, and had got everybody in trouble. After dark they went at it again and got a quantity of black, grubby honey.

Five hours; 10½ miles; elevation, 6,100; morning, 50; noon (?); night, 65.

August 15.—Sent men back to last camp to bring up *potio* loads we had been forced to leave. From the top of the mountain we had, the day before, seen a patch of green grass back among the hills. We went toward this. A very high wind blew. Going over a grassy shoulder of the hills, single file among some thickets, Cuninghame ahead, suddenly a bushbuck doe sprang out and stood sidewise forty yards away. Cuninghame dropped flat, his arms over his ears, and I, firing over him, put a .405 in her shoulder. Very hard animal to get, as they are mostly invisible in heavy cover. I have a buck and want a doe.

The green country on the slopes below the mountains we found inhabited by great herds of game, but extraordinarily wild. Through the thin growth of small trees with which all this country is sparsely covered we could see them disappearing at the mere first small glimpse of us. This puzzled us, but we gradually evolved the theory that game usually depend on *hearing* and *smell* rather than sight, but that when the two former senses are nullified by the wind, then they revert to the other. In fact they dashed off in exactly the headlong manner of game that has *winded* a man. This theory of the substitution of one sense for another was fully proved by the fact that next day, no wind blowing at all, we went back to the same place and found all the animals very tame. They could now revert for protection to their usual senses of smell and hearing, so that the mere sight of us did not alarm.

Zebra, impalla, topi, kongoni, waterbuck, and many Bohur reedbuck, Tommy, and Robertsi were there in numbers, but we saw little of them beyond the dust of their going. By extraordinary stalking I wounded a topi at 180 yards badly enough to cause him to turn off from the herds. While following him I had a most interesting experience. In a shady little grove without underbrush stood a reedbuck, a graceful pretty creature about the size of our California deer. His head was up and he was staring at me. My course led directly toward him. He did not move. Nearer and nearer I walked, bolt upright and in plain sight, expecting every minute he would bound away, until I was within five or six yards of him. Then, as he did not move, I quietly turned aside and *walked around him* about ten feet distant, and left him in his cool green shadow, still staring. And then, just a few yards farther on, I came across a family of sing-sing, some lying down, some standing. They, too, stared at me, in noble attitudes like a lot of Landseer's stags, until I was within thirty yards. Then I caught sight of my topi and fired at him across the sing-sing, and they vanished. All this was under the shelter of woods where there was no wind. Killed the topi at 200 yards.

After that we spent a long time trying to get near enough to a topi herd to procure one or more of the four we needed, but in vain. Finally after the fifth hard stalk I took a couple of shots at them running at about 200 yards, but missed. Also failed at a sing-sing doe at about 300. Again owing to high wind. We then started back to camp. When two miles from there ran across a few topi stragglers. These animals, so universally visible in the open, became almost invisible in the bush, even at short range and to the gun-bearers. Where *never* molested, as in this country, *both* topi and zebra are mostly found in the light brush. They come out into the plains only occasionally, as do impalla.

These topi were travelling somewhere. We cut in ahead of them and then sat down to let them get near us. Killed one dead in its tracks at 148 yards, and another, ditto, at 237. Left all men to bring in skins and meat and hurried toward camp to lay out a kill for Mr. Blackmane. It was now near five o'clock and we hoped to find some animals near the water. Sure enough, a herd of topi and kongoni were there. Crawled on my belly 100 yards in burned grass, emerging like a chimney sweep, and put a bullet in a topi's shoulder at 160 yards. He gave a bound past a small bush and out the other side. Dropped him with another shot, and found I had *two* topi. The first had fallen dead behind the bush, and the second had been standing there and leaped out as the first went down. Left one for lion bait, and whistled men out from camp to carry in other. This made us rather more meat in hand than we needed for immediate consumption, so we set every one to making jerky. New one on them, but it came out excellently, and we have ever since kept a piece or so about us to chew on. Makes a fine emergency lunch.*

In the evening driver ants started to march through camp. When driver ants start to go anywhere everything else has to stand aside. They are said to eat everything but tin. We headed them off with a line of hot ashes, and then laid a thick barrier of more hot ashes around them, leaving an appropriate exit in the other direction. Dolo got down on his hands and knees, shut his eyes, and was led by another man back and forth all around the donkeys. He carried grass on his head, muttered charms, and when he had finished claimed that his beasts were now quite safe from the *chop*. A donkey died in the night, and we heard leopards about.

Morning, 58; night, 56.

August 16.—Nothing doing at our lion kill. After examining it we went on to the green patch again where our wind theory for wildness was well worked out. Ran against a fine bull eland and killed him with one heart shot from the Springfield. He was a very fine trophy, but was otherwise an unfortu-

---

* This supply of jerky lasted us through the whole trip and into the elephant country. I do not know why sportsmen do not use more of it.

nate old warrior. He had one blind eye, carried a
healed broken jaw, and had lost the end of his tail!
The skin on the back of his neck was two and one
quarter inches thick! While the men were attending
to the trophy, and pending arrival of meat porters, I
took fine close-range pictures of topi and kongoni.
Back to camp by noon.

Late in the afternoon Cuninghame and I went out
to lay poison for leopards and I had the luck to knock
a Bohur at 120 yards with the .405. Feasted high.
Eland tongue is a real delicacy. Two more men sick.

Morning, 55; noon, 78; night, 58.

August 17.—Took a parting look at the lion bait and
then set off over the low pass into the other valley.
Left Dolo, the donkeys, and the sick men. Instructed
them to go back to Windy Camp, where, be it remembered, some time ago we left two sick men, two
sick donkeys, and twelve loads—and to bring up the
lot. We left Dolo six men as help.

Down the slope of the valley beyond the pass the
grass was very high and wearisome, and (in spite of
soot) we were glad the country behind us had been
burned. Many reedbuck leaped from their beds and
bounded away, showing only heads and horns. Then
Cuninghame saw a big roan standing in the shadow
of a little thicket. He was 208 yards away, but by
luck I managed to centre his shoulder offhand. Ran
into the thicket. Found him there, and brought

him down at close range as he dodged through the bushes. Fine prize, and a big one. He had been wounded by a Wanderobo arrow in the neck, and the wound had suppurated so badly that we were afraid to use the meat.

Farther down the valley in burned country again we struck buffalo spoor. Told the men to turn sharp to the left up the slope of the mountain to where some green trees indicated water. There they were to pitch camp. Meanwhile, we tracked the buffalo some miles across the burned area and into the thicket, only to have a fitful wind whip around on us at the last moment and send him off when we were within a few yards of him. Returned to find safari camped at a pretty green spring high up on the the slope of the hill, with clear water, green trees, and a far outlook. Rained a little. Heard lions.

Morning, 58; noon, 85; night, 68.

August 18.—All the scrub and small trees hereabout are full of small green parrots that chatter and scream and fly about; and monkeys; and brilliant plaintain eaters, the most gorgeous of created birds.

We started at 6:15 and marched across a sort of opening from our interior valleys through the border mountains that led to the open plains. Across this mouth was a hill corresponding with the one we had left at our last night's camp. About three miles out we crossed a dry stream bed with tall trees and ferns, and advanced beyond it over a burning. Two animals stood side by side on the black soil among the bushes. Glasses discovered them to be roan. I sneaked as near as I could and dropped the first in his tracks as though he had been struck by lightning. The other ran, but stopped an instant to look back, and him, too, I knocked down in the same manner. Distances 252 and 347 yards. Cuninghame and two men remained to attend to these, while I skirted the hill, about halfway up; for these were all buck, and I now much wanted a doe to complete my collection. A half mile farther on I saw below me a herd, and counted nineteen. This is assuredly the greatest roan country in Africa. At 260 yards I knocked my doe out with one shot.

We camped near where I had shot the first two, in a grove of great green trees with a spring of clear water, and the hills behind us and the plains before. Late in the afternoon when the sun was low I strolled among the lovely high green trees and enjoyed the ibises, the many reedbuck—and the rhino!

Morning, 57; noon, 72; night, 64. Sent back men for extra loads left at the camp two days back.

August 19.—Went very early along the edge of the watercourse in the hope that a bushbuck might stray out beyond his cover. Luck was with me, for I ran on two so busily fighting each other that I dropped them both at forty-five yards. Great prizes. Luck is with us here.

Returned to camp and we had a serious talk over our situation. Our transport is seriously crippled. So many donkeys have died that we are now quite unable to move forward except by relaying. This condition is going to get worse instead of better, unless we are willing to abandon a portion of our valuable equipment or some of our trophies; neither of which we want to do. Each defunct donkey leaves behind him not only the two loads he has been carrying, but also his saddle, pack-sacks, and two sheepskins that have been in use as his saddle blankets. The Wasonzi told us that at the old slave-trading post of Ikoma, now a German government post, some distance to the south, we could buy any amount of donkeys. They said that there are Indian trading stores also.

After discussing the situation thoroughly it was agreed that Cuninghame should take a very small safari and strike directly south until he cut the track from Arusha to Ikoma. At Ikoma he was to mail letters; get information as to lake transportation, elephants, buffalo, etc; copy or procure whatever maps the officials might have; get some *potio;* and buy some necessaries and a few luxuries to celebrate on, a list of which we promptly made out. In the meantime I was to proceed slowly in a generally northwesterly direction, searching out routes and water. When, in the course of time, I found likely game fields or other items of interest, I was to camp. At the present camp

—where we now were—we could leave two men and all spare loads. They were to stay here until Dolo and his outfit returned and until Cuninghame got back from his recruiting expedition. As soon as I knew where my permanent camp was to be, I was to send back here as many men as I could spare. These would at once serve as guides and as help in moving forward the spare stores. Then the outfit was to join me at my "game camp." Cuninghame picked six men, Kongoni as gunbearer, Soli as personal boy and cook, and M'ganga as diplomat and chief interpreter. Dolo has six porters, Sulimani and the Toto on the trail. There are two sick men back at Windy Camp, and two are to be left here as keepers. That leaves me fourteen.

Since these hopes and plans are now fresh in the readers' minds, I will here insert Cuninghame's notes of his expedition. They are chronologically a bit misplaced, but they give a very vivid idea of the vicissitudes of African travel, the reliability of African information, and the uncertainty of African plans.

CHAPTER VIII

CUNINGHAME'S JOURNAL

LEFT Roan Camp at 7:00 A. M., August 20th, for supposed water near the Gaboti River, bearing 208°. Marched till 3:00 P. M. and struck the Gaboti River. Could never get two bearings off marks at one time. Country all trees and low lying—compass giving trouble, not working freely. Dumped men and hunted hard for water till 5:30. Found no game, no birds, and no sign of a spring. No rises to get a view from and bush hopeless. Returned to men and made for nearest point on Bololedi River. Men about tired out when I fetched up at river at 8:15 P. M. Found water and two lions. No camp made but lay down on the river bed with good fire and plenty food and water. Men marched twenty-four and three quarter miles, and Kongoni and I must have covered over thirty miles.

August 21.—Left Bololedi Camp 7:00 A. M., having previously determined my position (with a new compass) as about one mile downstream of the marked standing water. Set a course and knew I ought to cut the Ikoma track. Did so in half an hour, and having made certain it was the right path, held on to it. Marched two hours and only got one chance of taking any bearings anywhere. Soon after thought I could see with glasses Nalaro Rock. Took sights and found I was correct. Distance about twelve miles off. When near Gaboti standing water (estimated by watch as no bearing whatever obtainable) found a sort of dry reed bed, but no sign of Gaboti River, no game, no sign of standing water, and nothing but bush. Held on to track for three more hours, when suddenly saw Nalaro Rock about two miles ahead. A real hard country to steer through as you very rarely see anything but bush and trees. Passed Nalaro and made Londani River at 3:00 P. M., still on track. Found no standing water anywhere and started digging. Got a little water three feet down. Men very done up. Sun hot. Distance marched twenty-one miles. Am inclined to think Gaboti standing water is dry now, and that this water is only found two or three months a year. No game at all here but half a dozen Tommy.

August 22.—Stayed the day at Londani River. Men willing to go to the *boma* on the principle of the carrot in front of the donkey, but I decided to hunt for water in event of my having to bring donkeys back by this road. Found sufficient water in one hole under root of big tree and made it secure against game and cut a way down to it from the bank. Shot two male Granti* for meat. Saw large herd of wildebeeste on other side of river some four miles west so concluded there must be

* Robertsi (?).

plenty of water in holes down the river some miles. No game whatever near camp. Heard lions far distant last night. Blew half a gale from sunrise to 11 A. M.; after that clouded up, a cool wind started again 5:00 P. M. and blew all night.

August 23.—Marched twenty-eight miles and made Ikoma *boma* at 5:00 P. M. Found Londani River perfectly dry; had to dig for water. Only one official in residence, only two rotten *dukkas*,* one an Indian and one a Swahili. Found next to nothing in them, but *mericani* † and wire. Not a donkey ever heard of in the district! Sharp rain shower at 6:00 P. M. Turned in very disgusted with everything.

August 24 (Sunday).—Went and reported myself to the Fortress (!) at 11 A. M. Found the "gaoler" could speak quite fair English. Talked for quarter of an hour and then he suggested I should see him in the office at 1:30 on Monday, as he was very busy over nothing all Monday morning. I left, but sent him a note at 5:00 P. M. about porters, food, guides, etc., suggesting that he might get a move on in the morning by issuing the usual instructions to *askaris*. Got verbal message back: "To-morrow at 1:30 P. M." Felt rather amused over it all.

August 25.—Went up again at 1:30 P. M. and the guard refused admittance till 3:00 P. M., saying that the

---

* Shops.
† White cotton cloth.

bwana had issued orders he was going to sleep till 3:00 P. M. Sat down at front door till three, when bugles blew and nothing else happened. Saw my man at 3:25 in his office. Gave him the correspondence,* which he read, carefully returned to me, and said never a word. Found he had not acted on my letter to him *re* porters and food for guides. Got him to give the necessary orders at once. Porters (fifteen) certainly available; food *very* scarce owing to failure of last year's rains; Wanderobo guides most unlikely to procure, and if obtained would bolt in a day or so. After I left him I got M'ganga to go and hunt the *askari*, who was sent for the derobo, and promise him 10 Rs if he brought me two derobo by to-morrow night.

Maps unknown here. The office had only one traced map of very poor character on the district only. No maps procurable at Shirati, Mwansa, or Arusha. The only way to get any is to apply to Daressalaam. We must make a copy at Shirati if possible.

Mail and post. Stamps unknown here. No regular mail service. Officer sends his mail when he likes to Mwansa and will accept ours at our risk. Will give them to-morrow. Mail to be sent off in six days and occupy six days to reach Mwansa.

Steamer time-table.† Nothing known about sailings. Says that the dates are continually being altered. (This

---

* Letters from Berlin, etc., instructing all officials to aid us.
† Victoria Nyanza.

cannot be so.) There are two steamers arriving each month at Shirati! One from Kisumu from the north, and the other from Mwansa (the south); dates unknown. Lake steamers call at the new port Musoma, three days south of Shirati.

Supplies at Arusha. Believed to be good for native *posho*, as there is a big population around. Condition of European supplies unknown. Supplies at Amala River district unknown, but *posho* probably procurable, as natives plentiful up to four or five days east of Shirati.

Big game license. *Not* obtainable at Shirati, but only at Mwansa and Daressalaam. We may be able to arrange this by deposit at Shirati. There is no telegraph or cable there.

Elephant, Buffs, etc. As the officer never shoots any game at all, he knew nothing whatever about it, not even the names. Local niggers report elephant somewhere in Ungruimi country south and north of Amala River. M'ganga has the information.

Fly areas. All along the Amala River cattle fly and sleeping sickness fly, but *G. palpalis* not supposed to be badly infected. Risk for safari very slight indeed. Risk for animals considerable. Tsetse fly around Ikoma recently and seems to be arriving from nowhere and spreading everywhere all along the northern boundary districts; hence scores of Masai and local native stock is beginning to die (in odd places) all over the country. All this is quite recent and nothing much is known about it scientifically. The only area known to be perfectly free is the Serengetti Plains.

Donkeys. Unknown here. At Shirati a few at 80 Rs and over. Plenty at Iramba province, near Galano Boma. This place is about ten days south of Ikoma and three days south of Mwansa, and it would take about ten days to buy ten donkeys from local chiefs at 15 to 20 Rs per ass.

Musoma (see small map) is a new deepwater steamer port of eight months old. Going to be *the* port of the future, and already many stores and one European *dukka* is established.* *All* European safari requirements reported to be had there.† One official in charge. Mosquitoes very bad there. Kisumu steamers calling there after Shirati and Mwansa regularly.

Spears. Very few and the poorest quality; only saw three.

Porters. Wages at rate of 17 cents‡ per day or 5 Rs per month, with *posho* daily extra. No blankets or kit whatever. Wanderobo wages at rate of 20 per day —or as per arrangement.

August 26.—Porters arrived; only three loads food *posho*, which is all that can be obtained, which same is most unfortunate, but this district is really most im-

---

*These glowing accounts proved to be considerably modified by facts. See p. 250.

† Untrue at that time.

‡ 5⅔ cents our money.

poverished owing to failure of last year's rains.   At
5:30 two Wanderobo arrived and I questioned them
closely, but could not get much out of them.   M'ganga
said that I had better not say too much, but get them
off on safari and then make a *shauri* as to their accom-
plishments.   Sent the mail to the *boma*, and the German thought that N. T's. letter would not reach
Nairobi *till September 20th*.   Dine in the Fortress to-
night at seven o'clock.

Officer's name Lieut. G. Giehrl.   Clear out tomorrow without fail.

August 27.—Started at 6:30 A. M. and marched sixteen miles to camp marked on map with two Wanderobo as guides.   Camped at their kraal and found it two
miles from any water, which water was in holes in the
Grumenti River.   On the march met the deputy
Wanderobo chief and he said that we had inexperienced
guides (as I quite well thought) and that we were to
ask for better ones, and if we did not get them to wait
till he got back early to-morrow morning when he
would try and fix up a good *shauri*.   Found it useless
to try and improve on the two men I have already,
so after two hours' talk decided to march to Barakupess water to-morrow.

August 28.—Started at 6:00 A. M. and marched
nineteen miles to water near Barakupess.   Hardly any
game except a few topi.   Shot one near water for
meat.   Difficult water to locate, and I have not yet got

a sight of the two Barakupess hills, though they can't be five miles off.   Intend striking due east for Dolo's camp to-morrow.   Derobo seem to know this country like a book and showed me two waterholes on the march.

August 29.—Started at 6:00 A.M. and marched twenty miles to Dolo's camp.   Map all in error for the last two and a half days.   Saw lots of wildebeeste and topi three hours from camp.   Shot one topi at camp.   Found Dolo and eight donkeys alive.   Received S.E.W's two letters, and shall start off again to-morrow on his track.   Hope to just manage to carry *everything* off.

CHAPTER IX

AUGUST 20.—Cuninghame and I parted company at daybreak. I set out by compass, bearing for a river called the Bologonja, described by savages as running. Went for miles over rolling burnt-out desert on which roamed a few kongoni and eland. Then saw the green trees of my river, walked two miles more—and found myself in a paradise.

For three miles we continued on down the river outside the tall trees that constituted its jungle. Then we saw three lions, but they got the wind of the safari and decamped. I chased them a half mile, but nearly ruined my ex-broken ankle, and had to stop from sheer pain. Then we turned aside and made camp.

It is hard to do that country justice. From the river it rolls away in gentle, low-sloping hills as green as emeralds, beneath trees spaced as in a park. One could see as far as the limits of the horizon, and yet everywhere were these trees, singly, in little open groves; and the grass was the greenest green, and short and thick as though cut and rolled; and in the broad hollows were open parks.

The Bologonja was indeed a clear stream, running over pebbles and little rocks, shadowed by a lofty, vine-hung jungle of darkness, coolness, little gray monkeys, and brilliant birds. When we had pitched our tents inside this jungle we found ourselves in a green room full of charming, intimate voices. No hint of the fierceness of the equatorial sun reached us. Yet twenty steps brought us into the open where we could see the rolling green hills with their scattered little trees, and distant mountains here and there to the north, and the high, noble arch of the cloudless African sky in which the sun burned all day long unobscured. And then twenty steps back again to the stream—running water in a land of little choked springs, of rare green slimy pools, of rock pockets fouled by game, and of long leagues of unmodified, unmitigated thirst; crystal clear water in a land of silt where from year's end to year's end one never hopes to see the bottom of his drinking cup for the mud! Just to sit under the palm leaves where the breeze sounded like on-coming rain, watching the shimmer and refraction and shifting of the waters, was a marvel and a joy. March on four days more, perhaps away from this stream? Not any! This was good enough for us!

In the afternoon I strolled over the fine green hills and revelled in the sight of the game—black herds of wildebeeste, like bison in the park openings, topi everywhere, zebra, hartebeeste, Tommy, oribi, steinbuck, impalla, reedbuck, and others. Out of the lot

I picked a kongoni at 237 yards after missing one at 180, buck and doe oribi at 50 and 120 yards, and a wildebeeste at 353 yards.

Never have I seen anything like that game. It covered every hill, standing in the openings, strolling in and out among the groves, feeding on the bottom lands, singly, or in little groups. It did not matter in what direction I looked, there it was; as abundant one place as another. Nor did it matter how far I went, over how many hills I walked, how many wide prospects I examined, it was always the same. During my stay at the next two camps I looked over fifty square miles. One day I counted 4,628 head! And suddenly I realized again that in this beautiful, wide, populous country, no sportsman's rifle has ever been fired. It is a virgin game country, and I have been the last man who will ever discover one for the sportsmen of the world. There is no other available possibility for such a game field in Africa unexplored. I moved among those hordes of unsophisticated beasts as a lord of Eden would have moved.

But to get back to the day: the animals were on this afternoon a little curious and a little shy. At moments they were as tame as cattle, again they were as wild as horses in pasture. In some circumstances the most conspicuously marked animals seemed quite invisible; and in others the most craftily neutral tinted stood out as plainly as striped banners in a breeze. At times the mere sight of the crown of a helmet over a bush would send them flying with a thunder of hoofs that fairly made the earth tremble, again, I actually had several hundred animals trek solemnly toward the sound of my rifle to investigate for themselves what it was all about! Most of the time they hardly looked up from grazing when they were not *too* near.

Four hours; 9 miles; elevation, 5,200; morning, 64; noon, 80; night, 73.

August 21.—Heard wild dogs in the night. I got up in the black night, ate my solitary breakfast by the flicker of a fire, and then, just as the first milky gray was seeping into the darkness, I started out for a walk. The ground was not to be seen at all, nor the objects near the ground, only the tops of trees like ghosts. We stumbled and moved slowly, feeling our way. All about us we could hear beasts snorting at us, like mettlesome horses stamping on the earth; or perhaps we heard the short swift rush of them as they dashed away. Only when they moved could we see them, phantoms, bits of the same dim substance of all the rest of the world. They were puzzled at us, and curious, and very near.

And all the time the flames were spreading in the sky, the fierce, hot red and copper and orange flames of the African sunrise. They reflected on the earth. We could see a little better, guess a little more. Then

CONSTRUCTING ONE OF THE STOREHOUSES OR "CACHES" IN WHICH WE
HAD TO LEAVE OUR SURPLUS GOODS

ONE OF OUR STOREHOUSES OR "CACHES" COMPLETED

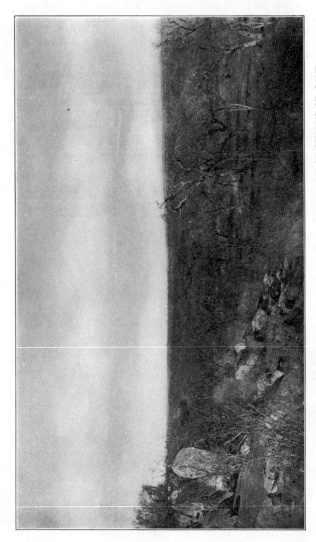

TYPICAL COUNTRY SOUTH OF THE BOLOGONJA RIVER.   THE HAUNT OF SWARMS OF GAME

all at once some dilatory god threw over the switch, and it was light!

Never shall I become accustomed to the magic of this phenomenon. Whenever anybody, white or black, happens to be near me, I remark upon it to him; and generally gain slight response.

Went first to look at the lion kill (nothing), and then up the small bushy ravines on the chance of seeing his lordship. Found where he had killed an eland with twenty-four inch horns. Saw sign of greater kudu.

The country rolled away before us in wave after wave of low, sparsely wooded green hills. The shallow valleys between were without trees, and grassy as so many cultivated parks. The eye followed them a mile or so, to come to rest on the low slopes of more hills, covered scatteringly with more little trees. In the bottom lands were compact black herds of wildebeeste, grazing in close formation, like bison in a park, and around and between them small groups of topi and zebra—two or three, eight or a dozen—moving here and there, furnishing the life and grace to the picture of which the wildebeeste were the dignity and the power. And every once in a while, at the edge of a thicket, my eye caught the bright sheen of impalla, or in the middle distance the body stripes of gazelle, or close down in the grass the charming miniature steinbuck or oribi. These were the beasts, of course, we were certain always to see; our daily familiar friends, the crowds on the street attending to the affairs of the veldt. And as we wandered farther up the valley, or along the bordering ridges, we could see also in all directions down through the trees other scattered animals who had not joined the crowds in the valleys, hundreds and hundreds of them.

In a little open flat I found a Tommy (very few of them here) with a fine head, so I dropped him at 157 yards. His horns proved to be fifteen and three eighths inches (good ones in British East Africa about thirteen inches). At the sound of the shot a lot of game across the valley decided to come over and see us, which they did, single file, and at a dignified pace. They filed by, 400 to 500 yards away. There were fifty-two eland (how's that for a sight?) accompanied by about one hundred zebra, a few topi, and kongoni, and eighteen wildebeeste.

Then I returned to camp and rested until two o'clock, when I took a different direction over the hills, and to my wonder found the game as continuously abundant there. From the tops of the swells it was particularly pretty to look over the tops of the trees to the green flats like courts, and the wildebeeste grazing on them.

At this time we run across a great multitude of game returning from a waterhole. The fact would be evident enough to any one within earshot. A great chorus of zebra barkings, persistent, shrill, over-power-ing, led one to the right spot.   Then we saw the long procession of the beasts returning from the water to their accustomed businesses.   The great majority of them plodded along the trail single file, adhering strictly to the path, looking neither to right nor left, being soberly respectable as suits the average middle age of any body politic.   But alongside capered the youngsters, kicking up their heels, racing back and forth, biting at each other.   And always they were aided and abetted and urged on by those striped clowns— the zebras.   Rank after rank, they went by, each with his kind—the wildebeeste, the hartebeeste, the many topi, the eland, the impalla, and all the little flanking gazelles—and so over the rise of the next hill.   Each as he topped the ridge against the western sky stood out sharp-cut, a silhouetted miniature, then dipped down the other side out of sight.   From the direction of the waterhole rose lazily a great cloud of dust where yet other hundreds of beasts were awaiting their turn, or rolling luxuriously after their thirst had been assuaged.

Then we followed over the rise, to witness the gradual fanning out of the procession.   A little group dropped off to right or to left, and fell to grazing. Others kept on over yet more distant hills.   Within the half hour the great herd had broken into hundreds of little groups, scattered over many miles, and count-less hills and valleys.   Again the green lawns were covered with the black wildebeeste.

It was now time to turn home. The sun was low and the shadows long. It is not well to be out in the first dark of Africa. The nightfall is hungry and dangerous; though the dawn is fed and safe. And when the sun dips below the horizon, darkness comes as the dawn comes, swift and sharp as the fall of a sword.

Here under the equator the sun keeps very regular hours. The difference between his rising or setting times in summer and winter is only about twenty minutes. One can count on about six o'clock, morning or evening, for those performances. It is very handy. One does not have to estimate the sun as "an hour high"; he simply looks at his watch and *knows* it is an hour high. That is fairly important when one wants to know when to turn campward.

Very reluctant to break up this peaceful scene, I killed a topi at 243 yards for ourselves, and one at 208 yards to send back to Dolo when I dispatch my relay to-morrow. Then Memba Sasa and I circled to cut the stream some distance below camp. Near the river the trees are thicker on the hill. Here we caught a glimpse of sing-sing. Did some very careful slow stalking and got within 150 yards all right. Difficulty was to make them out, and to get a shot through the thick stuff even then. I had to wait nearly half an hour before I made out the buck's shoulder clear enough to shoot. Dropped him in his tracks at 160 yards. The herd crashed away, of course, but one doe paused to look

back, and I got her at 215 yards.   This made my pair.
Hiked back along the river and sent out men hastily,
for it was now near dark.

Saw little game, and *no game trails going to the water*
at the river!   So there must be water out on the plains.
Many grouse, however, and some green parrots and
gray monkeys.   A Baganda man, named Maliyabwana
("the white man's money"), brought in a long string
of fish.

Morning, 63; noon, 73; night, 70.

August 22.—Last night Memba Sasa reported with
slight fever.   Gave him quinine, and told him to lie by
to-day.   Instructed Ali to pick me out a porter to visit
lion kills with me, and added, "one who will not run
away."   Overheard the following:

Ali: "You will carry the *bwana's* other gun.   If you
run away you will get *kiboko;* if you do not run away
you will get three rupees.   If the lion makes *kalele*, do
not run away; the *bwana* will kill him.   If the lion runs
at you, do not run away; the *bwana* will kill him.   The
bwana has killed many lions.   *Bass!"*

Sent back all the men but two to bring up a relay of
goods from the last camp—"Dolo's Camp."

I myself started for the lion bait just before daylight, shouting as I passed a command for the temporary gunbearer to follow.   I heard him behind me,
but did not look back at him for a mile or so.   Then,
behold!   It was Memba Sasa!

Of course I cussed him for disobeying orders, but he swore earnestly that he was all over his fever; felt strong.

"And perhaps that man will run away," he added. "Ali told him too many times not to get scared." Good psychology.

However, nothing doing at the kill. I crossed the river and toiled to the top of a high cone hill for the sake of compass bearings and a sight of the "lay of the land." I have a strong desire to strike south into the heart of the plains to see what I can see. Found Chanler's reedbuck up there, and roan at the base. The climbing was rather hard, consisting of loose round lava fragments partially concealed in the grass.

From the summit I could see pretty well in all directions. The north-and-south hills through which we had marched from Windy Camp and the Wasonzi were plainly visible far to the east. North were many hills and ranges. West, and very distant in the blue, I made out an escarpment—two or three days distant; the Mara River must run below that. Our own river, the Bologonja, flowed northwest in the general direction of the Mara; I could follow its course for some distance by the green forest line. That must be the direction of our marches when Cuninghame returns. It looked to me as though we might, farther down, cut loose from the Bologonja and across the triangle to hit the Mara lower down. But my chief interest was

to the south.   As far as I could see, the same type
of country persisted—rolling green, sparsely wooded
hills and shallow valleys.   The eye was stopped by a
sort of height-of-land ten or fifteen miles away—not
hills, but a higher rise of the rolling country.   A bold
outcrop of big rocks offered absolutely the only landmark; and as water was more likely to be among them
than anywhere else, I took their compass bearings, and
resolved to strike first of all for them.   Through the
glasses I saw thousands of head of game.

Returned to camp on the same side of the stream,
but saw comparatively little game there owing to the
state of the grass.   There were, however, a number of
topi, Bohur reedbuck, and impalla.   Got my needed
Bohur doe with the .405 at 107 yards.   Near camp
caught sight of a queer-looking black hump sticking out
of the tall grass.   When near, it suddenly unfolded into
a cock ostrich and departed.   We found twenty-eight
eggs.   Only a dozen or so were covered by the bird;
the rest were scattered out a few feet, as though they
had been kicked aside.   This is the slovenly habit of
the ostrich.   Took one egg, but it was bad; no omelette!

In the afternoon I took one porter and went out
with the intention of taking game pictures.   The sky
overcast, however, and the game had a fit of being wild.
Speaking of pictures, some time back I heard Ali ex-
plaining the camera to some *shenzis* as follows:

"The *bwana* looks in the box; and when he sees what he wants in the box, he makes it go *click-click;* and when he is at home and wants to see that thing again, he looks in the box and makes it go *click-click*, and there he sees that thing even though it is far away."

This is so good an explanation that I have adopted it. By letting savages see the image on the ground glass and then telling them this, I can get them to pose.

Found six good water-pools some miles "inland."

On our way home we jumped a buffalo cow with a calf a week or so old. She trotted away across the open hills, buffalo fashion, nose straight out, slowed down to baby's capacity as a traveller. Just as she began to calm down, she ran plump into Memba Sasa. Off she went again very frantic, and, as luck would have it, she tried to cross the stream at our camp ford! The whole camp boiled out to receive her. Poor old buff!

We spent the short evening each in his own fashion, I in my canvas chair smoking, staring into the soft darkness or the shifting flames; the men squatted on their heels around their tiny fires, eating quantities of meat and cornmeal, and chattering boisterously. Outside our little dome of light the night businesses of the veldt went forward. Only the most formidable or the most insignificant creatures raised their voices, except in alarm or warning. Lions roared; insects hummed and chirped. Out there in the dark was a different world from that in which we moved so freely during the daylight hours; a dangerous, tragic world. Next day we would find evidences of the fact. I have seen killed by lions the remains of every sort of creature except buffalo and rhinoceros. Lions are said occasionally to kill even buffalo, though rarely.

I had this evening a long camp-fire talk at the gun-bearers' fire. I tried to describe to them the different sorts of big game we have in America. It was very difficult to visualize for them such a creature as a grizzly bear; he was so entirely outside their experience. I should like to see the mental image my dilution through the Swahili left in their minds. In turn they told me of their own peoples, and their childhood, and the *bwanas* for whom they had carried weapons.

Morning, 61; noon, 73; night, 70.

August 23.—Off at the first gray of dawn before I could see about me. A very high wind came up soon after sunrise. In the hollows I found the game fairly tame, and spent much time sneaking close for pictures. Took a half hour to go 100 yards, an inch at a time, but was rewarded by some excellent photos. A beast much nearer the type of the true Neuman's hartebeeste* than that of the Naróssara country is found here. Thought we had him from British East Africa, but that must be a hybrid race. This is a smaller animal, so light in colour that he looks like a ghost, long legged, and

---

*The hartebeeste in B. E. A. is now described as a separate species called the Nakuru hartebeeste. Whether this can be referred to that species, or is something new, I am not quite certain. I shall hereafter call him Nakuru for convenience.

with quite a different head.   When in a herd with the ordinary Coke's hartebeeste he is easily distinguished. And believe me, he is shy!   Where everything else is tame he is most difficult to approach.   He evidently does not take anything for granted nor believe what other animals tell him.   Wariness is evidently the nature of the beast.

After taking my pictures I cautiously laid down the camera and dropped one at 242 yards.   He got to his feet, and I laid him down again.   Off went everybody, of course.   I held absolutely motionless, and, as often happens, many beasts did not locate me, and came circling back.   Among them were two Nakuru. I sat perfectly still for a long time, and at last they fed within range.   Missed first shot at 262 yards, but got into the shoulder before they went.   A raking shot finished.   Very much pleased with the acquisition of these specimens, I sent to camp for porters, and set about taking trophies.   While doing so three marabout showed up.   I fired three shots, and got two.   A herd of zebra ran over the hill ahead of the porters and stopped within fifty yards of me.   How they did go when they got my wind!

On the way to camp had the luck to find a small herd of Nakuru hartebeeste asleep behind cover, and actually got close-range pictures of this shy beast.

Spent the afternoon labelling specimens, writing, etc., as for some days my ankle has been so bad that I often have to stop and "writhe a bit." Made nine miles.

Morning, 60; noon, 79; night, 72.

August 24.—Having resolved to loaf, I ate breakfast by daylight for the first time on this trip. Did various small jobs until my relay safari came in from Dolo's Camp about eleven o'clock. Had them put down their loads and rest, with instructions to pack up in an hour's time and follow my blazes down river. Intended to move merely to a fresh camp at the base of the hill from which I had taken my bearings. They reported Dolo back at store. Four more donkeys and the other mule have died.

Marched three miles to foot of hill Memba Sasa and I climbed, and there camped in the river jungle, clearing ourselves a shady place for the purpose. I had just lain down for a rest when to me came one of the porters in great excitement; he had seen a leopard asleep. Grabbed the .405 and followed. Sneaked quietly through the green undergrowth and the thick green shadows. Finally, through the leaves, we saw below us, about forty yards away, a gliding, silent, spotted creature. I caught the tips of ears, and blazed away. Made a good shot through the brain and killed—a hyena! However, it was a fine one, and nobody could tell who the spots belonged to in that thick stuff, so we did not laugh much at the porter.

Then Memba Sasa and I went scouting. Killed

a zebra for lion bait at 230 yards with a shoulder and a raking shot. Saw quantities of game, as usual, in the same sort of country we had been hunting in, including *both* Nakuru and Coke's hartebeestes, separate and distinct, the former as wild as ever, the latter big, red, and curious, as usual.*   Killed one of each, took both heads, hung the meat in trees, and returned to camp. Coke's 105 yards; Nakuru in high grass at 130 yards; two shots, one miss, one hit.

About midnight a pack of baboons travelling along the course of the stream blundered into camp, and there *was* a fine row. Evenings rather dull and lonesome; no light to read and nobody to talk to. My Swahili† is now about as good as any one's, so I sit at the gunbearers' fire a good deal, and we all swap yarns.

This march 2¾ miles; elevation, 4,950; morning, 61; noon, 79; night, 73.

* Saw some apparently hybrids.

† Of course I mean the porters' crude Swahili, not the complicated coast language.

CHAPTER X

AUGUST 25.—Every book on African hunting, and every African hunter worthy of the name, will tell you that a lion will never in daylight attack a man unprovoked. There is no blither warrior than the lion when he is given due cause to fight. You can stop or turn a charging elephant, a charging buffalo, or a charging rhinoceros by pounding him hard enough; but not a charging lion. If he once starts for you, you must kill him. Furthermore, a comparatively slight annoyance will sometimes cause him to charge; you don't need to wound him. But unprovoked and out of hunting hours he is supposed to be a peaceful citizen. To-day I had one experience that apparently was an exception. I struck out to the southeast, merely because, from the top of the kopje, beside the big distant rocks, we had seen some smaller outcrops striking up above the bush only four or five miles away. They looked nearer— from the top of the kopje. When we came to walk the distance, we found it considerably more than we had anticipated. Down the long gentle slope of the hills, across the valley, up the long gentle slope on the other side, and so repeat. In each valley and on every incline we found game. In one little burned patch a steinbuck lay crouched down close, its ears folded back just like those of a dog that considers himself especially virtuous.   In grass the little antelope would bave been perfectly concealed.   Evidently it considered the fact that the grass had been burned as an extraneous detail for which it could in no manner be held responsible, for it held its position as rigidly as though it had been completely hidden.   As a matter of fact it was in plain sight.   To such lengths will habit carry the conventional-minded!

We reached and examined the rocky outcrop.   Then quite idly we turned down the valley in which we stood.   Along the centre of the valley ran a shallow dry watercourse in the bottom of which grew various sorts of brush.   This brush strip varied in width from nothing to 100 feet.   Memba Sasa and I took one side of it, while Sanguiki and the two carriers took the other.   We had no very definite ideas.

For it is great fun quietly thus to follow one of these little brushy ravines.   You never know what will pop out next.   It is no good to raise a row and yell and throw stones.   If you do that, everything gets out far ahead.   But if you just sneak quietly along, perhaps occasionally tossing a pebble into the likely looking thick places, you will have lots of fun.   In the first place, a cloud of little birds are always rising, strange little birds, with only the satiny sound of rushing wings in common.   Some of them are brown and sober-minded, and some of them—the various sun-birds especially—are the gaudiest and most glittering of created beings outside the insect world. Some have tails three or four times their own length, and some have no tails at all. Near water-pools they are incredibly numerous, so that the aggregate of their tiny weights bends down quite good-sized saplings. Some have a good deal to say about the situation and some are disdainfully silent.

Beside these little fellows are many larger birds. Grouse whirr away, or rocket high; guinea fowl, consulting each other anxiously in clucking undertones, dodge ahead; hornbills swoop aloft; little green parrots buzz about in a sort of cinematograph fashion; an occasional profane ibis—profane in language though "sacred" by name—flops off with a string of oaths.

Gray or green little monkeys gallop away ahead, or clamber up things to take a look. Baboons bark hoarsely, run a little way, climb up something, shake the foliage violently, and disappear. The souls of aviators awaiting human incarnation buzz aloft on the tiny aeroplane-like bodies of huge beetles. Butterflies like flowers cling to the tiny twigs of bushes; and flowers like butterflies seem always on the point of flight.

And of animals there is no end. Some tiny antelope—a dik-dik, an oribi, a steinbuck, a bushbuck—is always scrambling madly away from fairly beneath one's feet only to dive headlong into another bit of cover where it hopes for better luck at remaining concealed. And occasionally some mighty crash brings one up all standing, every muscle taut, every sense alert. Then, if all is silent, comes maneuvering, cautious reconnoitering, a scouting for a sight either of the beast or his tracks. Or, if the crashes continue, a scurrying to and fro for a point of vantage and reasonable safety. Probably it is an old rhinoceros disturbed at his nap, or a stray buffalo. If you are hunting neither of these creatures—and we are not—your whole desire is to avoid an encounter. To do this, however, means no unwise policy of concealment. It is well to see your beast as soon as possible in order to know how to pay due respect to his choice of routes.

One practical word of advice: when engaged in this harmless and pleasing pastime, do not carry your lightest gun in your hand. If anything unexpected happens, it is well to have your heaviest armament where it is handiest. For that reason I was carrying the .405.

We wandered along down this valley for two or three miles; and were just beginning to think the sun hot, when we came to a slight widening of the brush patches. Sanguiki and his men were out of sight across the ravine. Memba Sasa had angled fifteen or twenty feet to the left with the purpose of looking down a hole. Suddenly I heard to my right a tearing scramble and crashing of small brush.

TYPICAL HUNTING COUNTRY IN THE NEW REGION

WHERE THE BIG LION POPPED UP IN MY FACE—TAKEN FROM THE SPOT
WHERE I THEN STOOD

SEE PAGE 133

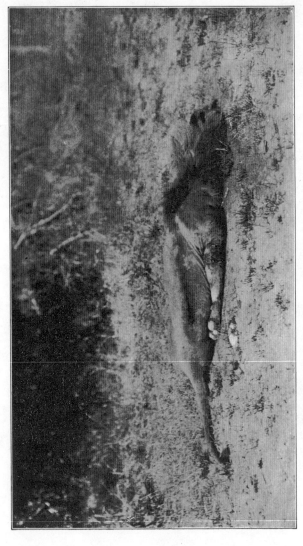

THIS LION WAS KILLED STONE DEAD WHILE IN FULL CHARGE. HIS ATTITUDE SHOWS WELL THE SPEED AT WHICH HE WAS GOING

So vigorous was this crashing that I thought it must be either a buffalo or a rhinoceros. The banks of the ravine immediately at hand were almost perpendicular and perhaps eight or ten feet high; but both upstream and downstream, and about twenty yards apart, game trails had been worn to a good grade. I ran directly for a point midway between these game trails. My thought was that from this vantage I would be able to see the beast whether it continued in the bed of the ravine, or whether it climbed out by either of the trails. This looked like a safe plan, for no rhinoceros or buffalo would attempt to scale that steep bank.

A big maned lion leaped to the top of the bank right in my face!

I was just four yards from him. In the fraction of an instant that he paused to assure his balance I recovered from the shock of surprise, swung the bead of my .405 on him, and pulled the trigger. It would be exceedingly interesting to know just the actual lapse of time between the appearance of the lion and the first shot. In reality it must have been exceedingly short, for the beast was caught between the landing from his leap and his spring; he indubitably intended to attack, knew just where we were, and was out to make a fight of it. Yet I apparently had time to notice a great many little details, such as the fact that the lion had an unusually fine mane; that the mane was so erect between the ears as almost to point forward; that his eyes looked round rather than elliptical. Later Memba Sasa told me:

"I said, 'Will the *bwana* never shoot!'"

Nevertheless, before the lion had even tensed his muscles for the next effort that would land him on me, the first bullet took him. It was an exceedingly interesting example of how rapidly *and comprehensively* the human mind works under excitement.

The .405 Winchester delivers a blow of about 3,300 foot-pounds; and this animal was so near that the velocity was in no way diminished by air resistance. The largest buffalo I ever saw was knocked right off his feet by a shoulder shot from it.* This lion did not lose his balance, but the force of the blow thrust him sidewise as a paper box is blown by a violent gust of wind. That he was not knocked flat seems to me remarkable. Perhaps the highly organized nervous system of the cat responded instantaneously so that the muscles reacted unconsciously and at once. I yanked the lever of my rifle down and back and put in another. The bullet entered just two inches from the first. I was shooting for the heart; the head shot on a lion is always uncertain.

This second shot again thrust him back so far that he toppled over the edge of the bank and down into the ravine.

I ran to the edge. He had recovered himself and

---

* He didn't stay down!

was again scrambling up the steep side, growling horribly. My third shot broke his foreleg. Steadying, I raked him from end to end. He rolled over on his side still growling and roaring, biting the ground. I watched him closely for further trouble, but after a moment he died. Memba Sasa was standing close to my left elbow, the Springfield cocked, five .405 cartridges spread ready fanwise in his left hand.

There succeeded the brief dead pause that always seems to follow a lion row. Then we shouted. The cry was instantly answered by Sanguiki and his men. They had probably been standing with held breath awaiting the first definite indication of how the fight was going. Certainly there must have been enough to listen to, what with the repeated detonations of the heavy gun and the snarls and growls of the lion.

We tried to carry the dead lion into the shade, but were unable to lift him. Therefore we constructed a shelter of boughs. A lion's skin is a tricky affair, and must be handled immediately and carefully. He was a magnificent creature with a thick long black and tawny mane, better than any other wild lion I ever saw, and almost equal to a menagerie beast.* Never expected to get anything so good. Stood three feet seven inches at shoulder; nine feet three inches straight

---

* In mane. In physique a wild lion is almost always bigger than a menagerie lion.

line measurement in length. Very heavy beast, must have gone well up between 500 and 700 pounds.

Then Memba Sasa and I began to figure over the incident. A wounded lion, or a cornered lion, or even a lion that has been followed until he has become annoyed, will attack practically every time. But what had induced this old fool to pop out at us so savagely? We were walking along attending to our own business, which had nothing to do with him. In my African experiences I have, up to now, seen 103 wild lions; and Memba Sasa has, of course, seen many more; but this was the first instance of its kind for either of us. So interested did we get that we determined to back-track the beast.

The trail led us immediately into a dense, low, shady thicket. Bending half over, we crawled cautiously in. A low snarl and the half-guessed yellow of a gliding body warned us that the bower—for it was a bower, a shady, pleasant, cool little arching bower—was already occupied. Crouching low, I peered as hard as I could, but did not succeed in getting another sight of the beast. We crawled in farther.

A dead zebra lay on its belly, all four legs stretched back. Evidently it had been dragged bodily by the head or neck. Think of the strength required for this feat! We examined it. Except for the marks of its killing, its skin was unbroken. A wide swath through the brush led us out of the thicket and fully

150 yards into the open. There the kill had been made.

"Memba Sasa," said I, "he did not attack without reason. He had a good reason. We spoiled a *n'gnoma* (party). He had here his meat and his *bibi* (woman), and he did not intend to be disturbed."

So, after all, even this was not a case of a lion's attacking entirely unprovoked! We left the carcass of the zebra as bait for the lioness.

Near home, just before we dipped to cross the stream to camp, Memba Sasa let out a peculiar sort of howl. Before we had gone 200 feet every man in camp was there, most of them with their faces whitened, dancing wildly the lion dance. It was quick work.

Spent the afternoon caring for the trophy, paring it down, doping it with alum water, and finally stretching it in a huge frame, which we hoisted in a tree. Made a very mild joke, which lasted the camp some days. One of the Swahili porters was bragging that he liked any kind of meat, lion included. I knew him to be a Mohammedan.

"Very well," said I, "I will take you with me hereafter, and you can *hallala* the next lion." *

The crowd caught many fish. Walked 13 miles; morning, 58; noon, 84; night, 71. Call this mother's birthday lion.

---

*As is well known, the Moslem must *hallala*—cut the throat—of any animal he intends to eat while the beast is still living.

CHAPTER XI

AUGUST 26.—Returned early to the thicket. Had the lioness several times within a few yards, but could not get a sight of her. The zebra was pretty well eaten up. This in spite of the fact that the dead lion's carcass lay within eighty yards. Evidently conjugal affection did not go so far as to destroy appetite. Several hundred carrion birds sat around in neighbouring trees, but they had not yet ventured to the feast. I have many times noticed this peculiar action. The birds could clean up an ordinary carcass in five minutes, but will often leave a lion untouched for days, though they cannot bear to go away.

Then beat down the ravine for some distance, and cut across the hills home. At one place a herd of zebra departed over the hill. A spoiled child of a colt, not having seen us, refused to be hurried just because the elders chose to go off in such a hurry. Anxious mamma, at the top of the hill, uttered impatient and worried commands. He toddled along, his eyes half closed, his ears laid back crossly, replying every once in a while with a sulky, petulant bark. So busy was he in having his own way that I got within a few yards of him. And then how he flew! "Mamma was right after all!"

METHOD USED IN DRYING LION SKINS

MARABOUT STORK

A TYPICAL OSTRICH NEST. THE BIRD WAS ENGAGED IN COVERING ONLY
THE GROUP OF EGGS IN THE CENTRE. THE OTHERS WERE
APPARENTLY KICKED ASIDE AND LEFT TO ADDLE

Crossed the river high up and came to camp on the other side.   I found a little flat bordered by palms and the abrupt downslope of clay, where saline deposits had lured right out into the open that rather solitary and most invisible little creature; the Bohur reedbuck; so that I saw them, twenty-six of them, cropping and licking away like deer, each ostentatiously independent of the other in order to convince chance passers, like ourselves, that spite of this apparent herding, they had not abandoned their principles.   Had to stop and bandage my ankle in order to get on at all.   The thing is very painful and is turning black.   Hard to walk, but the country is too fascinating to permit any one with a wiggle left in him to stay in camp.

Reached camp at noon.   A slight rain came up, and we rigged a very funny shelter for the suspended lion skin out of everything waterproof we had.   About four went out for camp meat.   Soon got within range of topi across a ravine, and dropped two before they got away, 182 yards and 197 yards.   Swung around and again climbed the hill above camp in hopes of a Chanler's reedbuck doe, but did not get a shot at the two I saw.   Game very tame to-day.   Winds baffling and aggravating.

The men working on the skins are always fine to hear, one crooning a short falsetto solo, and the others chiming in with a swinging bass refrain, under their breaths, busily.

Twenty-one miles' walking; morning, 58; noon, 80; night, 72.

August 27.—Took tent without fly, cook load, bed and men's load, three men, without burden, and staff, and with this small safari struck nearly due south into the supposedly waterless country. Had waterbags, and plan was, if no water was found, to return next day.

For seven miles we continued in the same type of country, the ridges and rolling hills rising imperceptibly toward a sort of low system; and for seven miles the game continued as abundant as ever. Then came recent burning with only a few animals. I had laid my bearing for the outcrop of rocks seen from the camp hill. Got to this, and began to hunt for water. There seemed to be none in the immediate vicinity, but a mile distant, in a queer wide depression full of grass and with a conical rocky kopje in it, I at last found a tiny pool that a little digging turned into a spring. No shade and the water not very good, but we hung blankets over the tent and boiled the drinkables.

After a short rest I went out after the first necessity, some animal for meat. Missed a reedbuck twice, and then downed a topi with two shots at 212 and 127. Very high wind and hard to hold on. Left the men with the meat, and with the gunbearers pushed on as rapidly as possible to scout the game and water prospects to the southwest. We had a heap long walk, got down the next watershed and found a dry water-

MY RECONNAISANCE CAMP IN THE REGION SOUTH OF THE BOLOGONJA RIVER

SEE PAGE 141

ZEBRA, HARTEBEESTE, AND WILDEBEESTE IN THE NEW COUNTRY

ZEBRA, TOPI, AND WILDEBEESTE IN THE NEW COUNTRY

course.   Many game trails, but no fresh tracks and no
game but giraffe.   All waterholes drunk or evaporated
dry.   I presume the game ranges in here abundantly
right after the rains.   High wind, constantly shifting,
lost me a fine impalla head on the way home.   Hit him
and stalked him four times, but each time the wind
whipped behind me and finally I lost him in the bush
(number four to get away this trip).   Sun terrifically
hot.   It is evidently impossible, because of lack of
water, to do anything to the southwest.

In camp I found the meat-safe had been left.   In
this country of many blowflies, and where health is a
precarious matter at best, this is serious.   Called up Ali
and the cook, and settled conclusively on the latter as
the culprit.   Fined him 6 rupees.   Vast silence in camp all
evening.   Saw several tsetse; a strange place for them.

Nine hours; 23 miles; elevation, 5,200; morning, 62;
noon, 84; night, 68.

August 28.—Off at six o'clock to scout the southeast, in which direction we had heard lions roaring.
Laid out a zebra for bait and flagged him to keep off
the birds—167 yards.   Topped the ridge, and came into
a country of long, down-sloping, parallel billows, grown
thickly with small trees, green grass dongas in the
bottom.   Loads of game; as much as back at the river.
Found several waterholes over here, but all fouled by
the game.   Finally came to a dry stream whose bed
consisted of sheets of smooth rock and boulders.

Among these were several big reservoirs of good water in locations inaccessible to the game.   We followed it up for some miles.   Found some klip-springers.   There are no cliffs hereabouts for them to spring on, so the poor deluded beasties live down in the stream-bed and there leap "from crag to crag."   Came on one suddenly, and startled him so that he fell off into a pool and had to swim ashore.   Here also saw bushbuck and roan.   Giraffe numerous.

Swung back along the broad low crest of the height-of-land.   Game tame.   About 3:00 P. M. and to northeast of my landmark rocks found a lovely spring of clean, cold water with low palms, and blue lotus flowers, and flaxen high grass all around.   Some strata set knife-edge fashion prevented the game from getting at it.   This looked good, so I sat down and sent a man with instructions for Ali to pack up and move over here. While waiting I shot a Tommy for meat (about 100 yards), and took compass bearings to locate the water. Tsetse all along this ridge.   Saw rock hyraxes to-day and sing-sing.   Got interested in counting game, and made a tally of 4,628 head, all day, actual count. Beautiful, quiet, and peaceful sunset over the dark and illimitable plains.

Ten hours; 20¼ miles; morning, 58; noon, 85; night, 66.

August 29.—Spent all day scouting to eastward and southward.   Loads of game, and another water—duly

WILDEBEESTE

A MORNING NAP
SEE PAGE 143

HE STOPS IN CONTEMPLATION
SEE PAGE 144

HE DEPARTS
SEE PAGE 144

mapped.   Same character of country.   Killed a good
warthog on the run at sixty yards, and missed a good
impalla, just at noon, at about 100 yards.   Beat many
dongas and counted 1,539 head of game before nine
this morning.   Then quit: too much work.   Sun very
strong.   Determined this as a cracking game country;
mapped it carefully.   Easy to get lost, as the twist of
the country is peculiar, and there are no local landmarks.

Ten and a half hours; 24¾ miles; morning, 56; noon,
100; night (?).

August 30.—Got results on our lion bait—in the
shape of eleven hyenas and a leopard!   The latter
leaped into the top of a low tree—a fine silhouette
against a saffron dawn.   He looked at us, leaped down
again, and disappeared before I could get a shot.   The
hyenas were of all sorts—big, little, and medium; red,
gray, and brown.   They vanished sullenly, at the last
moment.

We then swung on a circle toward our base camp at
the foot of the hill.   Across the valley saw a rhino
browsing.   Slung the .405 over my shoulder, took the
camera, left the men squatted, and sneaked down on
him.   A little ravine lay between me and him, and I
took two at twenty-five yards across this.   Then I let
myself down into the ravine, raised myself with great
caution on the other side—and found myself so close to
him that I could not get him all in.   Waited patiently

until he moved to the next bush, and then got a fine portrait.   After this I tossed two very small pebbles toward him, not enough to alarm him, but sufficient to cause him to move on.   As soon as he was far enough away I climbed out of the ravine and slipped along after.   Dogged his footsteps for half a mile, dodging from bush to bush, and occasionally getting some new pose.*   At last he emerged on the open plain.   I whistled sharply.   Instantly he whirled and started toward me and I snapped the final film of the roll.   Deposited the camera quickly on the ground and gave him a careful shot in the outside of the shoulder.   No chance to dodge in the open, and I had no desire for him to close.   This turned him at about thirty yards and he went off with a slight flesh wound.

Nothing remarkable then happened until we were quite near camp.   Then I saw a lioness moving across a small flat of grass in the valley.   Hurried down there, but she had disappeared in a donga where I knew it would be useless to follow her.   However, I happened to glance to the right, and there was another loping slowly along about 125 yards away.   Opened fire with the Springfield and got in three beautiful shoulder shots you could cover with your hand.   This slowed her up.   A fourth shot, as she turned, just cut into her tail, saving a miss but doing no damage.   She then

---

* These pictures did not turn out as well as I had hoped owing to the fact that I had, because of the easterly wind, to take most of them toward an early morning light.

HE WANDERS STOLIDLY AWAY
SEE PAGE 144

JUST BEFORE THE RUSH
SEE PAGE 144

turned at bay in a small thicket. Followed her with usual precautions. She thrust her head up ten yards away, got two .405 bullets in the chest, and collapsed. Took lots of hitting this one. While the men skinned her I went outside and killed camp meat in the shape of a topi at 180 yards and another at 210. Just outside camp got a wildebeeste at 231 yards. Thus closed an eventful morning.

Had just finished lunch when in came Cuninghame. We *were* glad to see each other! Ikoma proved to have no donkeys, no Indian stores, no *potio*, no water except in holes, not even one nail! A single German official occupied a battlemented stone fort with three lines of barbed-wire defences. Cuninghame brought back fourteen naked savages as porters, and two Wanderobo as guides. The porters are Wakoma, well-formed, strong copper men, quite naked, with pleasant faces and a happy disposition. They carry their loads by means of shoulder straps made of bark. Why this does not cut their shoulders in two I am unable to say. Cuninghame and I sat in the shade and swapped news all the afternoon. He brought back one tin of butter and a few German cigars. We also took our first drink of whiskey by way of celebration.

Four hours; 13 miles; morning, 56; noon, 89; night, 72. Donkey safari also came in.

CHAPTER XII

AUGUST 31.—Took a walk with Cuninghame, who was very keen to see the real Nakuru hartebeeste in the flesh. We saw plenty of other game, but found our beasts only after a long walk, six of them, looking ghost-like and as though on stilts. As usual, they were very shy. Repeated stalks brought me only within long range. Here I wounded one. There followed a long chase over the hills and into the burned country—I slipping along under whatever cover there was, trying to keep concealed; and the hartebeeste always taking alarm just before the favourable moment. Missed three times at long range; then landed the animal stone dead at 411 yards. Tied my handkerchief to his horns and slipped after the others. They were at this point joined by a second lot of a dozen or more. Through the thin bush managed to get a doe at 200 yards, and another at 160. These three specimens were most interesting. The first buck was clear Nakuru, light in colour, long of leg, and small in body, with the long horn base and the converging points to the horns. The first doe was as plainly a hybrid with Coke's hartebeeste. The second doe was a good mate to the buck.

Of course I had long since lost track of Cuninghame

and the men. They could not begin to keep me in sight and at the same time remain concealed themselves. I attached pieces of paper to the horns of the specimens, blazed a way out of the scrub with my knife, and took up my back track. By means of a few rifle shots and much whistling we got together. The sun was now high and hot. After measuring and comparing to our hearts' content, we skinned the trophies, divided the meat, and returned to camp. Our "little stroll" had turned out to be fifteen miles of hard, fast going!

Another donkey had died. Reorganized packs. Out late to look for marabout at our lion kill (two and a half miles more), but found none. Saw some bushbuck.

In the evening M'ganga was evidently a great social success with the Wakoma, as he elicited shouts of laughter from their campfire. M'ganga is quite a wonder as a linguist. He talks fluently Swahili, Masai, Monumwezi, Wakamba, Wasonzi, Wakoma, and Ungruimi. Our two wild men, the Wanderobo, got restless, as they generally do, and wanted to go. We gave them permission—if they cared to do so without wages. They promptly departed into the howling wilderness without food, and most certainly without clothes.

Morning, 66; noon, 84; night, 74.

September 1.—Off at 6:15 ahead of the safari,

following the course of the river. Character of the country remained about the same—rolling, thinly wooded green hills to the left, with wide green valleys between; the river, with a narrow strip of high trees; and higher hills some distance back on the other side. Many tall, slim palms with tufted tops, growing singly and in groups. About a mile down we saw a baboon family or tribe of fifty or sixty that had not yet arisen. These animals rest in the tops of the tall trees, so as to escape the leopards. They take a good grip with their hind hands, hump up in a furry ball, and sleep. The main lot discovered us and made off; but one old gentleman, undisturbed by the noise of the exodus, slumbered on all alone. When he did wake up and discover us below him, he uttered some shocking language.

About four miles on saw a big bull eland and a cow feeding together in a glade between two ravines that here come into the river. By crawling some distance I got within range, and gave him one in the point of the shoulder. He leaped forward. My second shot was intercepted by a tree. Third caught him running, other shoulder, at about 200 yards. Then I made two good running shots through timber at about 300 yards, and he came down. Left the gunbearers to care for him and went on down and made camp among the date palms by the river; twelve miles. Sent men back for meat and loafed. Got hold of some fly-blown meat, and am not well, for the first time on this trip.

Elevation, 4,600; morning, 66; noon, 89; night, 73.

September 2.—We knew this stream flowed into the Mara River, so considered it useless to follow the two sides of the triangle. Therefore when we judged the time right we took compass bearings and struck across on the hypothenuse.

For some distance the country remained the same, then the hills increased slightly in height, the grass turned high and brown, and in the creases between the hills were strips of dense jungle through which we had to chop a toilsome way. The prospect was exceedingly beautiful, for one could see far abroad, and the winding green strips of jungle patterned the country. But it was very hard work. Almost no game. Plenty of pool water in the ravines. Marched and marched, and at noon found ourselves near a lone rock kopje at the end of a rise of land. This was an excellent landmark, and we took bearings by it for a week or so hereafter. We could thence look back across billowing oceans of scrub trees and grass to where our hills of the Lion Camp showed dim and lone and blue. To the south the ocean-like plain led to infinity. To the west was a long pearly escarpment running unbroken toward the north. Somewhere between us and it must be the Mara.

Here near this kopje was some game—zebra, topi, hartebeeste, and a lioness that looked at us from a distance. We had no time for anything but business, for

although it was a certainty that the Mara was somewhere ahead, no one could guess how far it was even
likely to be. We angled on in our probable direction,
struggling over hills tangled high with grass, chopping
our way foot by foot through the too-frequent wide
jungles. In these jungles the forest was not only fine
and high, but it was also tangled, dense, and broad.
Very hard work for me, as I was still a bit ill, and the
sun was very strong. At about three o'clock we left
Sanguiki to tell Dolo to camp the donkeys, and to come
on next morning; we feared the hard work would kill
our few remaining beasts. At five o'clock we had not
reached the river, though we knew it could not be far
ahead. Cuninghame and I separated and began to
look for water wherever we saw palms. At last found
some beautiful clear pools filtered through gravel to a
delicious coolness. It was alkaline but not undrinkable.
When the safari came singing and shouting in, we
camped. The more tired out your African is the
louder he sings.

No sooner was camp made than we were treated to
a smasher of a tropical thunderstorm. One of the
Wakoma stood out stark naked in the rain, his arms
upraised. To every clap of thunder he shouted back
an answer in a loud tone of voice. When the storm
had died he still remained, and would promptly catch
up and answer each and every diminishing peal. He
was a fine sight, as he was revealed by the flashes—

the upright pose, the rain streaming from his glistening body, the flicker of his metal ornaments. M'ganga, later appealed to, said that he was the official Thunder Lord for his people. He was saying, "Go away! Go this way! Go that way! You like to sit on high hills! There are no high hills here! Go to Ikorongo: there are high hills!" He had also put "medicine" in a tree in camp. I asked M'ganga if he himself believed in this. He grinned quietly, and replied: "Well—the rain has gone."

Ten and three quarter hours; 25¼ miles; morning, 62; noon (?); night, 72.

September 3.—Instructed the men to remain until the donkeys appeared, and then to pack up. Cuninghame, the gunbearers, and I pushed on to find the river. Found it within a mile, but so far inside a dense jungle that we were glad we had camped where we did. We turned sharp to the right and with some difficulty made our way through the mile-wide jungle of the ravine by which we had camped, and found ourselves in open country again, with game. Here the riverside jungle narrowed to a mere strip. We pushed our way through it and looked down on the Mara. It was a real surprise. Flowing as it here does between high banks the eye passes across it easily to the hills beyond. As a consequence one expects only a small stream. As a matter of fact it was here fifty yards wide, and with a deep, strong, swirling brown current that indicated

great depth. No swimmer could cross it. It is several times the size of the Tana, for example. At this
moment it seemed to be in flood, yet the swollen
current may be a normal condition for all I know.
Certainly the rainy season is long past. Farther upstream it widened to a quarter of a mile, but even there
proved unfordable. This is the river from whose
lower reaches near the lake come persistent reports of
the amphibious beast "big as a crocodile, but with
long hair." There may be something in it: the report
comes from a great many independent sources. One
white man of otherwise mild imagination claims to
have wounded one. We did not see any!

We rather gave up the notion of slipping across to
where we had heard some lions, and turned north.
Here we saw topi, Nakuru hartebeeste, zebra, reedbuck,
impalla, and oribi, and a number of sing-sing. Among
them was the noblest buck I had ever seen. Had
with us only the .405, as this was a scout not a hunt;
but I took that. He proved very shy, and—as sometimes happens —there was too much game; it served to
warn him. At last, seeing that I would get no nearer,
and that he was next due to skip out entirely, I made a
very careful estimate of the distance as 400 yards, set
the sight up four notches, sat down, and let drive. By
the sheerest fluke in the world the bullet took him
through the heart—411 yards. His horns went thirty-
four and a half inches with a spread of twenty-eight

inches. A twenty-six to twenty-eight inch length is considered extra good.

We then sent for the safari and made camp right in the middle of an isolated thicket, cutting ourselves burrows and chambers in which to set the tents. The sun here is very powerful at noon. Rather seedy, so rested. Cuninghame went out to look for a possible way across the river, and to shoot another beast for our complement of meat. Shortly he sent in a topi. Returning later, he reported finding islands and possible bridge route five miles up. Saw giraffe and eland.

At dusk the Wakoma came to us in a body.

"We want to go home," said they.

This was a facer, as we would not get far without them. They seemed to have no complaint, but only to have become restless and uneasy. Their minds, however, were quite made up. First, we spread out a big blank book, called each man up, asked him his name and the name of his Sultan, making a great and elaborate pretence of writing him down. All this very deliberate and slow, so as to get them well impressed with the seriousness of the occasion. Then we told them that we would send them back in twelve days, when we reached the tribe of the Ungruimi. After that we called each man up by name, asked him if he individually insisted on going home, and on receiving his answer caused him to stand aside from the group. Thus singled out not one had the nerve to say he would

go.   Then we dismissed the lot without further *shauri.*
They appeared quite satisfied.

Dolo drifted in, reporting another donkey dead.
Heard leopards, lions, and hyenas.

Elevation, 4,100 feet; 8 miles; morning, 51; noon, 91;
night, 78.

CHAPTER XIII

SEPTEMBER 4.—Left Dolo and the donkeys—six remain—and went up river to Cuninghame's bridge site. Kongoni and I deflected to the right to get some meat for (a) Dolo and Company, and (b) the men we were sending back to the Simba Camp to bring on the stores we had had to leave. The game had a wild day, but after a little trouble I got within distance and laid out two topi, one with two shots at 260 and 217 yards, and the other with one at 227. We then cut across country and caught Cuninghame just as he was making camp in a thicket.

Tackled the river. Some tall slim palms grew at the very water's edge opposite an island. We felled several, the tops of which caught the current so that they were swept away, but finally got one to stick against the island. A boy swarmed across it carrying a rope. Thus we had communication established. By felling other palms and dragging them we finally made a teetery sort of footing. Crossed the island to look at the other branch of the river. It was more of a problem because there were no palms on the island, though plenty on the other bank. A volunteer managed to swim over, at great risk. He caught a rope and made it fast, and others soon joined him.   Two hours of labour then bridged the other channel.   Then Cuninghame and I took our guns and went to explore for a camp site on the other side, and the boys went fishing.   We stooped and crawled by hippo trails for half a mile— and found we were not on mainland at all, but on another island with the bulk of the river still ahead! Furthermore, this arm could not possibly be bridged: it was altogether too wide and swift.   Scouted both ways and found a possible ford, but even there the water was running fast and deep.   Natives could get across all right without loads, after which we would string a strong handline and cling to that.   While Cunninghame was attending to this, I agreed to return and scout farther up the river for any other easier way.

Went some miles, enjoyed fine, broad-beaten hippo trails, and returned about dark.   Had one interesting experience.   As I was going very silently through a dense green jungle, I stopped to admire a giant guinea fowl strutting about in a tiny glade.   Suddenly some animal incredibly swift and active made four great bounds and grabbed at the bird.   It just escaped.   So quickly did the beast rush that actually I could not make out what it was until it stopped.   Then I saw it to be a baboon.   I had no idea they could move so fast. He sat on his haunches gazing philosophically after the escaped bird, and I could fancy him saying, "Missed, by gosh!"   I found no ford.

FISH FROM THE MARA RIVER

ONE OF THE CHANNELS OF THE MARA RIVER

CONSTRUCTING A BRIDGE ACROSS ONE OF THE NUMEROUS CHANNELS OF
THE MARA RIVER

SEE PAGE 155

Cuninghame and men back late and wet. They had strung the rope, and had got across through water breast deep over huge slippery boulders, only to find themselves on a third island beyond which the river flowed ten feet deep and forty feet wide. There was nothing for this but a block and tackle, but first we had to get a line across. By means of many tosses from the ends of long poles Cuninghame at last got a knot to jam in a palm root. A volunteer went across on this and made fast. Then they left it until to-morrow.

Heard Kongoni express the situation thus:

"When we had finished the bridges we thought we had caught (*kamata*) the river; but it turned out to be only a *toto*." *

One and a half hours; 5 miles; elevation, 4,200; morning, 66; noon, 84; night, 68.

September 5.—Crossed the river in two hours by (a) three bridges, (b) a deep ford with handline, and (c) by block and tackle. Slung the loads over first with the pulley, then lowered the rope to water level and dragged ourselves over hand over hand. Some of the men, notably the Kavirondo, were quick and handy; but others spluttered and ducked and kicked and splashed something wonderful! We camped on the high ground the other side, and proceeded to dry out. Left the rope in place for our return.

After lunch Cuninghame and I scouted across a

* Baby—young one.

high grass plateau with a few scattered thorn trees. Here were again marvellous swarms of game. I should be afraid to say how many we saw in that short walk, mainly topi, zebra, hartebeeste, and wildebeeste, but with a very fair number of Tommy and oribi. Shot a zebra at 207 yards for camp meat.

Walked 8 miles; morning, 60; noon, 90; night, 70.

September 6.—Set off on a compass bearing for a reported swamp close under the escarpment. There we hoped to find buffalo. We are now in a triangle framed by a bend of the river and the escarpment, twenty miles by eight or ten. Followed the bearing for a while, then were turned aside for some miles by persistent lion roaring. After a bit ran out of game and into high grass, so gave that up and swung back to our original plan. At this place shot a Tommy three times at 123 yards before he left his feet, though he did not move twenty yards. This ended a long streak of pretty good shooting, for I have killed fifty out of the fifty-three animals last shot at. Now I came due for a rotten spell of two or three days, attributable possibly to noon marching and great heat. After quitting work from twelve to four for a few days I got back my luck.

We slogged along doggedly over the open country toward the escarpment. The game steadily diminished. About five o'clock I just scraped a wildebeeste and got no further chance, so camp was meatless. We have had no trouble finding water heretofore, and anticipated none so near the escarpment; but not a drop was to be found even in the most likely places. Everybody hot, tired, and dry after a hard march. Things looked mean; but finally we found two gallons or so among the stones of a donga. Energetic digging developed barely enough to get on with. Saw three Wanderobo who fled wildly, and would not be persuaded near us at all. An old man later proved more friendly and allowed us to give him a shoulder of Tommy, in return for which he gave us the valuable information that there was no other water, but that the swamp was just below. A heavy storm with wind and rain swooped down on us in the evening.

Nine and a half hours; $20\frac{1}{4}$ miles; morning, 51; noon, 96; night, 71.

September 7.—Followed the dry donga down to the swamp. It was a beautiful green jewel set in wooded hills, about three miles long and one mile wide. Its tall reeds swayed and rustled in the wind, and here and there gleamed patches and glimpses of water. In this dry and parched country it was a refreshment to the eye and a delight to the spirit. Its shallows should have been alive with the little waders, its deeps with water-fowl, its whole area vocal with the delightful cries, squawks, whistles, and eerie calls of the marshland; overhead should have wheeled innumerable birds stooping to its myriad insects. There were none of these things. Not one living creature did we see. It was the abode of dead stillness. Wondering, we tramped around the head of it. There were no tracks in its mud nor through its grasses. A half-dozen small green mounds elevated six feet above the surface proved to be springs, with the water standing in pools or gushing out from their crater-like tops. This water was strongly mineral (perhaps arsenical?) which may account for the absence of life.

At any rate this was a disappointment. The swamp was here all right: ideal in size and location to have accumulated all the buffalo of the region. Only it was the wrong sort. At least that was knowledge; so we jotted down the fact, and prepared to return. Having nothing else to do with the day we resolved to drive a coarse grass swale for lions. Sent messengers to camp to turn out the men, and sat down to wait. Somehow they mistook their orders and spoiled the beat.

"Let's get out of here," said we disgustedly.

So we returned to camp, packed up, and got under way at 10:40. It was no time of day to travel, but we were anxious to get on. Took a compass bearing that should bring us to the river a short day's march below our bridge. On this course we found the swells of the plains broke in rough stony points, with flats and turret-like kopjes below. In one of these, about noon, we saw three lions about 200 yards distant; but, without actually running away, they kept ahead of us, and we could not get even a snapshot at their gliding yellow bodies

in the thin scrub. Pretty hot and winded we stopped
a few moments, then went on. Very strong sun.
Game came in streaks, first a barren country, then
plenty of it. Thunder was brewing in all directions.
We are now approaching the Little Rains. The day
starts overcast, soon clears to a hot noon and afternoon, then gathers at dusk to great piled clouds and
peals of thunder and jagged lightning and a tremendous downpour *somewhere*. Sometimes it *hits* us;
again we see it in the distance.

Toward four o'clock began to think of meat. I
missed a waterbuck at long range (about 350 yards),
and then a hartebeeste twice at about 200 yards. Soon
after struck tangling long grass with a high hill beyond,
and apparently a grassy donga between. Looked like
a long distance yet, as evidently we must surmount the
high hill before we could come to the river. Then we
marched to the donga—and found it the river, big and
deep as ever, but with here no trees to mark its course.
One of those happy surprises that do not often happen.
Camped thankfully in the middle of a shady thicket.

Hunt 6 miles; march also $11\frac{1}{2}$ miles; $5\frac{1}{2}$ hours; elevation, 4,100; morning, 68; noon, 96; night, 73.

September 8.—Started up river across country, as the
stream here made an obvious bend. Shortly ran into
an immense herd (fifty or sixty) of sing-sing, and stalked
them nicely, but did some rotten shooting, as it took me
eight shots at 200 to 250 yards to get the two does we

wanted for camp. Just couldn't hold steady. Loaded the meat aboard the men I had kept free of loads for the purpose, and struck across after the safari. Country the same as usual, and I saw heaps of game. Found a human skull very much chewed, and was interested to see how thick the bone was, and how few convolutions the brain cavity showed. Some Wanderobo hunter dead of thirst, wild beasts, or disease. Caught the safari at 10:30, and almost immediately after saw another beautiful sing-sing only slightly smaller and of the same type as my other good one. He was shy, but by careful stalking got within 260 yards and downed him. At noon we came to the river, had lunch, and set about crossing it in reverse order to the former process. Two hours saw us at our old camp. The fire had been through since we were there and the ground was black, but our thicket uninjured.

Five and one half hours; 14½ miles; morning, 59; noon (?); night, 74.

The net results of our crossing the river at this point, then, were as follows: The open country below the high abrupt escarpment is about twenty miles long by about ten in its greatest width. It is cut by a number of watercourses, some of them wooded, but none normally containing running water. A very thin growth of thorn scrub covers what may be considered open, grassy, rolling country. Here and there are low, rocky, circular outcropping hillocks crowned with green thickets. This, I should say, is the peculiar character-istic of the place—that the thicket growth is on the summits of these small hills instead of in the hollows. The thickets are nowhere continuous, and one can always march around them. There is little water to be found along the escarpment or in its ravines. This is probably because of the volcanic character of the country: the water sinks below the surface. At the westerly end, the country breaks into rocky points and buttes. The poisonous swamp is already described. The bench is uninhabited, though native tribes are numerous atop the escarpment. Sleeping sickness is prevalent among them. Game is extraordinarily abundant. We found it in the easterly and middle portions; but undoubtedly it shifts location according to the feed. We saw probably ten thousand head, and of course examined a very small part of the stock. It comprised the following species: wildebeeste, topi, zebra, impalla, oribi, dik-dik, warthog, Bohur reedbuck, sing-sing, Thompson's gazelle, Coke's hartebeeste,* lion, ostrich, buffalo, crocodile, hyena. Saw also signs of rhinoceros. Probably also could be found eland, stein-buck, roan, giraffe, and bushbuck, although we did not happen to see them. Altogether it is a wonderful game field.

* Saw no Nakuru on the west side of the river.

CHAPTER XIV

SEPTEMBER 9.—Down river through the freshly burned country to our base camp. Here we found Dolo and Company, together with our relay safari, all right. They had backfired, and were quite safe. Loaded them all up, and after an hour's delay went on. For a short distance we enjoyed the good walking of the burned country. The game was still there. I suppose it had gone into the woods while the fire raged, and now was enjoying charcoal as a diet—together with the very roots of the grass. Then we struck higher hills, deeper ravines, chaparral, forests, little open glades of high grass. It was very pretty and intimate, but hard travel, for we had to chop and twist and double and turn to get on at all. However, we did get on, and at noon emerged from that strip to the green open hills again. Camped in the middle of a thicket; and found ourselves just across the river from our camp of day before yesterday. In the afternoon Cuninghame went fishing (we have had plenty of fish ever since striking the river), but I loafed. Assured our own meat by killing an oribi, but the men had to fall back on jerky because I missed a waterbuck. This, however, ended my spell of bad shooting. Dolo reported that while we were gone he had to shoot two cartridges at hyena. I'll bet he was delighted at the chance, for he has been longing for a decent excuse to let off that old blunderbuss. Heavy storms in evening.

Five hours; 13 miles; elevation, 4,000; morning, 64; noon, 92; night, 74.

September 10.—We now struck inland across a big bend in the river. Travelled in rolling open highlands all day, with new blue landmark mountains getting nearer all the time. In them, our Wakoma said, live a tribe called the Ungruimi. From them we hoped to get food and men. At first the country was burned, then beautifully green. As we drew nearer we could see that the mountains were crowned and patched with defined thick groves of forest trees; and beyond them, singly, fantastic cones and knobs. The character of the footing soon appraised us of the reason, for the rocks became volcanic and slag-like, and the ravines abrupt and eroded. At times the rocks, and consequently the soil, were a clear mauve in colour. The game, which had been abundant, now thinned. Therefore we got busy and killed two Nakuru hartebeeste at 180 and 237 yards. Reached the river again at about noon. At this point it runs over a hill and down a long slope between the high countries with a great dashing and hollow roaring among the tall trees of its bed. Little cone hills 100 feet high surround us close, and the forest-patched mountains peep over them. In the afternoon Cuninghame went out and shot at a hippo: we need cooking fat badly. Of course we cannot tell until to-morrow whether or not he landed.*

Overheard the gunbearers discussing why it is that game is always wild when you want meat, and tame when you don't. Says Kongoni: "When the *bwana* goes out for *nyumbo*, then all the animals run and tell all the *nyumbo*, and then the *nyumbo* are very frightened, but the other animals are not frightened."

Two donkeys died. We have now four survivors. Rained hard in evening.

Six hours ten minutes; 16 miles; elevation, 3,650; morning, 60; noon, 92; night, 74.

September 11.—Started out ahead of safari to look for Cuninghame's hippo. No hippo; but beautiful early morning views of the soft folds of the mountains over the way with their caps of forest and their cañonfuls of dark woods. Along the river the gorgeous flowering trees and bushes are coming out, red, yellow, white, and purple. The air of morning is always very clear after the evening's rain. There are also millions of industrious, loud insects.

After an hour the river bent away from us down through a mysterious strange country of little blue cones and craters rising singly from slate-gray distance, and we turned sharp to the left along the steep side of

---

* Although hippo trails proved that at some time these animals are very abundant, there were at present almost none to be seen. I think at times of flood they may drift down the whole length of the river to Lake Victoria.

THE IKORONGO MOUNTAINS FROM THE EAST

HUT OF THE UNGRUIMI. THE ROPES THAT HOLD THE THATCH ARE
TWISTED OF GRASS

AN UNGRUIMI GRANARY

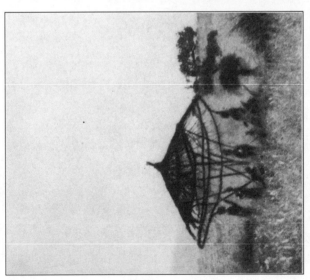

THE FIRST STEP IN BUILDING A HUT. THE ROOF IS
RAISED FIRST AND THE WALLS BUILT UNDERNEATH

Ikorongo. We were at the head of a long easy slope to a distant stream, and could look across to another range about eight miles away, with a fine table mountain in it. After a time we struck into a beaten broad path, and so about eleven came to the village of Ikorongo, and saw our first Ungruimi.

The village consisted of scattered houses, each with its *boma* of thorn or young euphorbia shoots, and its little flock of granaries, like children about it. The houses are large and neat, made of a stout wall three or four feet high, and a high-pointed thatched roof through which the centre pole projects. This is triumphantly topped with an empty gourd from which sometimes little palms are growing. I suspect this latter is less from a sense of æsthetics than as a charm or magic. The granaries are exactly similar except that they are taller in the walls in proportion to their height, which is in the walls seven or eight feet by four or five in diameter. They are rarely perpendicular, so they stand about in drunken fashion as though coming home from a debauch. The grass roofs are held down by heavy twisted grass ropes thrown around them negligently with quite the air of a garland.

The people keep chickens, dogs, goats, sheep, and the fattest, finest humped cattle I have seen out here.*

They raise a sort of rape called *m'wembe* which they

---

*This place is in the extreme limit of the tsetse country; in fact, I found several abandoned villages where the deadly fly had of late years extended its boundaries.

store in their granaries and beat into flour as required in a mortar made from a log.   The men are exceptionally well formed, smooth, lithe, well developed, with torsos a sculptor could take entire as models.   They are about *café au lait* in colour, shave their heads to taste, and have keen, intelligent faces.   Their lips are often thin, and their noses fine cut, which gives them a reminiscence of one retroussé Irish type.   The women are remarkable for the strength and graceful power of their bodies rather than for any beauty.   I have never seen better set-up, arched-ribbed, deep-chested creatures anywhere.   Unfortunately, living in the lower elevations, they have not the firm, high breasts of the mountain people.   Their expression is engaging and they are not shy.   They wear a sort of skin half garment, metal anklets, wire armlets, and many beads, but do not burden themselves like the Masai.   The men wear a cotton cloth shoulder cape, blanket, or nothing as they happen to please.   Their ear lobes are stretched; they wear small armlets and well-made bead belts, white with red patterns.   These latter are particularly effective.   They go unarmed except for a short sword, but I saw a few spears of a unique pattern.

The bow is their weapon of chase.   The method is to drive the game toward a row of bowmen squatted beneath tripods of sticks!   They use no other blind!†

The children of both sexes go naked quite until about

---

† Possibly it is necessary only to break the human outline.

ten years old. In fact the first of these people we saw
was a string of a dozen girls, each with a water gourd
atop her head, and a string of beads around her neck.
They smiled sweetly on us, and passed unabashed.

We made camp beneath a tree, and soon received a
visit from the elders, rather fine and dignified old
savages, and a number of the younger men, one of
whom spoke good Swahili. It developed that this
village was under rule of a sultan across the valley, but
that he kept a son here to see to things. The Swahili-
speaking youth was the son. He said he had learned at
Shirati where for three years he served the commissioner
there—as cook! He was a bright-looking boy, with a
piece of Mericani as his sole garment. He disappeared,
and shortly returned wearing (1) a tarboush on the
front of which were sewed two cogwheels from a clock;
(2) *two* white duck coats, the larger underneath so both
would show; (3) a yellow and black striped footman's
vest; (4) a patched old pair of checked breeches; (5)
spiral puttees; (6) wrecked shoes; (7) a red handkerchief
around his neck; (8) four other red handkerchiefs hang-
ing from his belt. We had then no doubt he was the
Prince. We ended by engaging him as guide and interpreter for this country, and he is now on our staff.

Our *shauri* ran about as follows:

First—how many loads of *potio* could we buy?

"Two."

"Get them."

He disappeared. Presently in came singly and in groups women from the various houses carrying each her contribution. These varied in quantity from a peck to a mere handful, but each swelled the total until the quantity was made up. We paid at the rate of one half cent per pound.*

Second—could we get porters?

"Not here, but at a village across the valley."

"All right, you can take us there to-morrow."

They then, as usual, begged for meat, so I went out with one man as guide. He took me across the river and through rich bottom lands where fed hundreds of their fat cattle, and so over the swells of the valley, but all we saw were three oribi and two Nakuru hartebeeste that skipped as soon as they saw us.

A feature of this country are the long safaris of driver ants. They are like a twisting brown rope several inches in diameter, moving steadily onward, with their big *askaris* guarding the flanks. I stepped one fifty-six paces long! Think of the millions of individuals!

Beautiful sailing moon in the evening. Four and a half hours; 10 miles; morning, 64; noon, 92; night, 74.

September 12.—An omelette for breakfast. An old savage brought in about thirty eggs in a half gourd. Being not exactly sure of the customs of the country, I asked the chief's son, our new retainer.

---

* Equals one sixth of a cent our money.

"Well," said he judicially, "you look at them all to see if they are good; and then—well, you have money —you have lots of money."

Took the hint. Eggs worth one rupee for forty.

Broke camp and struck straight across the valley. A little beyond where I hunted yesterday came to loads of game, so the savages are right as to its being here. Shot at a topi at sixty yards, and Kongoni said the bullet went a foot in front of him! Found my sight had been knocked way over. Hit another at 150 yards by aiming in front of him, but even then too far back, so that although he was very wobbly he did not come down. Cuninghame came up and I borrowed his gun. Just then saw some wildebeeste the other side of the wounded topi. Now a wildebeeste's tail is the surest road to a sultan's favour,* so I did something foolish—left a wounded beast afoot to go after another. Killed the wildebeeste very prettily at 328 yards, and turned back to attend to my topi. It had gathered strength and was walking away. It had a walking fit, in fact, and never paused for five and a half miles. It joined and went through much other game; and as the other game was unhurt and curious they prevented me from getting near enough for a shot. Indeed I had a very hard time to keep track of it at all, and finally lost it. Then I struck back for home and by sheer accident ran on it newly dead! It

---

* They are used as fly whisks.

had walked at the same steady gait until it had dropped. And one of the strangest features was that the two of us, although we had gone five and a half miles, ended within 200 yards of the spot we had started from! Left one gunbearer and took the other. Got in to the village in an hour. Found a large central hut and a half-dozen smaller had been swept and garnished for our accommodation. As the huts were brand new, we took possession, though we pitched our tents under a big tree. The old fellow we at first took for the sultan was an individual as little like a negro as any I have yet seen. His features were aquiline, his lips thin, and his face lined with lines of humour and shrewdness rather than merely of old age. He was like a Sioux Indian, or rather a weather-beaten old New England fishing captain. He wore simple, heavy brass armlets, a bead necklace, a plush carriage robe, and very heavy small brass rings in his ears. A small steel chain passed from these across his forehead, thus easing the weight, as it were. He smoked a unique pipe, with a long engraved steel mouthpiece and bowl, polished like silver, neatly bound with hide at the bend. A slave carried a reclining steamer-chair.

With him was an oily looking, sly youth of eighteen, speaking fluent Swahili, dressed in fez, *kanzua** and tarboush, and supplied with a slave and ordinary camp-chair.

---

* A night-gown sort of garment.

TYPICAL N'GRUIMI HUTS, AND THEIR DRUNKEN LOOKING GRANARIES

THE MOUNTAIN RANGES EAST OF MYERU'S

MYERU—THE OLDER AND YOUNGER. MYERU "PÈRE" IS HOLDING THE HEIRLOOM PIPE

SEE PAGE 173

We adjourned to the shade. It turned out that the young man was the sultan. The old fellow was his father. Asked why thus, he replied, through an interpreter:

"I am old and not strong, and like my chair and my pipe, and not to work. So I make *shauri* with the Deutsche that my son be sultan." Abdication, in short.*

We went into the matter of men and *potio*. Twelve loads of *potio* promised, and seven men. This took two hours of talk. It seems the Germans have undertaken a new port at Musoma (on Victoria Nyanza), to take the place of Shirati,† and they have sent their native *askaris* in even this far and drafted all the ablebodied men. They must require a lot, to have cast through the thickly settled lake peoples to this remote place.

The *shauri* was diversified by the time-honoured rupee trick, the opera hat, and Bachelder's sword cane. We also tried to buy the old man's pipe. No go. At last said the old man:

"The great master, when he came to Shirati and called in the sultans" (fifteen years ago, Cuninghame says), "wanted to buy this pipe. But when I die then my son will smoke it."

---

* In view of subsequent similar arrangements I am inclined to think that the German policy has been to depose the older chiefs in favour of their sons in order that the government might the more readily handle them. As all parties seem happy and satisfied with the arrangement—whatever it is— the transfer must have been diplomatically made.

† Owing to the encroachments of sleeping sickness at the latter port.

True example of an heirloom, a very unusual thing with negroes.

I was very much amused, too, with a lot of women working with hoes. They plied them vigorously in unison to a song, and every once in a while held them aloft like standards and went running around in a circle, shrieking at the tops of their lungs. Certainly they took their labours lightly! After a time they dropped their hoes and danced down to me, clashing their heavy anklets in time to their chant. One damsel was the leader and did a *pas seul*, better not described, while the others did a background chorus. She ended the show by kneeling in front of me and sorting out from some fold of her garment a tiny and unsuspected infant. Thank goodness I had my camera on my knee, so she could not put it in my lap, which was apparently her intention. Of course the *shauri* ceased while this row went on. Then the sultan made a very slight motion of his head, and they vanished. He is boss, all right!

Ended by presenting him a safety razor and two blades with a promise of magnificent gifts when his part of the contract should be fulfilled.

Targeted my rifle, and readjusted the sights that had been so badly knocked over.

Ate before a wonderful prospect out across the sweep of the valley to hills that turned amethystine in the evening light. A woman with a wistful and pathetic expression came and knelt before us holding out in two toil-hardened hands a bowl of milk. She continued kneeling there quite humbly while Ali took the milk, nor could we get a word out of her, nor a change of expression. We put a whole string of blue beads in the bowl, and she bowed very low, and arose and vanished.

Five hours; march $7\frac{1}{2}$ miles; hunt $5\frac{1}{2}$ miles; elevation, 4,300; morning, 70; noon, 80; night, 64. Heavy rain and thunder in evening.

September 13.—Cuninghame is consumed with a desire to scout for elephants in some far western district, and I am equally desirous of exploring to the south. As it is desirable to do both, we have agreed to separate for three weeks, meeting at a rumoured ford on the Mara. When we came to make up chop boxes, found we were short of some things, so had to wait today while men went back to relay up what the dead donkeys ought to be carrying.

Ali came to report:

"There is no tea, there is no oatmeal, there is no sugar," said he—three essentials.

Said I ironically, "Have we plenty of anything?"

"Yes," said Ali innocently, "plenty of soap."

Cuninghame went off to another village in hopes of recruits, I out for gift meat. Of course everything was very wild. Missed a wildebeeste in high grass at 350 yards, then dropped a zebra at 280. Turned him over to a rejoicing swarm of savages, and went home by a détour, just to enjoy the groves of red-flowering trees. They are quite large, with no leaves now, and decorated all over with pompoms from which depend feathery streamers, all of the finest scarlet, without a trace of pink or yellow tone in it.

In the afternoon visited the palace yard, where I achieved great popularity by means of the rupee trick, a few small gifts, and a number of simple jokes. A minute infant with a tremendous corporation I christened "Bwana Tumbo," which was received by all with roars of delight, and I think the name will stick. We had quite a sociable afternoon-tea sort of time.

Returning, I saw people coming in with the meat. One group consisted of father, mother, and small boy about four years old. The latter carried proudly on his head a very tiny piece of meat. He was getting "all nice and bluggy," just like papa and mamma.

The water safari of women went through camp, each with a gourd on her head according to size of bearer, the very tiniest little girls having small gourds holding a pint or so. They went by very straight, single file, paying no attention to the remarks of the porters.

Cuninghame back at three o'clock with no luck recruiting. The evening was enlivened by an *n'goma* at the palace. They had two drums, a deep one and a shrill one, and they played varied tunes, and chanted in unison until they got excited enough. Then they

yelled. M'ganga, his conventional soul outraged by
the row, went up and told them they must stop, that
the *bwanas* wanted to sleep! For sheer nerve that took
the cake, but he got away with it. He might have
been speared, but they actually called off the festivi-
ties!

Morning, 62; noon, 71; night, 66. Rain in evening.

September 14.—Sent eight men back to help our
donkeys with stores. Cuninghame took fourteen
and went elephant scouting for three weeks. I took
nine regular porters and six savages and struck south.
We were also accompanied by half a dozen of the sultan's men for meat. Shortly I got a chance and
dropped two topi before the little herd drew beyond
range. Passed many houses,* and so out across a
beautiful green plain about four miles in diameter.
Wildebeeste and topi in great numbers were all about,
but very wild, due probably to being driven by the
savages.

Myeru's head man with two followers had kept on
with us, although most of the rest of his men had
dropped back with the meat. He still lived in hopes.
Now he moved up to my elbow. With painstaking care
he pointed out to me each perfectly obvious herd. I remained impervious to hints. About noon he sighed

---

* This country must have been long at peace, judging from the number of
isolated homes built out everywhere. That it has not always been so is
sufficiently proved by the ruins of old villages perched high and fortified
in the rocks.

deeply, salaamed, and sadly departed for the Sultan Myeru's village, followed by his henchmen.

The growth surrounding the round grass plains proved to be scattered small trees with white trunks, like poplars or birches. Below them the grass grew short and green, like a lawn; and over the grass were scattered white and pink flowers. We wanted to camp near the plain in order to examine the game thereon. Fortunately a short search brought us to a waterhole. We pitched camp beneath the shadiest of the little trees.

Very hot at noon, as the air is moist. At 3:30 went out scouting. Enjoyed the walk, and saw plenty of game, but of only a few species. Parenthetically, these few are all there are to be had in this especial district. Wildebeeste lead—I have nowhere seen so many; topi a close second; and zebra a bad third. Also there is a fair sprinkling of impalla, oribi, and, in one place, roan. Dropped a zebra at 250 yards with three shots, as lion bait; and topi at 130 as camp meat.

March four and a half hours; 10 miles; hunt, 5 miles; morning, 64; noon, 84; night, 71.

CHAPTER XV

SEPTEMBER 15.—Last evening the lions began roaring very soon after dark. They were somewhere to the westward and a considerable distance away; but their reverberating calls carried distinctly to us. There were a number of them, and they were doing what I used to call "curate-response" roaring. That is to say, one would begin just before his predecessor left off; so that a continuous pulsating volume of sound rolled across the night. It was a good deal like a long freight train crossing a peculiarly resonant bridge; or the droning of a distant twelve-inch shell.

From the first heavy sleep that falls on the tired tropical voyageur—when sleep visits him at all—I was aroused by a burst of noise. Raising myself on my elbow, I found that the beasts were much nearer—say at the top of the low ridge a mile away. They were monopolizing the whole world of sound. Even the insects seemed to have fallen into the dead silence that prudence or terror had imposed on the rest of the veldt. I tried to make out how many of the lions there were, but was unable to distinguish clearly; I thought there were three. Then, in spite of myself, I fell into a doze. The magnificent organ tones persisted in my consciousness; became fantastic; mingled with dreams; faded into distant thunder.

I was jerked back from sleep by a roar that seemed to shake the tent. The men were chattering together in subdued tones; and I could see against my canvas the flickering of replenished little fires before the men's tents. This one mighty roar had for the moment terminated the concert. A dead blank silence had fallen on the world. Leaning on my elbow, I listened intently. I could for a moment hear nothing. Then came the sound of a steady *lap lap lap* of a beast drinking. They were actually watering at our little waterhole just outside the camp-lines!

There was nothing to be done; and no particular danger. The situation was interesting, that was all. In about ten minutes the lions withdrew. I fell asleep again; but through my dreams I could hear them occasionally, voicing their satisfaction—or dissatisfaction —as they slowly retired. Never before had I heard lions roar so persistently.

Next morning, eating my breakfast as usual before daylight, I talked it over with Memba Sasa. We agreed it was about time to go lion hunting. Memba Sasa thought there were four of them. Subsequent events proved him correct.

We took with us every man in camp, with the exception of the cook and Ali; just in case we might have to beat cover. The game had drawn close about us in the night. Within the first 200 yards I counted twenty-six topi and wildebeeste. For three hours we ranged and quartered the undulating hills. There was plenty of several sorts of game; but no lions.

"Memba Sasa," said I, "if we find lions here, it is just luck. There are very many waterholes and very many pieces of cover. Lions could drink anywhere, and lie down anywhere; and unless we had great luck we would not run across them."

While I was saying these words a lioness thrust her head up from a clump of small bush twenty yards ahead of us. Some of the porters saw her first, and raised a great fuss. I had the .405 Winchester in my hand and immediately took a shot at the middle of her chest. She flipped backward off the ant heap on the top of which she had been lying. A flying shot missed her as she fell. She whirled back from the edge of the thicket and charged at me, snarling with rage, but before she had hit her stride three rapidly delivered shots stopped her.

Almost the same instant a male lion emerged from the other side of the thicket and trotted slowly away. Evidently he had not seen us, but the noise and row had disturbed his siesta, and he was going to a more peaceful locality. We thought we caught a glimpse of a lioness just ahead of him; but could not be sure.

We trotted along after, trying to strike a happy medium in speed that would take us near enough to catch the beast's attention, and still leave me wind enough to shoot straight. I had exchanged the .405 for the Springfield, for I expected the first shots would be at fairly long range. Inside a few hundred yards the thin bush ceased. We emerged on a tiny open plain, grown sparsely with sapling-sized trees, on the other side of which were more thickets, perhaps a quarter mile away. Here the lion caught sight of us and stopped abruptly. The lioness, too, came to a halt and turned sidewise the better to inspect us. They were then about 150 yards distant.

We stopped next one of the small saplings. Memba Sasa moved up next my elbow. At what stage of the game the rest of the men took to the trees I do not know. Pretty promptly, I should think. At any rate, those trees fairly rained niggers after the row was over.

I waited a few moments to steady down after our short run. The two beasts held their positions, side on, staring back at us. When my heart had quit thumping I took as close a shot as I could at the lion, and hit him very near the middle of the shoulder. With a snarling growl he leaped straight up in the air, then turned to bite savagely at the wound. The lioness did not stir.

My attention concentrated on the wounded beast, I threw back and forth the bolt of my weapon in order to get in another shot before he came to himself. I was on the point of taking aim when Memba Sasa touched my elbow.

"*Angalia bwana, simba m'kubwa sana*" ("Look, master, see the very big one!"), he breathed.

I looked. From behind the screen of thin bush to the left sauntered the most magnificent wild lion I had ever seen. His yellow mane hung thick and long halfway to his knees, and extended far along his back. His head was up, and his sleepy, wise face expressed dignified surprise.

It is well known to African hunters that wild lions rarely carry heavy manes. A good proportion of the adult males are of the maneless variety; while those that have manes lose a great deal of them in thorns and in the bush. No wild lion ever quite equals in this respect the pampered and sheltered menagerie specimens any more than the latter can compete with their wild kindred in size. At this time I had killed and helped kill seventeen lions. Of that lot seven were males; of the males two were maneless; and of the other five only one had a fairly decent mane, and one what might be called a really good mane. But none equalled the lordly old chap who stood before me. It was very bad sense to "take on" one lion before settling with the other; but the temptation was too great. I put a Springfield bullet in his shoulder, too.

At the report of the rifle the lioness charged like a flash. Nobody had said or done a thing to her. She just wanted to prove that line about the "female of the species," I suppose.

Already I had two wounded lions on hand, but evidently it was necessary to acquire another. My bullet checked her nearly short up, from the mere shock of impact. Out of the corner of my eye I had seen the first lion, recovered from his catfit over being hit, swing into his stride when the lioness started. Memba Sasa was snuggled up to my elbow, chanting low-voiced a sort of war song of his own. With my left hand I snatched from him the .405, at the same time passing the Springfield behind my back. He seized it in almost the same motion with which he handed up the other gun. Good old Memba Sasa! Here, as always, he played the game!

When I got back to camp an hour or so later I tried to put down in my notebook exactly the sequence of events. I put down something; but when a few weeks later I start to write this journal more fully, subsequent recollections that float across my mind, fragmentary but very vivid, make me doubt whether I can reproduce in my own mind an accurate sequence. Therefore I will not try to put down in what order I shot at those lions, nor where each several shot hit. I do know that I shot at each of them in turn as it seemed necessary to keep them checked. It was a good deal like pushing eager puppies back into a kennel yard, first one, then another, then another, then the first one back at you again. A later count of cartridges expended showed that from the two rifles I fired eighteen shots.   Five of these were expended on the first lioness, and four on the big one after the main battle was over.   So I must have used nine cartridges to stop the charge.   Of these I missed one.

It was absolutely necessary to keep cool; and I was scared enough to do so; for I realized that if for a minute fraction of an instant I allowed myself to lose my grip, I would be stampeded.   After all, in a really hot corner, when a man is in a certain danger of his life, he is too busy to analyze.   And it is the man who analyzes who gets rattled.

At any rate, we shot nine times, we shot pretty fast, and we shot accurately.   That is solely because we had to.   I used the two rifles alternately, for I had some sort of notion of keeping both magazines full.   Memba Sasa went on crooning his war song, and loading like a machine.   The second lion collapsed early in the game and about 100 yards away.   The lioness came close in, but was crippled for keeps at about fifteen yards.   The big lion had stopped sixty yards distant and was sitting on his haunches staring about him.   He had been badly hit, but was in no immediate distress.   I have a notion that he had not yet located us behind our little sapling, or perhaps was a trifle dazed by the impact of the bullet, and had charged with his two companions, following their lead.

Now I am perfectly aware that a wounded lion charges.   Exceptions are so rare as only to prove the rule. But I have always cherished a theory that even a wounded lion can be bluffed out, provided the man does the charging first, before the beast can gather his faculties. Here was a heaven-given opportunity to try that out.

So I took the .405, stepped out from our sapling, and began to walk steadily toward him.

If I had stood still in his sight for the instant necessary for him to see what I was, he would have come in; for he was hurt and angry. But he had not that instant. Holding my rifle ready for immediate action, I advanced on him at an even gait. He saw me at once, and fixed on me his great yellow eyes.

He sat thus absolutely still while I covered about half the distance between us. In my mind I had fixed upon a certain little bush twenty yards or so from the lion as the point at which I should begin to shoot. When I still had half a dozen yards to go, the intentness of his gaze broke. He began to act exactly as a dog does when he is embarrassed, glancing down, now to right, now to left. At twenty-five yards the pressure became too great. He suddenly turned and bolted! And I missed a hasty shot at him as he ran!

Mind you his nerve was not broken, for within 100 yards or so he rounded to in a small clump of brush, whence he charged desperately. Only, as I say, the pressure was too steady and too persistent for so nervously organized an animal to endure.

We had no difficulty in locating the spot at which he had stopped. He was growling nastily in his throat; loudly, in crescendo, on the intake of the breath; slowly, with a sort of gurgling undertone, as he exhaled. The leaves concealed him. We walked forward to within thirty or forty yards then began to edge to right and left a few inches at a time, trying to get a sight of him. It was very nervous work. We dared not get off balance for a single instant.

How long exactly this lasted I do not know. The beast was lashing himself up: and his growling and snarling were working up to the point of explosion. Suddenly, so suddenly that for a fleeting instant I was almost paralyzed by the surprise of it, he broke from the cover and launched himself at us.

This is, in my opinion, the supreme moment in a hunter's life, the moment when, all preliminaries at an end, the lion makes his direct and deadly attack. The little unessentials are brushed aside. Only remains the big primitive idea to fill all a man's mind—kill or be killed. The preliminary maneuverings have made him nervous and jumpy enough to scream aloud; but now all his faculties fall into battle array. He becomes deadly cool. Each of the few movements necessary to bring his weapon into play he executes with what seems to him an almost deliberate precision. A smouldering, repressed emotion fills all his being; it is not exactly anger, but something like it, rather a feeling of antagonism, a pitting of forces and skills. He delivers each shot with an impact of nervous force behind it, as though he were to strike with his own hands. "Take *that!* take *that!* take *that!*" his mind seems to itself to mutter; though of course he has really no time nor attention to waste on articulation. And beneath all this is a great wary alertness that sits like a captain in a conning tower, spying cannily over all the situation as it develops, poised ready to plan competently for the unexpected.

Excited, in the usual sense of the word? No. But alive to the uttermost of all his faculties at once? Yes. That is why the moment is supreme.

I killed that lion with three shots, the last delivered at eight paces. He was considerably slowed by his previous wounds, but he made a gallant fight. Each blow stopped him short; but he gathered himself and came on. He rolled over at last: stone dead.

Returning, we found the first lion dead when my second shot had caught him just under the chin. I do not know just which rifles did what, except in the case of the first few shots, as after one or two shots I always handed them back for reloads, desiring always as full magazines as possible.

The row must have been appalling, though we had no chance to notice it, for every beast was snarling and growling and roaring without limit, and the rifle fire was pretty rapid. Fired five shots from the .405 at the first, and seven .405's and six Springfields at the second lot. Hit number one four times, the smaller lion twice, lioness twice, big fellow seven. The smaller lion has an ordinary mane, but the big fellow's is so thick and long that I could hardly get the alum water to run down into it, even by parting the hair. These two are far and away the finest wild lions I have ever seen either in the flesh here or as skins in London.

All the rest of the day and far into the evening was spent in preparing the skins. On the way home saw a few guinea fowl, the first for a long time. When we went to take our flag off the lion bait this evening we found the savages had made way with all the meat! They left the flag.

This camp is infested by a yellow and black striped fly, with a loud buzz, that occupies about a cubic foot of air space in which he hikes frantically back and forth in zigzags. And you cannot hit him; it's been tried.

Rigged a sort of jury tent to hang the skins in. Heard leopard and hyena and lions far off; but I think we have the lot near here.

Morning, 60; noon, 90; night, 72.

CHAPTER XVI

SEPTEMBER 16.—Spent the morning in a long scout to the hills southeast. Saw much game of the three species, with a heavy run of wildebeeste, of which I got some good herd pictures. From a height we looked down on another country similar to our own, with three of the bright green plains in sight. On each fed black herds, and through our glasses we could make out savages stalking across. Near camp I killed a wildebeeste for meat, at 172 yards. After lunch took my chair in the shade and wrote for a while. When I came to get up I found it absolutely impossible to straighten my back. The muscles refused to work, and the slightest movement even of an inch or two was accompanied by severe pain. After an hour, by slow degrees, I managed to help myself upright and got into camp. There sat in my chair. Unable to reach out or down, even to get a saltcellar, without the most severe pain. I could, however, sit quiet in a chair with no more than a bad ache, so I did so, and watched a beautiful sunset with clouds of mauve and a very blue slate. No temperature, and appetite fine; so conclude it is like a bad stiff neck, only just below the small of the back: probably lumbago. Got to bed ridiculously, an inch at a time, lying on my side on the tent floor, and worrying my clothes off *poli-poli.**

Morning, 62; noon, 90; night (?).

September 17.—Bad night owing to severe aches. Found this morning the curious fact that ordinary body movements, such as rising and walking, are ordinarily conducted by a certain limited amount of will power sent out automatically by the brain. I say "Rise," and the brain repeats the order to the muscles. Then if the muscles are out of order, they fail to respond, send back a sharp pain message, and the brain tells me, "You *cannot* rise." But then if you take charge yourself, instead of leaving it to automatic action, and concentrate your will on each and every separate movement necessary to rise, you can do it. All you have to do is to break firmly through the pain protest. As soon as I found that out, I resolved to move camp, for the possibilities of this place are well scouted. No temperature, appetite good; no reason for *not* moving except the ridiculous one that it hurts like blazes. So I got two long sticks, and started out to do one step at a time. Very tiring work, of course, both on account of severe pain, and because of the extra expenditure of will power. But then, one needn't go so far. We crossed the green plain, entered another birch-like strip of woods, and came to the other

---

* This attack was probably due to congestive chill. I still have traces of it, nearly a year later.

stream bed that I knew must flow past Ikorongo. And there, placed to order, were two zebra. When I came to abandon my two sticks, and hold a rifle out, however, I found that the position and weight seemed at first prohibitive. However, I got it level at last, managed to hold it steady for an instant, and downed the zebra at 225 yards (Memba Sasa stepped it). Put a flag on him, went on a bit, and made camp. Saw one lone Nakuru hartebeeste near camp, the only one in the whole country, I think. Got out my chair and sat down! Rested all afternoon, while the gunbearers scouted certain country I designated. They reported roan on a hill, not much game, and no other water as far as they went. In the evening I sat by the camp-fire and watched some wierd, bat-like birds wheeling and turning rapidly and silently overhead. They looked like imps of darkness, for their wings trailed long fluttering feathers, like the conventional devil's wings.

Two and one half hours; 3 miles; elevation, 3,950; morning, 62; noon, 86; night, 72. Rugee's birthday. Drank him a silent toast—in tea—and wondered where the good old boy is.

September 18.—A very aching and restless night. Was called a half-hour earlier than usual to allow time for the slow process of dressing. Found my condition much the same, except that the pain goes into the hip-joints as well. However, got my sticks and we went to look at the lion bait, which was untouched.   A little farther on I jumped a Bohur reedbuck with a most remarkable head.   Fortunately he stood long enough for me to go through the very slow process of getting into position, and I managed to land him in the ribs just back of the heart.   About 100 yards.   It did not stop him, however, but slowed him down so we could keep him in sight.   Stalking was, of course, out of the question, but I kept after him until he went over a little hill.   Arriving at the top of this, I saw him below me, loping heavily along, and by good luck hit him again at 125 yards.   He is a real prize, and also this was meat day.   After this ran into some oribi in grass and missed them eight times, but as they are next to dik-dik for smallness this did not depress me, in the circumstances.   Shortly after saw an impalla.   Could not get near him, but was willing to take a chance.   Missed first at about 250 yards.   Then he partly faced me, and I broke his hind leg.   Then hit him in the ribs at 317, which was sheer luck.

Meat enough assured, I returned to camp, after three hours.   Retired to tent, and had mosquito canopy up account of flies.   Wrote log and read.   Hard to get comfy, as any position aches, and any change of position hurts like blazes.

About four o'clock the sky overcast, so I resolved to scout a bit down river.   That would finish what I wanted to know about this country, and enable me to work back to Myeru's.   Made a two-hour walk, and had a flurry of rain, but found no good prospects.

The nature of the country is most beautiful, and I must try to describe it.   Conceive a perfectly flat green lawn of indefinite extent; the grass short as though mown; nowhere, even next the trees, growing into high ragged clumps.   Plant this lawn sparingly with small trees with white trunks, like birch trees, far enough apart not to spoil the open appearance, but thick enough to close in the view at quarter of a mile.   Then scatter over this lawn flowers that grow flat to the ground, with barely an inch of stem to support them, so that they give the impression of having been scattered fresh cut.   They are four petalled, velvet in texture, the exact shape and size of a wild rose.   Most of them are white, but a very few range in colour from deep red to pale pink.   Across the sweeps and flats they lie spangling the turf sparsely; but in tiny depressions they are as though drifted.   In addition to these are occasional other flowers, high growing, with stems, some flesh coloured, some bright red and upstanding, some orange and yellow, and some with feathery leaves trailing vine-like along the ground.   But they are not abundant enough to modify the effect of the others which always remind me of one line of Omar's: "star-scattered on the grass."

Just before camp I ran across the same lone Nakuru hartebeeste I had seen in the morning, and warned by

AN EXTRAORDINARY EXAMPLE OF STRETCHED EAR LOBES. THIS
MAN CARRIED A LOAD FOR US THROUGH A THICKET COUNTRY

THE WHITE AND PINK FOUR-PETALLED FLOWERS

SEE PAGE 194

their growing scarceness that I might not collect my one remaining specimen, I put a .405 in his shoulder at 122 yards.

Our savages are very keen for used cartridges, and this being larger than the Springfield, was to them an especial prize.

Usual storm in evening.

Morning, 66; noon, 87; night, 70.

September 19.—A leopard hung all night near camp, and we had hopes of him at the bait, but found it devoured by hyenas. Packed up and were off at 6:40. Safari could beat me all hollow travelling, for while I can now abandon one staff and have taken to Mr. Bachelder's cane, it is very tiring and painful to move at all, and any little twist or unexpected hummock drops me as if I have been shot.

The display of flowers in crossing the valley seemed even more beautiful than that of yesterday. Passed two villages, whose head men came out to speak to me. The latter one followed me to Myeru's begging meat, but I had my own men to think of and could not turn off to hunt. He carried two unfortunate chickens intended as a bribe, but as he soon saw I did not purpose answering his plea, he thriftily bartered them to the men instead.

At one place, while watching the antics of some very large gray monkeys, I happened to glance down and saw a lot of peanut shells! I rubbed my eyes and looked also for the pink lemonade. It seems that peanuts are a staple of the country. Bought some and had them roasted.

At the end of three and a half hours got in to our old camp and found Dolo, Sulimani, the Toto, all four donkeys, and the eight men all well and very glad to see us. The sultan, having duly impressed me before by his gorgeousness, now appeared in a blanket.* He had seven loads of *potio* ready out of the thirteen promised. I called him up and very firmly informed him that unless the other six were forthcoming by evening he would get the price only, and no backshish. This stirred him, and I saw messengers running off in all directions, to return at the end of a few hours followed by a slave or so bearing a greater or lesser amount of meal. By eight o'clock all was in but two loads. He sent word that was all he could get. I, sitting among pillows, sent a stern message that the rest must come or no backshish. About nine he brought in the last, which he said had been prepared for his own household. I counted out the thirteen rupees payment, added five rupees and a folding knife, and left him satisfied.

One of our men is greatly given to decoration. The other day he found some white tree pollen with which he daubed his face in a manner ghastly to behold. This evening he appeared with the feathers of the in-

---

*This seems the frugal custom of most Central African sultans. One dazzling appearance, and the finery is put away.

tended gift chickens stuck every which way over his head, like Tom o' Bedlam. Shot a lucky topi near camp at 232 yards.

Three and a half hours; 10 miles; morning, 67; noon, 85; night, 71.

September 20.—Have had a lot of fever among the men of late, and had to hold an extra clinic this morning.* Left Myeru's at 6:40 after considerable *manena* with the savage porters, who as usual wanted to quit. Got them going by combination of threats and promises. Long march, or it seemed to me long, down the length of the hills, then over, through, and between the smaller cones, kopjes, and ridges with which the system ends. Lots of green parrots that fly very fast with a rapid, whirring, quail-like method of going. Native villages everywhere, and isolated *shambas*. Country open and grassy, with rock outcrops and little groves and scattered trees.

I had my canvas chair carried for me, and rested in it often. At one point the safari caught and passed me, thus resting, and went on over the hills. They evidently thought I was safe for a while, for no sooner were they over the summit than they threw down their loads. It was still an hour till rest time, and this was sheer impudence. By luck I happened to go on very shortly and caught them at it. Then I waded into them, striking at their shins with my stick. They

* The official time for doctoring is just before the evening meal.

knew themselves in the wrong and dodged here and there, laughing considerably, and trying to dodge in under my blows to get hold of their loads. This was an easy matter, as I could not get around in very lively fashion. Then they went off down the trail at double quick time, and never offered to lay down a load until the very end of the journey—a tremendous march. It shows what they can do when they get to it.

We saw many villages and houses perched up in the hills. At one place the people were just starting to put up a new house. The skeleton of the roof was being raised on the end of a centre pole, a good deal like a big umbrella. After it was in place they proceeded to fasten the sides beneath it. These people drive all their flocks inside the houses at night. It must be warm and cozy, to say the least! Twenty or thirty animals, a dozen human beings, no ventilation whatever, and a tropical climate!

At last we stopped on the wide slope of the last hill, which dipped down to the Mara River and then gradually up again to the escarpment twenty miles or so away. It was one of those wide sweeping views peculiar to our southwest and some parts of Africa, with small slate-blue kopjes rising from milky distance, and then the dark ranges. I made camp in the guest camp of the village, or collection of villages belonging to a sultan named Missambi. The main house had no side walls, but instead a sort of picket fence halfway up, like an old-fashioned summer house. I had my ground sheet, bed, and box put in here, and I could lie on my cot, fully protected from the sun, get all the breeze, and watch the lights change and soften on the ranges. The only objection to it as a camp-site was the fact that the nearest water was about a mile distant; but that is usual with African villages. The women have to carry it; and I suppose woman's time is considered valueless.

After what was to one in my condition a pretty hard march, I did not feel a whole lot like social persiflage; but that was part of the job. Therefore I propped myself up in my bed and gave Ali the signal to let in only those in authority. They came, the elders of the village, grizzled, dignified old men, followed by slaves carrying offerings of eggs, milk, native flour, and peanuts. They greeted me formally, and told me the sultan had gone to walk around, but that word had been sent that I had arrived. I opened a long *shauri* for porters, giving my usual elaborate speech and offering one rupee a head bonus for each man brought to me who would do good *cazi* for a month. Then I summoned Ali and had him serve them coffee in the kitchen.

About an hour later, while I was writing the log, a small boy of about ten years old, dressed in a piece of snow-white Mericani and wearing a tarboush, came around. I glanced at him, said "hullo, *toto*," and went on writing. After a while one of the porters, passing, said to him, "What do you want here?"

"I want to see the white man, *mimi sultani.*"* This infant was potentate of a dozen villages!

Well, I had him in then, you may be sure, and we exchanged lofty civilities. He had quite an idea of dignity, stood very erect, answered in straightforward fashion, and spoke excellent Swahili. While we were in high converse a row broke out between Ali and the man supposed to carry water. The latter, a Wakamba named Mooli, I have been watching for a week, as he has been getting lazy and above himself. Now he was claiming it was far to water, he was tired, etc., although this was his *cazi*, and Ali was having difficulty in moving him. I yelled for him to shut up and do his work; and as he did not immediately move, got up and went out. He seized the bucket and ran downhill a short distance, then stopped and began to jaw at me.

This was rank insubordination, and every head was turned to see what I would do about it. My physical condition prevented the usual procedure, which would have been to knock him down on the spot; so I put into a command to return all the will force I possessed, at the same time looking at him sternly. It was much as one would compel a reluctant dog. He hesitated, then slowly obeyed.

---

* I am the sultan.

THE SULTAN MISSAMBI—IN WHITE—AND ONE OF HIS COURTIERS

THESE GIRLS ARE ALL THE AFFIANCED WIVES OF MISSAMBI. THE WHITE
PAINTING INDICATES THAT THE CIRCUMCISION CEREMONY IS ON
SEE PAGE 206

GRASS HUT NEAR MISSAMBI'S VILLAGE IN WHICH I TOOK UP MY
HEADQUARTERS
SEE PAGE 199

He took his *kiboko* badly, struggling and shouting at the men who were holding him; and on being released he jumped to his feet and started off downhill on a run.

"Where are you going?" I shouted after him.

He snarled something back in Wakamba, which I do not understand.

"He says he's going to Nairobi," three or four men instantly volunteered.

"Seize him!" I commanded.

A dozen porters started in pursuit, but he gained on them at every step. By now he was several hundred yards away, and at every moment nearing the cover. Two of Missambi's men, wrapped in goatskins, stood near. I caught their eager, questioning glance and motioned an assent. Instantly they dropped their robes and darted away, fine pictures of lithe, naked savagery. These people are certainly runners! They bounded easily; but within a half mile they had passed all my men, and within a few hundred yards after that they had seized Mooli. The whole lot surged about him in a frenzied, shouting mass. For a moment I was afraid in their excitement they might actually do murder; and I cursed again the wretched back that held me here. In a moment or so, however, they headed on the return to camp.

Everybody was super-excited, jabbering away madly, running here and there. I had on my hands a fine explosive mixture of savagery that might go off at any moment. It was no time for flash judgment nor quick action, that was most certain.

While they were covering the distance of the return journey I had Ali bring out my canvas chair, and established myself and it beneath the shade of a tree. Mooli's eyes were rolling. Two men struggled with him. Evidently he was about ready to run amok.

Began by asking him innumerable questions requiring a yes or no for answer; and insisted on getting that answer. At first it was difficult; but after a time I got his mind more or less focussed, which was what I was after. "You were going to Nairobi?" "Do you know the direction of Nairobi?" "Do you know that Nairobi is two months' safari distant?" "Do you know that on the road are many Masai who would spear you?" "Do you know there is no food on the road?" "Do you know that if you went to Nairobi you would go to prison for two years?" (Sheer bluff, of course.) "Do you know that even if you were to hide in your tribe the *askaris* would find you?"

This interchange took time, and gave an opportunity for everybody to calm down. At the end of it all the bystanders were calm and listening with the deepest attention. I could now venture on the didactic.

"You made *kalele* and ran away when you got *kiboko*. When a safari boy gets *kiboko* and deserves it he says nothing."

This is so true that a deep murmur of assent went up.

The community pride was touched. A general desire to say something became evident.

"Well, what is it, Fupi?"

Fupi: "This man is not a *zanzibari*:* he is a *shenzi*.†
This is his first safari. He does not know the customs of a safari."

By this I knew that one slight danger—that of mutiny—was past. The men, touched in their professional pride, were ready to repudiate the culprit.

I (grimly): "He will know more of them when I get through with him."

Nods of approbation.

Of course my usual procedure, and the one that would be expected of me, would be to inflict exemplary punishment with the *kiboko*. I did not, however, think the man would stand it in his present frame of mind. However, discipline must be maintained.

"If this were a real safari man, I should give him fifty *maramoja*." (Nods and whispers, "Yes," "That would be just," etc.) "But as he is not a safari boy I will be easy with him. If he ever again makes any more *manena* he gets twenty-five the first time and fifty the next. But this time I will merely fine him one month's wages. *Bassi! Now, take those pails and go get water!*" Off trots my wild man, meek as Moses, and he has been a good boy ever since.

---

* Professional porter.
† Savage.

Ali now rises and makes a short, formal speech. "The *bwana* understands safaris. The *bwana* has been on many safaris. When men do their work well, *bwana* is good; but when they do their work badly, then he is *kali sana*."*

Well pleased with all this because (a) this man needed stiffening badly, (b) it showed the safari men that I know my business, and, above all (c), the Ungruimi were present and heard, and the affair has helped my prestige with them.

I now retired to my cot. The sultan and his immediate suite crowded in after me.

Missambi is a bright, intelligent boy of twelve or thirteen, with a rather fine-cut face, big soft eyes, and engaging manners. He has been thoroughly educated by the Germans to read and write Swahili, and has been taken to Shirati and Ikoma for short residences. In consequence he knows a good deal of white men's institutions, and even described to me a bicycle, calling it a "*gharri ya quenda*"—"a vehicle for going." Evidently he has been trained by the Germans to rule under German supervision. His "right-hand man" and general playmate is a boy of about his own age, a youth with a broad, square forehead quite out of the usual negro type. His immediate influences are: first, a young man of about twenty-five or so, an eager, calculating, energetic, politic, rather truculent individual;

* Very fierce.

and, second, an elderly man of the old school, crafty, scheming, autocratic, cherishing a veiled hostility to the white domination, having no Swahili. Missambi, poor boy, was thus divided in mind between his naturally friendly disposition and desire to follow his orders and the strong influence the elders of his own family can always exert over a boy of that age. As yet he possessed little real authority over his people. His orders were diluted through the wishes of his two older guardians or relations. That they had any effect at all was due somewhat to traditional respect for the hereditary chieftain, but principally to the very genuine awe with which the Germans have succeeded in inspiring their savage tribes.

The old man visited me once, and only once. We exchanged formal speeches through an interpreter, proffered each other small presents, he made his salaam and departed. The younger man, however, was always about. He had an eye for the main chance, and got everything he could from money to medicine. That he did not get more was not for lack of asking. He was exceedingly officious, and on the surface eager to be of service; but I am certain that underneath the surface of things his influence was quite as strongly against us.

We did our time-worn tricks amid great applause— the opera hat, the disappearing coin, the sword cane, the image in the reflex camera, etc. Also, by a happy thought, I got out the scissors and cut out paper dolls —the sort done from a folded paper, all hold of hands. These were a great success. Each savage had to have a row of them. It was certainly a ridiculous sight— these armed grown men dangling little paper figures up and down in an *n'goma*.* After these preliminaries we got down to business. I wanted eggs, information, and fifteen men to carry loads. The eggs were promised at once; the information (false) was immediately forthcoming; the men would have to be sent for, but would surely be here to-morrow. I then instructed Ali to give them coffee at the cook camp. Thus rid of the lot, I enjoyed well-earned peace.

Memba Sasa and a savage had been out all afternoon scouting for alleged Uganda cob. He came in very disgusted, reporting nothing but impalla, and mighty few of them. I suspect the Ungruimi names for cob and impalla are the same; and hence the misunderstanding. So there goes one fond hope!

In the dusk of evening a weird and ghastly procession came down past us, eight or ten girls painted white from crown to toe and variously streaked in wavery lines. I asked Missambi about them, and he proudly told me those were his affianced brides, and that this peculiar decoration was of the nature of our engagement rings!

I am just settling to rest a bit when up come my

* Dance.

six savage bearers from Myeru's village and line up outside. Call an interpreter.

"What do you want?"

"We want to go home."

This is the usual sporadic outbreak, and I give them the usual reply:

"All right; go home. But then you get no wages at all."

As they have been with me some little time and have done considerable work, this ought to settle it. They hold a short *shauri*.

"All right," they decide; "we want no wages; we want to go home."

This was a facer; for I need every man I can get hold of. Nothing remains but to bluff. Of course I know nothing whatever of political conditions in this (to me) new country; but I can make a shrewd guess. I rise on my elbow and say sternly:

"If you go home now without finishing your *cazi* I will tell the *bwana m'kubwa* at Shirati, and he will send *askaris* and will take away your cattle."

The guess is a good one. They raise a wild shout, as though in derision at themselves, and, quite cheerfully, retire.

This happens every once in a while, and I think they merely want to be assured that they cannot go.

Then I treat a man for fever, another for too much meat, a third for an infected small wound, and a fourth for incipient ophthalmia. At last I have Ali bring water; and then eat. All natives are banished by the zealous Ali while this sacred rite goes on, both hands outspread, shooing them off: "Go away! go away! Cannot you see the *bwana* is going to take *chakula?*"

Cuninghame and I live very simply and are healthy in the *tumbo*. Quaker oats, treacle, coffee, and corn-cakes the invariable breakfast; meat, bread, and tea for lunch; meat, *one* other dish (either lima beans, rice, dehydro carrots, or corn), dried fruit, bread, and tea for supper. Not much in variety, but great in quantity.

I ate my meal, moved with difficulty to my little fire, and sat smoking and thinking thoughts until a heavy storm drove me in. The display of lightning was magnificent, great, wide, jagged flashes that went not only down and across, but even *up* in tridents!

Four and a half hours; 12 miles; elevation, 3,700; morning 65; noon, 90; night, 74.

CHAPTER XVII

SEPTEMBER 21.—I purported to-day sending back four of my own men, six of Myeru's men, and ten promised by Missambi to bring down the twenty loads I had left at Myeru's. Missambi had faithfully promised to have them here by six o'clock. Of course they were not on hand, and finally I sent off my ten in advance—it is a long round trip for one day. About eight o'clock the sultan came in, accompanied by a number of friends to whom he wanted to display the wonders.

"Where are your men?" I demanded.

He explained in great detail that they were on their way from another village. As it seemed necessary to be politic, I accepted this—although I did not believe it —and went through my gamut of tricks, ending, as before, by cutting out paper dolls. With these they were again immensely pleased.

Sent Memba Sasa to the river to look for hippo and fords. While he was gone I hobbled up to make a call at the village.

This, as seems usual with the residences of these Central African potentates, was less a village than a collection of a few huts occupied by the leading spirits of the government and by the bodyguard. The rulers appear generally to live apart from their subjects. At times this is probably just as well. I have gathered that Missambi is either the supreme ruler of all the Ungruimi or controls a majority of the villages. Certainly his sphere of influence seems much more extensive than that of either of the other kinglets to the south. The younger of the prime ministers had me in to look at a wife with a bad leg. It was a very bad leg, the sore reaching down to the bone. I gave him a small amount of antiseptic and directions, and instructed him to bring me at my camp a big water jar in which I would mix a quantity of permanganate. He seemed very grateful, and promised to bring the jar. For some reason he never did so.

The village proper, which is over the hill, is very large and scattered, and wealthy in cattle, sheep, goats, and *m'wembe*.

Returned home, and tried to get as comfortable as my aches would let me. Did some reading and writing, and enjoyed the landscape. Sent periodical messages to the sultan demanding men, and received always the same answer—that they were coming from another village. At twelve o'clock four of them marched in under charge of a head man, and I formally entered them in the books. Missambi now sent word that these were all that would come in from outside, but the others would be sent from his own village.

Memba Sasa returned reporting two practicable fords, but no hippo.

At one o'clock, as no more men had come in, I resolved on a change of policy. Armed the gunbearers and donkey men, and sent them up to the village with a peremptory statement that I wanted to see Missambi. He came, with his prime ministers. To him I spoke in substance as follows:

"You promised me ten men at daylight; it is now afternoon and only four have come. Either you are not acting right, or else you have no authority over your people. When I get to Musoma I shall tell this to the *bwana m'kubwa* there. If he thinks you have done wrong, he will send *askaris* and take from you many cattle and two of your wives. If, on the other hand, he thinks you have no authority, he will appoint another sultan who can make the people obey."

I delivered this, at greater length, of course, in a very stern and lofty tone. He listened, looking very miserable, much like a small boy on the verge of tears. I think, left to himself, he would have been quite amenable. His chief advisers, however, looked as black as thunder clouds, though they dared not say anything.

Having delivered the ultimatum—which was sheer bluff and quite unauthorized—I would listen to no reply, but dismissed them at once; and made a great parade of my armed forces!

In ten minutes four more men came; I took down

their names and sent them off to Myeru's with two of my own. Shortly after Memba Sasa came to me with the startling news that a white man had arrived at the sultan's. The only possible white man would be the German official at Musoma or Ikoma, both many days' travel distant, and I had never heard of their coming this far in. This was decidedly awkward after my recent bluff. Here I had been threatening in the name of the German Government; and behold! the German Government was on hand to repudiate me and resent my unauthorized use of it! I got out my glasses and tried to get a sight of the man, but could only make out his figure. I had Ali get out the one bottle of whiskey and the box of German cigars.

At the end of half an hour a young fellow with a wide hat and a green tie walked down the path. I hobbled out to meet him. We eyed each other curiously.

"How are you?" said I at last.

At the English he brightened perceptibly and returned my greetings. I suggested refreshments and led the way. He told me he had lost his safari two days before and asked if I had seen it. With him only a bow-and-arrow savage carrying—a bicycle! After a lot of sparring it developed that my man was not a German official at all but a fugitive trying to escape from such officials over the British border. He had killed illegally three elephants near Kilimanjaro—a two months' journey to the east—and had been dodging farther and farther toward the interior trying to find a spot unguarded. He had lost his men, but hoped to come up with them beyond the ford at Mara. He had stopped at the sultan's so long because he was afraid I might be a German official.

He was very furtive and uneasy, a young Boer with narrow, topaz-coloured eyes. Asked me if I was prospecting.

"No; shooting."

"You can't have much to do," said he contemptuously.

"Nothing much, except helping fellows like you along."

This cooked him. He departed in five minutes or so, going hard, followed by his ugly *shenzi* with the bike across his shoulders. He told me he would go to South Africa, remain there a while, change his name, and come back for the ivory.

"I buried it," he said, "and I don't care; I've made my money!"

As three elephants could hardly afford a very large fortune, and as his expenses would be heavy, this sounded like bravado.

Heavy rain at six. Back and legs still bad, and especially uncomfortable at night. There are many hyenas here. They howl around the sheep *bomas*, and each cry is instantly answered by a regular chorus of bleating. Morning, 68; noon, 90; night, 75.

September 22.—Loafed all morning. Missambi has recovered from his scolding, and has brought in eggs as a peace offering. My back and legs somewhat better. At noon, after lunch, while I was doctoring my various patients, the relay came back, with the loads from Myeru's; and almost immediately, to my great surprise, Cuninghame's safari topped the hill. I was indeed glad to see him, for I had not expected him for ten days yet.

It will be remembered that my back hit me about three o'clock in the afternoon: by ten next morning Cuninghame, *five days' distant*, was told all the details! I had often heard tales of how rapidly and mysteriously news travels in Africa; but I had never before had an opportunity of experiencing the phenomenon. Many explanations are offered, some of them pretty fanciful, ranging from telepathic dreams to drum signals. I have no explanation myself; but only a tentative suggestion. Often I have noticed how the native voice carries. Men working on hills on either side of a wide, deep cañon will talk away to each other all morning. In order even to attract attention I would have to shout very vigorously. Whenever a white man has a command to issue to a man at the other end of camp he invariably tells one of his boys to say it; otherwise he would have considerably to exert his voice. The native speaks loudly and clearly, but without yelling. I have heard it said that this is because the African has a more open larynx than the white man.

Since this is so, I can see no reason why news cannot be
passed along from field to field, cover to cover, village
to village, simply as a matter of ordinary conversation.
The fact that the conversation is carried on at a range
of several hundred yards instead of a few feet has nothing to do with the matter.   The possibility of this
hypothesis is aided by the further fact that the African has no fixed sleeping hours.   Somebody is always
awake and talking, just as somebody is always sleeping.
If it strikes the native as a good idea to sit by a fire,
cook up a little something, and talk, he does so whether
the hour is 2 A. M. or 2 P. M.   And it must be remembered
that in this country every little incident to do with so
strange a creature as a white man is a prime bit of
news.

In this way—or some other—Cuninghame knew I
was sick, and was told just my symptoms and what I
was doing for myself.   His first thought was of the
deadly blackwater fever—that hits the back.   So he
hastened to return.

His report was about the usual African thing.   The
elephants dwelt in a huge papyrus swamp where they
were absolutely inaccessible.   They came out once a
year.   Then, provided you could bribe several villages
of the Wirigi to take to the hills and keep away, you
got *one* shot.   Then all the elephants went back into
the papyrus swamp!   The country north of the Mara
is full of sleeping sickness, and therefore out of the

question. Two or three days' march west he struck a powerful chief named Walioba, who rides mules at 800 rupees per mule, and is generally a personage; and sold our last four donkeys to him—when we shall arrive— at 80 rupees. In his territory were buffalo; and Cuninghame had found out where.

We talked the matter over, then resolved to store the bulk of our goods here with Missambi; to strike directly south in search of a river called the Ruwana or Rubana where several people had told us many lions were to be found; and then either to return here or to Walioba's.

Accordingly we spent the afternoon making up loads, interrupted by occasional heavy showers.

Morning, 65; noon, 95; night, 70.

CHAPTER XVIII

CUNINGHAME'S REPORT

SEPTEMBER 14.—Departed Table Mountain Camp 7:00 A. M. and marched sixteen miles (see map) to Mitomeris. Passed prospector's camp en route and had a half hour's chat with him. He was working for some German mining company and seemed not over hopeful of his results. Had been there six months and knew nothing whatever of his locality, not even where Shirati was or his own position on the map. Bright boy, this. Camped at big village named Kiamburi, bought one load of *posho*, and found a man who has travelled much all over German East Africa and British East Africa. He reports elephant ahead in swamp, also cob, but no buffs. The cook guide has given me position of ferry all wrong, as there are *two* places named Jamawi, and the one on the Mara River so named is *not* the ferry place. Also have heard native rumours of quarantine from ferry to Shirati which require looking into. All natives go to Musoma for any business. May get further news at next camp. Shot one kongoni for meat (*B. Neumanii*).* Saw absolutely not a head of game during march, and only three Neumanii here.

* This refers to the type I tentatively call *Nakuru*.

September 15.—Departed Kiamburi at 6:00 A. M. and marched fourteen miles to camp near big swamp (see map). Located position, but map seems all wrong about the course of the Mara River. M'ganga found a friend who guided me here and gave me much news *re* a *simba** locality on the Ruwana River (see map). Also got much news *re* ferry but have not located it on map. Made a three hours' inspection tour in afternoon. Covered a lot of country. Found no elephant spoor except some a year old. Cob also reported here, but saw none and am sure none ever existed. Few topi, few waterbuck, one impalla. Mosquitoes start business at twelve noon and are very thick everywhere now (6:30 P. M.). No *anopheles* seen. Sun extremely powerful all day. March to another reported elephant swamp to-morrow.

September 16.—Departed 6:00 A. M. and marched twenty miles; made *shauri* en route at a village named Walioba (or that is the sultan's name). From him I got the following information: The elephants were *now* somewhere in the middle of the Masirori Swamp and meant to remain there until the river rose and flooded them out. Usually this occurs by the *end* of October or *middle* of November. They then come shoreward and out among the thorn trees. None has been shot or shot at for a long time. If you want to try to get one you must get some *barua*† from the

---

* Lion.　　　† Written paper.

Germans (which I could not quite fathom) or else Walioba will not give any assistance. If all seems in order to him, then he gives certain instructions to the surrounding *shambas* to retire or keep very quiet, and possibly you may get a chance for a shot. If a shot is fired that seems to be the end of all things, for either you get your *tembo* or they clear out and do not return to the vicinity for weeks. It is absolutely impossible to hunt in the swamp, and from what I have seen of it I quite agree. He reported buff locality five or six hours from his village. As there are *shambas* in close proximity these buffs are in all probability nocturnal in their habits. They dwell in thick bush, and natives are reported to be able to get at them, for they killed two for the Germans six months ago *after* the the sportsmen had tried to shoot two for themselves. This buff place may be worth inspection. After obtaining this information, marched on to the ferry and arrived there at 3:00 P. M. Sun very powerful and no breeze. On reaching ferry I got hold of the *askari* in charge after much *manena;** and having made a good march I hoped to get across to-day and camp on the north bank. No luck for me. The dugout (and there is only one) was not capable of holding more than one man and a *toto†* and the latter had to bale out for dear life during the passage. There is not another

---

* Chatter.
† Child

dugout left on the river as *every* native canoe has been seized and taken to Musoma or destroyed. This on sleeping sickness grounds. There is nothing left me but to march to Musoma which is reported sev(n hours' distant. Such is Africa and plans made therein. Apparently there are *no* cob in this locality. All the information *re* the "Suma" animal refers to impalla. I am quite certain now over this. Sitatunga certainly do inhabit the Masirori Swamp, as they have occasionally been seen by natives when fishing from their dugouts, but to get one seems absolutely impossible in so large and dense a swamp. Mosquitoes real bad again here at 6:00 P. M. Large scale map ends near this camp and small map not much use to work by. Sun very powerful again to-day.

September 17.—Left ferry camp at 6:00 A. M. and marched to Musoma. Pedometer registered seventeen miles but considered distance to be fifteen as calculated by pace and time occupied. This is a poor little place but some day may boast more than a name. Plenty of *dukkas** here, but nothing in them except nigger stuff.

I do not intend to call on the officer in charge, as there seems no occasion to do so. I can see no signs of a port being made but there is some gold-mining machinery lying about the place. I forgot to mention that the *askari* told me yesterday that there is no way

---

* Indian shops.

down the river from the western end of swamp, so you
must go around it as I did and camp as far as possible
from it. Water good in swamp. Quite a few donkeys
here at 100 Rs per head!

MUSOMA TO SHIRATI

By road, on ordinary marching, four days.
By dhow, ten to fifteen hours, according to wind.
Rates, 2 Rs each white man, $\frac{1}{2}$ R each native,
30 cents* each load. Can always rely on obtaining a
dhow in two days at Musoma. Quarantine regulations on and a doctor must pass all natives before the
dhow will take same on board. Have been hunting that
medicine man two hours, but cannot find him. Have
arranged for a dhow to take me across to-morrow as
soon as I can fix up matters with the doctor. No
porters procurable here, not even one. No *posho* procurable here except a little Mwanza rice at 5 Rs (50
cents) per load (same as Nairobi price!). Donkeys
do well and thrive here. No fly and all cattle look
fat and well. Have seen cattle in *shambas* continually
since leaving Table Mountain Camp. Everything
here at famine prices and no one ever heard of treacle,
dried fruit, and such like. Shirati is reported to be no
better in this respect.

September 18.—Found the doctor at 7:00 A. M.
and he informs me that practically all the country

* = 10 cents American money.

north of the Mara River is rigorously closed to white and black alike, and the only way in is via Shirati, by steamer or dhow. *Sic transit cupabi elafantorum.*

(Here Cuninghame heard of my illness and returned.)

CHAPTER XIX

SEPTEMBER 23.—We were ready to march at six, but Missambi's ten men—who had slept in the village—did not show up. Repeated messages failed to unearth them; so at seven we started on for Myeru's, leaving M'ganga to bring on the rest—when he could find them. Passing the "royal palace," we stopped and made parting bluffs at Missambi and his advisers, who were sullen.

There was some local dissension, and the truth of the matter is that Missambi had no real authority, though himself well-disposed.

Had my chair carried, and sat down in it from time to time. Much better; and the hills seemed to have shrunk since the down trip. Got some seeds of the red-flowering tree. Made the twelve miles in four and a half hours, and camped again at our old camp near the Sultan Myeru. He brought us in eggs and milk, two loads of *m'wembe*, and seemed glad to see us. We promised him meat on the morrow. As I did not feel up to it, Cuninghame went out in the afternoon and shot two topi for our own use. M'ganga got in at six-thirty with ten men, but different ones than we had listed before. They had learned the other men's names, however, so we succeeded in listing only three to report to Musoma as deserters.*

Morning, 68; noon, 88; night, 69.

September 24.—Off at 6:15, accompanied by .a retinue of *shenzis* for meat. The head man blandly informed us that the sultan had sent orders we were to shoot him four beasts! We replied that we were not under the sultan's orders, and that two would be enough. Shortly ran into a topi which I killed at about 150 yards; and then another. The bullet (150 gr.) at 180 yards entered right shoulder, dove straight down, came out halfway down inside of left leg, turned at right angles, went through right leg, and hit the ground between me and the animal. This is the most erratic bit of twisting I have known even the Springfield to do. We continued on past my lion camp and up between the *donga* and the range to the right. About eleven I killed a zebra for camp meat at 240 yards, and a half hour later we camped near the last waterhole on the hither side of a wide low pass between two tablelands. These tablelands form the dividing

---

*It seems that my bluff of the day before was not so far off the truth. The Germans take the greatest amount of trouble in following up complaints on the part of white men of desertion or bad treatment by the natives within their sphere of influence. This is as it should be, especially in a wild country, and adds to the white man's comfort and efficiency, as well as the natives' well-being and opportunities. The bugaboo of "forced labour," so called, seriously handicaps British administration. The native will not work unless he is forced to do so; but when once he is at the job he is perfectly contented. As labour is the first step in his education beyond what he has always been, it is as absurd to let him off his share as it would be to permit children to stay home from school at will. That is "forced labour," too, when you come right down to it. Humankind is all doing forced labour. Of course the corollary of proper treatment in every sense of the word is implied.

line between the Mara waters and those of the Ruwana.

Hard work to get shade, which the great power of
the sun makes very desirable at noon. Cuninghame
saw a roan and tried to stalk it, but was preceded by
an unsuspected savage who loosed an arrow at it about
as Cuninghame was in range. Quite a big lot of wildebeeste and topi here.

On the march, during a stop, our savages found some
water, and one of them brought a cooking pot full back
to his friends. Our own lazy men, instead of going
after their own, crowded around, dipping at it with
their cups. The savages did not dare object, but Cuninghame and I, vastly indignant, waded in and gave the
safari boys a lesson. I think the incident did much to
make us solid with the *shenzis*—that and lots of meat!

Six hours; 14½ miles; elevation, 4,000; morning, 62;
noon, 90; night, 72.

September 25.—We are so used to heat that now
when it is below 65 we hug a fire and complain of the
bitter weather. We started this morning up a wide,
flat valley, gradually rising to the dividing woods and
the clumps of trees atop. Literally thousands of head
of game, but very wild. It thundered away at bare
distant sight of us, leaving only a haze of fine dust.
The animals were mostly wildebeeste, with a great
many topi and zebra, some eland, impalla, Nakuru
hartebeeste, and one roan.

From the pass we were vouchsafed a view southwest over wide plains extending off into hazy distance, and some very dim blue mountains perhaps forty miles away. We thought to make out the winding course of the Ruwana. The day's journey toward this plain was through country very much like the outermost foothills of our Sierra Nevadas—low rolling hills, scattered high chaparral and buckthorn, rock outcrops, and little flat valleys of dried yellow grass with a terrific reflected heat.

About noon we caught sight of several small native villages, apparently deserted; and as we saw quite a few tsetse flies, we thought we knew the reason. The tsetse seems to be gradually extending its range, and crowding the cattle-raising savages inward.

Camped huddled in the thin shade of two thorn trees near a lone waterhole—which we found after some search—and endured the midday heat. At four, although the thermometer was still at 90, the sun had lost much of its strength, so we went out to look for meat. The astute reader of this has discovered that we require either one large, two medium, or three smaller beasts per diem to keep fed up. This is important, as we have little other food. We ourselves are now down to tea, sugar, rice, lima beans (nearly gone), flour, and a little dried fruit. Shot a topi through the heart, 210 yards. He ran in a short circle for fifty yards, then dove with a magnificent bound headlong into the middle of a small bush. Of course he was dead before he hit the ground. Shortly after got another topi through the heart at 80 yards.

In camp we found some of the local savages. They are like the Ungruimi in beauty of physique, but are taller. They called themselves the Wasunyi. From them we learned that the entire plain of the Ruwana is filled with people and cattle, and that there is little or no game. After a long talk, realizing fully that it would not be to their interest to deceive us, since they are always keen for meat, we decided that the journey would not be worth while and that we should turn back. One of the savages offered to go along and show us the water, an offer we accepted.

Six hours ten minutes; 13 miles; hunt, 4 miles; elevation 4,400; morning, 56; noon, 93; night, 78. Back slowly getting better.

September 26.—Back along the hills we came over yesterday, but at a lower level—about halfway up their broad, easy slope. For a short distance I paralleled the safari, accompanied by a savage, to get meat promised them. When I had killed a topi with two shots at 136 yards, he left me, and I rejoined the safari. Much game, but exceedingly wild. At the end of about three hours our guide showed us a sort of rock tank of water, and we encamped. The pool was inaccessible to game, so the water was clear and cool—a refreshing novelty. A rhino came out of the bush about forty yards away, snorted indignantly, and trotted off, his tail and head up. Found tsetse.

At three we went scouting over the hills and through the valleys, which here are stonier and more rugged than any we have seen for some time. All this country is well elevated, so that occasionally we get glimpses afar to lower levels. Much game, but still very wild. It is so abundant that you cannot stalk one beast without being seen by a hundred others, so shooting is very difficult. By sheer luck I managed to find a lone zebra lost from his friends, and calling for them in the most indignant fashion. Managed to sneak him, and downed him with two shots at 110 yards. A little farther I shot an oribi for ourselves at sixty.

Then we came to another valley in the green pastures of which grazed a big herd of wildebeeste. This lot I managed to stalk because I was above them, and got to within 250 yards, from which point I hit one in the heart. At the sound of the shot a cheetah that had been lying under a tree, probably waiting a chance for a calf, jumped to his feet and made off. Missed the first shot, but landed the second "running deer" fashion, through the heart, 200 yards—sheer luck.

While the men attended to these Cuninghame and I went to look for water and by chance stumbled on a craftily concealed Wasunyi "shooting box." It was no temporary affair, but had well-built *bandas*, racks for drying meat, etc., and could be found only by accident. They had been there recently, and were successful, for we found scraps of kongoni, zebra, waterbuck, and eland. Later we often came across these savages hunting, and while we never had a chance to see them actually at it—since they always ran when they saw us—we admired the lithe savage pictures they made, stark naked, armed with long bows, slipping from shadow to shadow. The usual method is to drive the game. The bowmen station themselves in the known routes and passes by which the beasts are most likely to go. No wonder the game is wild. It has probably been harried by untold generations. The few so killed amount to nothing; but the method trains the rest to run at sight. The zebra here are very noisy, keeping up a perpetual barking day and night. I suppose they have nerves.

The word *to come* in this part of Africa is *moochie*. I wonder if our slang word "to mooch about" came by way of early travellers from here!

Two hours forty-five minutes; $7\frac{1}{2}$ miles; hunt, 7 miles; elevation, 4,450; morning, 66; noon, 92; night, 77.

September 27.—Resolved to move camp a few miles to where I had killed the cheetah, as there seemed to be more game there. On the way we ran into a herd of fifteen roan, and I managed to down one at (about) 150 yards before they ran. Found a good shady thicket to camp in with a rain-water puddle near. Cuninghame and I went in different directions to scout.

We both had exactly the same experience: heaps of game, but if a single head caught sight of us and ran, every other creature went, too, without waiting to see what it was about. Then others saw them moving, and followed suit, until the whole country for miles was off. By luck I saw a wildebeeste looking over the skyline of a hill at me. I could only see his head and neck, and had to shoot standing, but landed him, by luck, at 211 yards. Dropped in his tracks, but when I went up I found him diseased! and so left him. On the way back to camp came on a zebra around the corner of a bush, and laid him out at 104 yards before he had recovered from his surprise. Cuninghame got nothing. At noon he was suddenly taken with an attack of fever that sent him to bed. Spent the afternoon writing, reading, taking care of Cuninghame, and being amazed at the men who "played soldier," just like small boys, with unflagging zest for a solid two hours, drilling with sticks for guns. Weather very damp and sultry.

September 28.—Cuninghame laid up with his fever, so I started off early and made a complete circuit of the hill where we had seen the roan the day before. The rocky hilltops are charmingly wooded in little thickets and groves, with openings between. Saw plenty of Nakuru hartebeeste and some duiker, beside the usual topi, zebra, and wildebeeste. Also caught sight of smoke from *shenzi* campfires about two miles away. Killed a topi for meat at 146 yards.

Returned to camp and found Cuninghame sleeping, so continued on for another beast for meat. Hit a Nakuru hartebeeste in the shoulder, but the bullet dove down, and I lost the animal in the heavy cover, though we managed to trail it some distance. Shortly downed another at 135 yards with three shoulder shots, all of which went way through. This ended my experiments with the 150 grain bullet. It is a killer, but its action is too uncertain, as a certain proportion go right through or dive freakishly. The 165 or 172 gr. much better.

Returned to camp to find Cuninghame much improved. M'ganga tells me some Kavirondos had come away down from their country to hunt, but hearing my shots ran away. They do not want to meet a white man, as they have come through the sleeping sickness belt just to the north, and are afraid of being shut up. Many flies here—fuss flies, buzz flies, and blowflies.

Nine miles; morning, 63; noon, 90; night, 79.

September 29.—Cuninghame announced himself as able to travel. While the safari were preparing I visited our bait, as two leopards had been calling there for three hours. We heard them go away, snarling, just before it was light enough to shoot. Saw a remarkably fat hyena, however. On the way back we jumped two wildebeeste, and I managed to get one running, three ex five shots, through the thick bush, at somewhere about 150 yards.

Marched by a good native path four and a half hours through passes in broken, hilly country, and emerged on a wide grass plain surrounded by mountains, with a remarkably rocky single peak in the middle of it. Many herds of wildebeeste, zebra, and topi grazed in the open, and from above we could see countless savages, singly and in numbers, trekking back and forth across it.

In the path we came across some very curious "medicine," to which all our boys gave a wide berth—first, an old cooking pot, then some ashes, then crossed sticks, a hoe, and a knife, strung out for ten feet or more. Memba Sasa said it was intended to kill an enemy, but Cuninghame kicked it all aside and saved some one's life, to everybody's open horror.

Near the rocky single peak I cut off to get meat, while the safari went on to find water and make camp. Got a topi with two shots at 250 and 200 yards; and another at 234. As we are now nearing the lake and have plenty of carriers, I tried for a desired wildebeeste head, but here all seem to be cows and calves.*

Had some difficulty in locating camp, so went up to a native village for information, and was met by the finest savage ever. He was a very big man, with a slanting feather in his topknot, armlets and necklace with danglers, a little square of goatskin edged with

* In this and the three other big park-like plains in the vicinity this was true. The bulls were elsewhere. Curiously enough there seemed to be no lions hereabouts. One would think they would follow the young calves.

steel beads over one shoulder, spear and shield, and anklets made to ring like bells at every step—a fine, proud wild creature. He jingled away in front of me and led me to camp under a big tree by the only waterhole. I asked my savage for eggs, and sat down to cool off. Noon sun very fierce in this country.

Our camp was on a gentle slope of the hill and about 200 feet above the plain that extended for miles. We could sit in the shade and watch the game herds at leisure. Was all prepared to get a picture of my savage when he should return with the eggs, but he came back rigged like a scarecrow in tattered old khaki! Cuninghame made the trip quite well, and shot a topi near camp, but was quite done up.

Askaris are out hereabouts collecting hut tax for the German Government. They count the huts in each village, lay out a stick for each hut, do them up in a bundle, and carry them out to the official at Shirati. The latter then calls in the sultans, produces the bundles of sticks, and says:

"Here are twenty-two sticks—sixty-six rupees *maramoja* or I'll collect from your cattle." There is said never to be any dispute as to the tally.

At four o'clock Cuninghame and I got our chairs out in the shade, unlimbered our glasses, and amused ourselves by scanning the plain below. Some topi and a single wildebeeste were grazing about 500 yards below. Suddenly they all scattered off at a great speed.

"Wonder what started them!" said Cuninghame. Then we saw a black dog about the size of a pointer. Paying no attention to the topi, he took after the wildebeeste. The latter loped easily, while the dog fairly had to scratch gravel to hold his own. It looked like a sure thing for the wildebeeste, but the dog was a stayer. Farther and farther they went until they became mere specks, and we had to take to our glasses. About two miles away the wildebeeste dodged and doubled, then ran through a herd. The dog never lost sight of the one he was after, and paid no attention to the rest. At last* the animal turned at bay, making short lunges and charges, which the dog dodged, trying to get in at the beast's hindquarters. Now for the first time we noticed a savage running like smoke across the arc of the circle the chase had taken. He was stark naked, a fine figure, and carried nothing but a bow and arrows. How he could run! We saw him stop and discharge arrows, though it was too far away to see them. The wildebeeste hesitated, and we saw the little black speck of a dog leap for his throat. They both went down in a heap; and Cuninghame and I stood up and cheered, though we were two miles away, and could see nothing without the glasses. When we sat down again it was over. The dog was sitting by the carcase, and the savage was headed for a lone bush to get materials with which to cover his prize for the

---

* The chase lasted forty-two minutes.

night. When the meat was "bushed" he and the dog started soberly for home. Now that was real sport; it made us and our long-range rifles look pretty cheap; and my only regret was that I could not get acquainted with that bully pup!

Fine Arizona-like light over the plains at sunset. Cuninghame and I solemnly drank the Memsahib's health in weak toddy; for to-day is an especial anniversary.

Four and a half hours; $10\frac{3}{4}$ miles; morning, 69; noon, 91; night, 77; elevation, 4,200.

September 30.—Last night M'ganga, who understands their language, overheard one of the *shenzis* say to the rest:

"We are now near home, and we have had plenty of meat and very little work. Let us run away, and let our wages go."

Had up the lot, lectured them, and gave the ring-leader ten lashes, which settled it. They were very awestricken over our apparently magical knowledge of their plans.

Marched high along the slope of a mountain, all rocky outcrops, boulders, huge cubes, obelisks, all sorts of strange and fanciful shapes. Across the valley, which lay dim and blue below, were rows of separate peaks, each a perfect cone, spaced like huge shark's teeth; and milky, indeterminate distances.

We passed three villages perched among the rocks,

each with its waterhole below, from which lines of girls, stark naked, were carrying water in gourds of all sizes.* About ten o'clock we deserted the slope of the mountain and struck down and across a bushy flat toward distant blue mountains in the west. At twelve, as we still had encountered nothing but bush, we set down the safari and scattered to find water. Nothing can describe the intense heat of noon in this country. Beats anything in British East Africa. Sun is very powerful, and the earth radiates like a grate. Thermometers do not begin to indicate it. After an hour's search found a pool of mud flavoured with dung (to which we are quite accustomed). Also saw ten roan.

About four o'clock I started for the necessary meat, though it was still hot enough to cook eggs. Found a perfectly open plain where were hundreds of topi and a few Tommy, but nothing else. Amused myself (although the beasts were fairly approachable) by long-range shooting at single beasts. First miss then hit at 320 yards, then two raking hits at closer range accounted for the first. The second took two at 330. Then I saw a Tommy that looked good and killed it at 211. Proved to be what is probably the record for East Africa, sixteen and five eighth inches. A thirteen-inch horn is *good* for British East Africa, and world's record is somewhere about seventeen inches.

---

* Why these people do not build somewhere near the water, I do not know. They almost never do. Perhaps they like to keep their women busy.

A beautiful lightning display in the evening. Cuninghame better, but pretty tired.

Safari, six hours twenty minutes; 14½ miles; hunted 8 miles; morning, 63; noon, 97; night, 78.

October 1.—Set the safari on a line toward a waterhole known to some of our *shenzis*, and started off on a slight détour to see if we could not get a wildebeeste head. Last chance, as the country now merges into the thickly settled regions near the lake. Saw just one, but him I got after a long and careful stalk, at 361 yards. Shortly after killed a Tommy, but could not find him in the long grass.

We now pass into the country of the Wiregi, leaving the Ungruimi. Journeyed across a plain grown with scrub. To our left volcanic hills of red, to our right the bright green wide expanse of a papyrus swamp called the Masirori. We headed toward a bold rocky peak lying alone. After three hours overtook the safari resting by the waterhole. Two savages had chased an impalla into the deep mud, and there killed it and were now triumphantly cutting it up. Saw a lot of game near here, including a number of sing-sing.

The rocky peak proved very interesting in the queer forms and immense size of its boulders and spires, in the queer trees, bushes, and cacti that sprang from every crevice, and from the fact that hundreds of huts were built high up in the strangest cracks and crannies. Often quite extensive stone terraces had been con-

structed to hold the buildings.   Water was a mile and
a half distant, and must all be brought in gourds.   The
granaries were perched rakishly atop boulders, and
goats skipped about.   People climbed atop big round
rocks and stood, upright and picturesque, to see us pass.
We rounded the corner and came to the headquarters
of a very wealthy and powerful sultan named Walioba.
As usual with these African kings, he did not live with
any great number of his people, but occupied a settle-
ment apart, together with forty or fifty of his courtiers,
soldiers, and their families.   A very large square house
was building, behind a strong stockade.   We marched
straight by to the guest houses.   These were nine in
number, eight of the ordinary size, and one fully twenty-
five feet in diameter—the biggest circular house we
have seen.   Its walls were plastered to a height of
three feet from the ground, and the space left open
under the eaves for a view out and for breeze.   A flag-
pole with cords stood before this.   Inside were two
benches made of sawn planks.   They were very crude
planks, but they were sawn, and that was a curiosity in
savage Africa.   Not only was the inside swept and
clean, but all the grounds were likewise swept and piles
of firewood stacked.

Immediately we arrived, strings of women came, bearing each a great calabash of water which she emptied
into a jar outside each hut, and then went away ($1\frac{1}{2}$
miles!) for more.   The elders, very grave and ornate

HUTS OF WALIOBA'S PEOPLE—THE WIREGI

A WIREGI VILLAGE, IN THE ROCKS

savages, then waited on us to inquire what else we would want and to tell us that Walioba had "gone away to drink beer," but had been sent for. These men were very intelligent looking, were dressed in khaki with silver buttons, and wore new military caps! All the rest of the population are the usual naked savages. We mentioned our needs as milk, eggs, *potio*, and repose. Very hot and oppressive day, and we felt done.

About three o'clock I strolled over to take a look at the royal palace, and on my way back saw a white-clad figure enter camp on a mule Now mules in this country are worth almost anything, so I hurried forward, but by the time I got there Walioba had dismounted and entered our house. The mule was a very good one, and carried a Mexican saddle and Navajo blanket! Think of that, a blanket made by savages in the Southwest United States used by a savage king fairly in the interior of equatorial Africa.*

Walioba proved to be a square, powerfully built man, of thirty-five or so, with a keen but typically negro face. He wore on his head a clean navy blue yacht cap with carriage-cloth visor. His clothes were white, clean, and in good order, consisting of a riding coat and breeches, leather leggings, and good boots. In fact, he was well turned out. He proved most friendly. Gave

---

* We could not trace this outfit; but gathered vaguely that it must have come from some American missionary the other side of the lake.

us men's food gratis, milk, eggs, etc. Before we had finished we had sold him our remaining four donkeys at 80 rupees each—when they should arrive. He also made tentative bargains with Cuninghame for a tent at 350 rupees, and a mule at 450, both to be sent from Nairobi. So he is indeed a wealthy chief. Added a load of peanuts to his presents, and offered us guides for to-morrow. We gave him a Marble folding knife as a starter. His real present, as is the custom, does not come until we leave for good. Bargained for ten loads of *potio*, which he promised to collect and deliver. At supper time he returned in a bright-bordered piece of linen, and a dress waistcoat, stockings, and pipe-clayed white shoes, but no trousers! He was much interested in Baxter's alarm watch. A most intelligent man who seems quick at the uptake and keen at catching a complicated *shauri*.

Rained. Mosquitoes extraordinarily bad. At dark they appeared in literal swarms, so that we were driven to our mosquito canopies and the men to suffocating smudges. Many of our people are down with fever, and we have a large clinic every night.

Four hours; 11 miles; we went six and a half hours; $14\frac{1}{2}$ miles; morning, 67; noon, 91; night, 73.

CHAPTER XX

OCTOBER 2.—Expected the usual long wait for the guides, but to our vast astonishment they were on hand before dawn, squatted at little fires and ready for action. Walioba is keen business. Sent back twenty men to bring on Dolo, donkeys, and loads from Missambi's. One *shenzi* porter deserted in the night. Walioba supplied us one of his personal entourage, who took the deserter's load as far as the next village, where we hired another at two cents per diem.

Marched seven hours through a broken country with many rocky outcrops and peaks. Passed cotton fields white with cotton and yellow and pink with blossom. Over across the valley we heard a distant native safari passing to the music of a flute. It was very mellow and pleasing. Stopped at a native smithy. The blacksmith was very hirsute on arms and body, most unusual. The bellows were two goatskins joined at the necks and pressed alternately to give a steady stream. He had pincers and a small hammer, and for anvils he used hard rocks of different sizes. At the time he was making a hoe, and fashioned the hot iron very skilfully. All the villages are built right among the rocks, the houses perched in the oddest places, with goats and small boys to fill in, although there is plenty of open country all about, and water is always distant. Our guides knew no Swahili, so we followed them blindly. They took us by all sorts of winding and devious paths, native fashion, and finally set us down, about noon, among some superheated rocks. After an interval a girl appeared with a calabash of water and about a bushel of peanuts, on both of which our men fell eagerly. She motioned us to follow, and went on, her wire "neck ruff" bobbing at every step.* Our boys shouted loudly with delight over having a "*kilangozi monumuki,*" a "lady guide." We followed her for an hour through some very hot places, down and out of cañons and ravines in the skirts of the hills. Then she stopped us in a nice little rock furnace and disappeared.

We waited. To us came a finely built, bright-looking, middle-aged man, with a deep bass voice, who spoke Swahili. He informed us that he was a widower, lived alone with his four children, and knew where there were buffalo.

Did he know where there was water and shade for camp?

Led us a mile into the bottom of a cañon and we settled gratefully into a good old-fashioned high forest, with looping vines as big as a man's leg, and thick

---

* These curious wire affairs are coiled like the mainspring of a watch and stand out eight to twelve inches.

THESE OUTCROPS ARE TYPICAL OF THE COUNTRY NEAR VICTORIA
NYANZA

THE WIREGI GUIDE FOR BUFFALO
SEE PAGE 242

shade. The water was milk-white with mud. The tea, coffee, soup, etc., all looked alike, but it was cool and did not taste of cowdung, which was a happy surprise. The "lady guide" disappeared before we had a chance to reward her; but next day an individual announcing himself her husband put in a modest claim. I forgot to say that three hours' back, from a height, I got my first view of Victoria Nyanza—a deep blue distant and narrow bay, with islands, bold headlands, and a sea beyond.

Seven hours; $14\frac{1}{4}$ miles; morning, 70; noon, 89; night, 78; elevation, 4,200.

October 3.—The savage was on hand before daylight to take us to the buffalo. He had a strong and well-made bow and arrows, and nothing else. Very keen, hard-working, good old boy, and we were strong for him. He had buffalo there all right, but living as they did in the midst of savages they were strictly nocturnal and retired to the thickets before daylight. Then in the thickets they would not stand and investigate their disturbers as do ordinary buffs—they know already by experience just what it is and have no further curiosity—but get out at once on the slightest disturbance. It was totally impossible to stalk them, of course. The savage placed us at points of vantage and tried driving them past us. Twice he succeeded, but the thickets were so dense that all we were treated to were a few thrills as the beasts smashed and crashed within twenty yards or so of us. At noon we gave it up, agreeing that it was interesting; but, barring miraculous luck, likely to prove unproductive for months. But the old man had worked so hard, was so keen, and really knew his job so well, that we gave him three rupees and a knife. Beside, he was rather a pathetic figure at the head of his two little girls and two little boys trudging down after water, and no *bibi** at all. A load of peanuts—sixty pounds—came in, for which we paid cash 3⅓ cents. Three more men down with fever. Morning, 68; noon, 88; night, 74.

October 4.—Many forest hyraxes calling all night, and the most shrill and pleasing chorus of insects. We returned to Walioba's by a route of our own, and saved two and a half hours' march, which indicates well the usual roundabout paths of the natives.

Contrary to usual belief, most natives are very poor hands at finding their way through unknown country. All subsequent travel follows the first man's route. Nothing is more aggravating than to follow the windings and twistings of a native guide. The shortcuts are obvious and apparently easy; yet it never occurs to any one of them to try a better route. Nor does it bring aught but confusion to suggest such a thing. If you have a native guide you must possess your soul in patience and be content. On the return journey, knowing the lay of the country, you can save your time and

* Woman.

WALIOBA'S "PALACE"

WALIOBA—"PÈRE"

AN EXAMPLE OF EAR STRETCHERS AND A GOOD ADVERTISEMENT FOR
THE KODAK COMPANY

WIREGI PORTERS FURNISHED BY WALIOBA. THE HEAD PADS ARE VERY
CLEVERLY TWISTED OF GRASS

distance. Nor is the average native worth anything in finding his way after dark. But, to give him his due, he can often get back to camp when the white man has become hopelessly confused in the chase of some animal.

Struck a stray topi on the way in, and downed it at about 200.

The cotton fields are full of pickers. I never cease marvelling at the way the women can stand for long periods, bent at exact right angles at the hips, preparing some work near the ground. Their backs are perfectly rigid and straight; as are their knees; but they never seem to tire.

Found Walioba in savage dress, and took a picture of him. He was most reluctant, and only consented when I promised to take him *maredadi** later. In the course of the afternoon Walioba père, the ex-sultan, called. He was a fine old boy, of the old African school, fat, with a deep, hearty voice, and a truly regal carriage. No modern clothes for him, but he looked and acted every inch a king. He called Cuninghame "Papa" in the friendly manner of equal to equal. All he needed was a leopard skin to sit on and a howling dance before him to realize the ideal African king.

Mosquitoes very bad after dark.

Morning, 62; noon, 89; night, 75.

---

* Dressed up.

CHAPTER XXI

OCTOBER 5.—Went out for a last hunt in German East Africa, as to-morrow we shall start on a direct march for the lake. It is African etiquette to shoot meat for your hosts also, so we were followed by quite a retinue, viz.: ten porters for our two beasts, and fifteen savages for that to be given to Walioba I and II. When we reached the game cover, an hour distant, we squatted all but three (to act as messengers) and went on less encumbered.

Game was plenty, but wild, which made it more interesting. By noon I had killed a sing-sing at 292 yards; a topi at 110; and a zebra at 281, and another with two shots, first about 275, second at 180. This finished the job, and also the shooting for this part of the trip. The statistics are as follows: Animals shot at 176; animals killed 152. To do this required 303 cartridges with which 241 hits were made.

Very muggy sticky weather. Saw a cliff village below a small precipice. On the top of the precipice sat a baboon calmly contemplating the children below him; they in turn were perched on lower cliffs looking down on us.

Men and donkeys came in from Missambi's at 1:30.

All afternoon getting ready to move. Walioba in good old African fashion has changed his mind about buying donkeys, so we have them still to sell. He has ready for us as porters eight of his Wiregi, fine, tall, muscular men, as all these people are. He has also been prompt in bringing milk, water, firewood, eggs, three sacks *m'wembe*, two loads of peanuts, guides, etc. Therefore we gave him an alarm clock, a pair of socks, some empty chop boxes with locks, and five rupees. The alarm clock in especial he is most tickled with, and makes it perform for any and all comers.

Heavy rain. A leopard leaped the defences of the "palace" and stole a sheep in the evening. Everybody out with fire, spears, and much noise, but the leopard got away with it.

Our Ungruimis made much *manena* wanting to return from here. After a long *shauri* we found that they feared being pressed into service by the Germans at Musoma, should they show their faces there. We solved the problem by counting out their wages and wrapping up each individual's in a piece of Mericani. These we promised they should have the instant they had laid down their loads at Musoma; so they could, if they so desired, seize their money and depart instanter. With this they were satisfied.

Did 13¼ miles; morning, 70 degrees; noon, 90; night, 70. Dropped 18 degrees in ten minutes when it rained.

October 6.—Off for the lake with the biggest safari

yet, viz.: our forty men and four donkeys and twenty-
one savages.   Many of our men are sick, however, and
all have light loads.

Struck the native track in two hours and paddled
down it at a good speed.   This country is all of granite
with wide valleys of granitic soil, bold mountains made
of masses of huge boulders, smaller rocky kopjes, and
curious single spires and needles fifty to a hundred feet
high sticking up all by themselves.   The growth is of
thin thorn and many openings—no forests such as I
had imagined next the lake.   Villages everywhere up
in the rocks, and the soil of the valleys cultivated in the
usual native fashion—with a sharp stick.   No game,
but many game birds, such as guinea fowl, bustards,
etc.   Water scarce and not very good.

We stopped, at three hours, at a waterhole for rest.
Some girls came for water.   Their garments are of a new
type, consisting merely of a number of brass wire rings
encircling the hips loosely.   Much traffic on the road,
men carrying reeds from the lake, natives on all sorts of
business.   These are the true lake people, tall, exceedingly well built, and as black as black.   Camped at
five hours ten minutes, $13\frac{3}{4}$ miles, by the roadside.
Water green and bad.   Sent men with pails and bags
over the hills to Mara Bay to bring us back the bare
necessity.   No washing to-day!   Temperature low, sky
overcast, but very steamy and muggy, morning, 70;
noon, 80; night (?); elevation, 3,400.

ENTERING MUSOMA ON VICTORIA NYANZA. OUR FORCE WAS HERE AT ITS
GREATEST, AS WE HAD TWENTY-FIVE SAVAGES ACTING AS
TEMPORARY PORTERS

THE "CHAIN GANG" AT MUSOMA IN CHARGE OF GERMAN NATIVE SOLDIERS

R. J. CUNINGHAME AND STEWART EDWARD WHITE ON THEIR ARRIVAL AT THE LAKE

October 7.—An overcast and sticky day to start with, clearing later. Off at 5:35 along the edge of Mara Bay, with hills to the left and high green papyrus cutting our view to the right. Hundreds of dragonflies about, with transparent wings across the ends of which were broad black bands, so that as they hovered they gave the impression of unsupported bodies accompanied on either side by satellites. The native huts were here built next the papyrus—where the mosquitoes must have been very thick. They had herds of humped cattle among which fluttered and perched numbers of white egrets—a pretty sight. Stone spires in monolith and square rocks like forts cropped up here and there, isolated, from an otherwise alluvial soil. The path was broad and well beaten; and indeed we met much traffic—natives going to market carrying loads of sugar-cane or *m'wembe;* coming from market with coils of brass wire, little packets of sugar or salt, strings of beads, cotton cloth or beautiful new red blankets; carrying huge bundles of papyrus stalks to use as building materials, or just moving about to see what they could see. They are a very black people, these lake dwellers, but beautifully muscled and most symmetrically shaped.

Soon we began to catch glimpses of a bold and broken coastline with promontories and islands, and in two hours passed by the old government post at Ita-banga, now abandoned. There still remains a substantial two-story whitewashed stone house, the wreck of orchards, and sisal fields. The town itself, of many huts, is still a very busy place, for here land the dhows and hence set forth the trading caravans for the Ikoma and Tabora country, below where we had been exploring. Here Cuninghame dropped back to try to sell the four last donkeys. We hated to part with them, for of the sixty-one animals with which we left Vanderweyer's these four were the sole survivors. However, we could not take them with us. Got 240 rupees for the lot.

Here for the first time I saw houses made of adobe bricks almost exactly like the old California article.

Arrived at the new post of Musoma about two hours later. It is situated on a long very narrow neck of land that reaches straight out pretty close to the mouth of Mara Bay. This land is very low except that at the inner end two kopjes and at the extreme tip a rocky knob mark the terminations. It is absolutely bare of trees or shade; we camped on coarse quartz sand and scanty grass. The "works" at present consist of a small stucco house and a customs shed near the end, and a wharf about fifty feet long made of loose stones dumped down. A government house and two forts (!) are in contemplation. A great many very neat huts made of the clean-looking papyrus stems, and a double row of Indian shops, represent the town. In charge is a German non-commissioned officer, styled by all (including himself) "Bwana Askari," and a German architect.

Several hundred savages are labouring at the public works, some free, and a great many strung together by chains passing from one iron collar to another. I am bound to say the chain gang seemed quite cheerful. Everything was being done by hand, and with incredible labour. Long files of men departed for the distant rock hill and reappeared, each carrying on his head a single stone. This he dropped to its place, and returned for another. Other files of men carried each a little basket of earth or sand. Planks were being sawn from the solid log by hand, one man atop, one below, dragging a rusty and dull old saw back and forth. Four men held a pile upright, two more supported a short ladder against it: a seventh, perched precariously on the ladder, beat the end of the huge pile with an ordinary sledge hammer. It looked to be impossible that this should bring results—nor did it seem to as long as I watched—but it must work, for I saw the pile in place two days later! Four men were required to drag one stone a mile. They laid it on a piece of wood, and either hauled on it or laboriously rolled it back on its rude carriage when it fell off.

Our first job, after making camp, was to prospect for a dhow,* in which to sail north to Shirati—the land journey was impossible on account of sleeping sickness. There were none in port, and no prospects of any for

---

* These craft are sailed by negroes, but owned by the Indian traders, who ply a busy trade in peanuts and rice as against the usual trade goods.

eight days. We were rather dismayed at that, but there seemed no alternative but to wait, for all the country north is full of sleeping sickness. In the meantime we had a *shauri* with Bwana Askari, a capable German of the lower class, with Kolb and Dill whiskers. He spoke no English and we no German, so all our negotiations went on in Swahili.

It seems that the *askari* who met us at Natron reported that we had killed a giraffe, and as that is illegal in Germany without a "greater license," we were to be arrested. The giraffe in question had been killed on the British side, and the *askari* should have known that, for previous to meeting him we had done no hunting on the German side. We explained this, and Bwana Askari agreed that the nigger had been officious, but took from us a deposit of Rs 300. We get this back later when the accusation is officially quashed.

Spent part of the afternoon writing to the Governor, the Provincial Commissioner, and the Customs, setting this matter right. At an Indian *dukka* bought a tin of jam, a bottle of lime juice, and some chocolate. For some time we have had only oatmeal, rice, tea, coffee, and sugar, and this purchase was intended to represent luxury.

A torrential downpour lasting an hour drove us in at three o'clock, and another lasted nearly all night. About half our men are down with fever, and Cuninghame has a slight attack.

The view up the bay from our camp is wonderful, with the long reach of the bay, and the different layers of hills and mountains reaching back and back to milky distance.

Four hours; 10½ miles; morning, 70; noon, 86; night, 68.

October 8.—A day of uncertain rushing about trying to get information of when we are likely to get away. A very small dhow blew in and went up the bay. We sent messengers after her and caught her when she landed at Itabanga. For fifty rupees her captain agreed to make one trip to Shirati, but could not make two. As the dhow looked inadequate for all our lot we made the men fall in and picked out those who were to stay until we could send for them. Hamisi, failing to show up, was found dead drunk on *tembo*.* Later when asked why he did not fall in with the rest, he replied that he had "sleeping sickness," an answer that saved him *kiboko*. Fined him one half month's wages.

About three in the afternoon I saw the black smoke of a steamer over the point, drifting down the wind. Joyfully we hastened to a height—to find that the "smoke" was a swarm of midges, a phenomenon for which Victoria Nyanza is famous. There must have been millions of them, for they were in appearance exactly like the voluminous smoke of a steamer that has just been fresh stoked. Once in the air they cannot

* Native beer.

come down until the wind dies, so their fate is most uncertain.

The "town" proved not uninteresting. The women of the government *askaris* parade up and down, Nandi mostly. They as a class are the only women in Africa who do not work, and they value themselves accordingly. Their hair is done elaborately, their ornaments are many, their patterned garment clean and new; but especially are they interesting for their airs of feminine coquetry. A very great—and very ridiculous—sultan was in making purchases. In his native wilds he was probably a fine-looking man. Now he wore a peaked helmet much too big for him, a light gray army over-coat that was the last word in misfits, puttees awkwardly wound, and huge brogans. An actor on the comic stage would be considered rather to have overdone it if he had looked so. This potentate was accompanied by his two favourite wives—in native undress—the bearer of the royal camp-chair, and a few miscellaneous *shenzis*. He was a canny old soul and did not intend being done, for he went carefully into every Indian *dukka* before making his first purchase.

A tremendous rain again in the evening, after the cessation of which we heard the sultan and suite returning home—very drunk. They howled and screamed and chattered at the top of their lungs; and nobody paid the slightest attention to what anybody else said.

Morning, 65; noon, 88; night, 78.

THE FOUR SURVIVORS OF THE DONKEY TRAIN. OF OUR OWN AND
VANDERWEYER'S, 59 ANIMALS DIED OF TSETSE

AT MUSOMA—THE ONLY SAWMILL IN THE COUNTRY

THE ENTRANCE TO MARA BAY, TAKEN FROM VICTORIA NYANZA

THE DHOW IN WHICH WE SAILED UP VICTORIA NYANZA

LOADING OUR DHOW AT MUSOMA FOR THE TRIP UP VICTORIA NYANZA

CHAPTER XXII

OCTOBER 9.—Packed up and sat down to wait for the dhow. She arrived about eight, and proved to be laden deep with peanuts and miscellaneous natives, all of which had to be unloaded before we could get aboard. She was the typical thing, high aft and low forward, so that she looked constantly on the point of making a dive; with one mast amidships and one huge sail on a yard. This was manipulated and swung about by the most fearful and complicated system of native-made ropes and wooden blocks. The crew consisted of four ordinary natives, and a more intelligent black citizen, who held the tiller. Fortunately the dhow is not a skittish creature and does not require quick handling. The crew put in its time sleeping or playing with a tinful of beads. When the skipper gave an order the proper man to execute it had to be searched for and waked up. Then the order was discussed in all its bearings. Luckily a dhow cannot be upset nor wrecked unless it hits a rock, and then it has to be a very big rock and the dhow going fast.

We got our loads aboard, and embarked the men one by one. The skipper had a sort of plimsoll mark of his own on which to keep his eye. We piled men on top of each other, squeezed them like sardines, at last got them all triumphantly aboard! We were much relieved at this—as were the men—for we did not want to leave them. There was no more room; but we still floated. Cuninghame and I occupied a flat, hard little deck right in the stern together with the crew and a jumble of ropes.

We cast off from the pier and poled ourselves out until we floated free. Then, and not until then, we raised the sail. Reason immediately apparent. The dhow refused positively to pay off, but nosed her way back into the wind every time she was coaxed out of it. Yells, confusion, excitement, production of two long poles to the end of which were fastened round pieces of wood—oars, save the mark! Thrice we vainly teased our way free, and thrice we came up into the wind. Then we hung on a hair of indecision, hesitated, paid off, and were away before the breeze. Fortunately the wind held fresh and fair all day. If it had not, heaven alone knows where we should have arrived or when.

The shores of Victoria Nyanza are deeply indented. In fact, the coastline is practically a series of long peninsulas and deep bays between them. Groups of islands of all sizes are numerous. Wherever the coast is not beaten by the seas it is fringed with a band of papyrus, sometimes thirty feet from root to blossom. The coast proper is rather barren and brown looking, with ranges of mountains, and the constant succession of rocky outcrops through which we had been marching. Nowhere are there forests; but the scenery is most beautiful in places. The water is a deep green. Crocodiles and hippos are common, and give a distinct feeling of incongruity to the open-sea impression.

Our little deck grew very hot at noon, but the breeze held; and by 4:30 we picked up the buildings of Shirati. Shortly after we landed. Nobody ever yet "made a landing" in a dhow. The sail is dropped while yet some distance out, and then the unwieldy affair is poked and punched in. Generally it goes to leeward, and they have to drop anchor and get ropes ashore and otherwise muddle about. By the time we were landed and had our loads ashore it was dark. We camped in an open place, and plunged into our mail, which had been sent down here for us. Rained in the evening. Lots of fever cases, among which was poor Cuninghame again.

Morning, 70; noon (?); night, 77.

October 10.—Shirati is a German Government post, situated on a long narrow tongue of land running out into the lake. This peninsula is 100 feet high, and bare of larger vegetation. The Germans have planted two avenues of trees, but they have not done well, and have generally a very sickly appearance. Near the water is a stuccoed and whitewashed customs house with two smaller houses for the Goanese officials a

short distance away. The way then rises to a square
stone fort of some size near which stands the District
Commissioner's building, long, low, and white, with
surrounding veranda. The other side the fort are a
dozen Indian *dukkas* and, in an open space, a roofed
shed for the native market. The second avenue of
sickly trees runs from the fort down the length of the
peninsula. A few scattered native huts, and several
more compact villages, make up the rest of Shirati. A
fresh breeze generally sweeps across the peninsula,
which keeps it reasonably free of mosquitoes and fever.
The sleeping sickness is bad only a few miles away; and
Shirati is soon to be abandoned.

We called on the District Commissioner and found
him a very pleasant, short, blond, and pink little man,
who spoke a little English. We had the wearisome
giraffe *shauri* to go over again.

Then we went down to the landing and tackled the
Customs. That took the rest of the day, for never
before in the history of Shirati had sportsmen gone out
from there. The babu had no precedents, no book, no
nothing to go by; and such a situation is very tough on
the babu. We made a good many of our own precedents on the spot, and got off fairly well.

Very hot and sticky, and a lot more of our men came
down with fever.

There is a species of eagle very numerous here and
well named Vocifer. He is the jolliest creature im-

aginable, for he is continually giving vent to perfect screams of laughter and joy so like the wild hilarity of the native women that at first I was thus deceived. And when one sees the joke they all see the joke and join in. This wild joyous cry is uttered on the wing or sitting. When the Vocifer happens to be in a tree, he throws his head back just as a person would do when laughing heartily. As the joke gets funnier his head gets farther back until it fairly lies between his shoulders with the open beak pointing straight up.

Morning, 71; noon, 90; night (?).

October 11.—Great difficulty to get firewood. We buy little bunches of it from the native women. Naturally there are no more evening campfires. In the early morning and late evening great flocks of the sacred ibis pass going to or coming from their feeding grounds. We spent the day reading up in the *Literary Digest*, and in writing letters.

Morning, 68; noon, 96; night, 75.

October 12.—To-day a boat was expected—though at what hour was unknown. At seven o'clock we packed up, as per instructions, and went down to the customs house. There we sat in the shade until 4:30. That is usual in Africa. A native in a dugout canoe fished just off the edge of the reeds for the same length of time, and apparently without catching anything; so we had no monopoly on the stock of patience.

At 4:30 the steamer came in and anchored. A small

boat brought a line ashore, and by means of that a lighter full of peanuts was hauled out by hand. We went with the lighter. The *Nyanza* is a small steamer, living quarters and engines all aft, freight decks amidships, small forecastle, like our Great Lakes freighters on a smaller scale. She is shallow and draws only about six feet. Awful little cabin with saggy and bumpy bunks. Live on the bridge, where meals are served. At about sunset we had completed loading the peanuts, and steamed an hour or so to Korangu, where we dropped anchor for the night. There is no night travel on Victoria Nyanza. Not much sleep. Too many natives aboard, too bad beds. A small group of some of the lake people were singing very sweetly in harmony; the first time I have ever heard Africans do anything but plain unison. A gorgeous night, with the reflection of the land in moonlit water.

October 13.—Korangu is surrounded, or rather backed, by high, dry-looking mountains, like those of Spain or our own Southwest. Visible is only one tin shed and a small house; though the captain told us a Seventh Day Adventist mission lay over the hill! We soon steamed away.

A remarkably hot day. The shores here are of bold high mountains; and many islands made for us a sort of inside passage, so that we lost the effect of the open sea. At one point we worked our way through a passage in which the channel was only 200 feet wide, with a right-

GOVERNMENT POST (GERMAN) AT SHIRATI. THIS POST WAS ON THE POINT OF ABANDONMENT BECAUSE OF SLEEPING SICKNESS

"BOLOGNA SAUSAGE" TREE. FROM THE WOOD OF THIS TREE IS BREWED THE POISON THE NATIVES USE ON THEIR ARROWS

A KAVIRONDO VILLAGE

angled turn; and here, owing to a misplaced buoy, we nearly hung up. This passage and one other are the only entrances to the Kavirondo Gulf. The latter is some sixty miles long, by ten or fifteen wide, and is practically a lake by itself. The mountains on both sides are very lofty, but set rather back, so there is a littoral. At the end there is a vast stretch of flat country—a continuation of the old lake bed—but at last the mountains close even this in.

Our intention was to land at Kisumu* and to look for Uganda cob at Kibigori, a place about twenty-five miles inland on this flat. We docked at Kisumu about sundown, with a good deal of flurry; and I easily saw why the captains of these lake steamers crack up. The climate and the nervous work are a combination to knock up anybody. At this point we got two pieces of bad news: The first was that Vanderweyer's donkeys are all dead. The other hit poor Memba Sasa. He got word that his father and his wife were both dead of plague; and that the Masai had seized the opportunity to steal sixty of his goats—a very severe financial loss for a man in his position. We decided to send him up by train tomorrow to see what he could do. I am extremely sorry, for I am fond of him. Slept (?) on board, as we had nowhere to go in the dark.

October 14.—Sent off Memba Sasa by early train. He wept at parting, and I felt like doing so. I shall

* Kisumu is the lake terminal of the Uganda Railroad.

not see him again. Then we spent some three hot hours on customs and on shipping out trophies and donkey saddles by freight. Also in getting our men all inoculated for plague, a job which did not in the least please them. It hurts somewhat. Cuninghame, like an old fox, headed off possible complaints by announcing that the inoculation was a sort of test; that those whom it made ill and unable to work would be thus proved plague-infected and must go in quarantine for fifteen days. As quarantine scares them to death we had no complaints!

Then we went up to call on the Provincial Commissioner, who proved to be the brother of that Horne we formerly met at Meru. This is a very tall man, so he is known as Long Horne, and the other as Short Horne. He was extraordinarily cordial, and sent off a wire to a man at Muhoroni asking about cob. Also invited us to lunch. We captured our men and made camp in an open space under a "bologna sausage tree."

Kisumu must be described in three parts: (1) At the water's edge are many huge corrugated iron structures representing goods stores, machine shops, customs, and shipyards. The ships are sent out in numbered pieces, and are here put together like a jigsaw puzzle. Then on the flat a little removed is a village of Indian *dukkas* and native huts. Then up on a low volcanic ridge are the houses and offices of the Europeans. These are pretty scattered, have gardens, stone walls, shaded streets or roads, and are generally quite attractive. The view out over the Kavirondo Gulf and the mountains and valley is very fine; and were it not for the climate the place would be very attractive.

The climate is bad, however. You see there many a big husky man; but his eyes are restless, his manner nervous, and his frequent laugh loud and forced almost to a note of hysteria. Plague is always present among the swarming natives; meningitis is creeping in; and sleeping sickness is so near that it is a dread and a threat. Doctor Moett, the medical officer, is immensely busy— and immensely pleased and interested. He set a dozen wire traps, caught a dozen plague rats, and left the lot by his laboratory door, pending investigation. When he went to look for them an hour or so later, they had gone. Only the empty traps! Summoned his boys.

"Oh, yes, we know where the rats are; we ate them; isn't that what the *bwana* caught them for?"

"And they were plague rats!" concluded the doctor pathetically.

Horne's house is in the middle of a lovely garden which would drive a garden lover crazy with its tropical stuff, and is a wide, cool, rambling structure with shady verandas. We had a good lunch, and Cuninghame and I were so pleased that after Horne had gone back to his office we remained loafing in his easy chairs. So later he asked us to dine, an invitation we accepted shamelessly.

Horne is very much interested in opening his district by means of good roads (in the native sense). He tried in vain to get the chiefs interested; and finally hit on the happy idea of a bicycle for each chief and an *askari* to teach him to ride. Now it is not unusual to see a naked savage hiking along in the depths of Africa on a glittering wheel. And every time he comes a cropper he gets out a thousand men or so to fix the road! There has been a good deal of interest for some time over a reported new animal in the back country. Therefore a certain official was more than delighted when two of his *askaris* came in to report that they had been chased by and had shot such an animal. Being an official he sent forth official commands that any dead animal found anywhere near that place belonged to *him;* and he sent out parties in all directions to search. After all these preparations had been made up comes a sad-eyed Indian.

"Please, *bwana*," says he, "I want 50 rupees because your *askari* kills my donkey."

As illustrating settler methods Horne told us of the man who was digging a well and ran into a rock twenty feet down. Drilled it, put in dynamite, but was unable to touch it off for lack of enough fuse. The usual asinine bystander had a bright idea. They arranged the detonators, rolled a big rock to the edge of the hole, stood at a distance and thrust it in with a pole. The rock failed to explode the detonators, but most effectually blocked the well! He also told of the man who put a rain gauge on his flat roof. After the first rain he sent his clerk up to read it. The clerk reported thirty-one inches. Disbelief; proof; investigation! It turned out that an *askari* was posted on the roof at night, and that the rain gauge's purpose had been mistaken by that *askari*.

CHAPTER XXIII

OCTOBER 15.—After a long wait and many excursions of inquiry we got a reply to our telegram. As cob were said to frequent Kibigori we packed up and set forth at 10:50. The march struck across the flat, and was exceedingly hot. No particular features to record except that the numerous groups of native huts were invariably located in circles of large shady trees, the result of the growth of stakes planted as palisades. The surroundings were exactly like those of the San Fernando Valley, so that the California readers need no further description. To the others I can only say—mountains on three sides, sea on the other, nearly flat valley with occasional low rolling ridges in the middle. Valley sixty miles by about twenty-five.

At the end of three hours we came to the edge of a barranca in the depths of which flowed a swift little stream. A fine, upstanding Kavirondo damsel stood knee-deep, busily engaged in washing out a flat basketful of beans. She had a string of beads about her neck, armlets, a leather string about her waist, and three mosquitoes. However, that did not seem to bother her. She chatted merrily to us, told us there was no

KAVIRONDO. THIS MAN WAS NEARLY SEVEN FEET IN HEIGHT

ALTHOUGH GENERALLY THE KAVIRONDO WOMEN GO STARK NAKED, WHEN THEY MARRY THEY HANG ONE OF THESE "TAILS" BEHIND

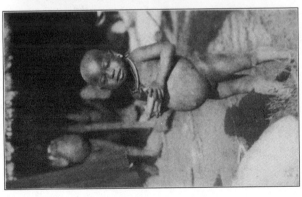

FULL FED—AND ABSOLUTELY SATISFIED!

KAVIRONDO GIRL
SEE PAGE 266

more water for sixteen miles, and passed up gourdfuls for our men to drink.

In the next week I saw many of these Kavirondos, men, women, and children. A majority of them were stark naked. Those that were partially clothed wore the garments as ornaments only. Since they know no harm in nakedness, they of course exhibit not the faintest trace of embarrassment or self-consciousness; so that in a wonderfully brief space of time one comes to accept the fact. One would naturally imagine that a totally naked people would be far down in the human scale, and would exhibit the lowest type of savagery. This is not the case Save for the one fact of nakedness they are rather above the average. They make very good houses, which they keep clean and the earth around which they keep swept. Their personal habits are cleanly. They raise a variety of crops, which they store in well-made granaries. In natural intelligence they seem to be above the average in the way of being quick to catch a meaning, take a joke, etc. Physically they are one of the finest races in East and Central Africa, tall, well proportioned, upright. The men are wonderful, with big frames, developed muscles, yet free from clumsiness. The women, too, are very fine, especially before the age of twenty-five or so; after which, as always in the low, hot countries, the breasts are apt to fall. Both sexes are fond of shaving their heads in queer patterns, which seem to have no uniformity and to signify nothing except the taste of the individual. All other hair on their faces and bodies is most carefully removed. Brass wire alone seems desired. It is worn moderately, only small collars, armlets, and leglets. The unmarried women wear nothing at all. The married women tie on a sort of tail behind made exactly like an old-fashioned bell-cord tassel, but very much larger. They occasionally carry also a small white goatskin burned or branded in stripes like a zebra. This probably has some especial significance, for when I tried to buy one I failed at any price.

"If I sell this I will die," they told me.

They are a friendly people, and it was a real pleasure occasionally to squat in one of their enclosed villages and jaw with them. Everything was clean and swept, nobody was greased and daubed (though many painted their faces), and there seemed a lot of spare hilarious good nature. At the very first it was hard not to be a little embarrassed at being surrounded by so many full-grown ladies without a stitch, but they were all so blissfully unconscious of anything out of the way that I ended by becoming so myself! Those who know these people well tell me that they are the most chaste of all the tribes.

Influenced by the damsel's information about water, we camped in an old cornfield at the edge of the barranca. There was no shade and no firewood; but we threw our blankets over the tents, and cooked with cornstalks.

Two and three fourth hours; 6 miles; morning (?); noon, 99; night, 75. Very humid.

October 16.—We were off by the first of daylight in order to avoid some of the heat. Passed many villages. From one of them came a wailing of many people that rose and fell in the wierdest manner. One of our Kavirondo porters told us that it meant somebody had just died. Saw a great many bustards and the beautiful golden-crested Kavirondo crane. Would very much have liked one of the latter, but did not dare shoot. The country was absolutely flat; villages and natives were everywhere, and no one could tell where a bullet would stop. We passed many people, and never ceased admiring their splendid physical proportions. One group of men with spears were all over six feet with deep chests and the developed muscles of the best Greek sculpture.

After six and one half hours' march (fifteen and one half miles) we reached Kibigori; and very glad to do so, for the sun is here very strong. We walked directly through the station and camped under a solitary tree on a height above the river. By five o'clock we had found and engaged two *shenzis* who claimed to know where cob are to be found. Rained hard late in the afternoon.

Elevation, 3,960; morning, 60; noon, 96; night, 74.

October 17.—We started out with our two *shenzis*, but before we had gone far we had collected a dozen, all anxious for meat. Villages everywhere, and the country not much broken. However, after tramping for some distance through thickly populated open landscape, we came to a narrow strip of "wild" country lying in the triangle where two streams meet. This was a very small bit indeed, and was composed of alternate small thickets and rolling high-grass knolls, with a narrow strip of forest along the course of the river. It was about a mile and a half long, by half a mile at its greatest width. Immediately it became evident that unless the cob was a particularly foolish beast we would never get near any of them with the procession we were dragging about. Therefore we squatted the lot on a knoll and told them to stay put. A hundred yards on we began to see cob in the very tall grass. They were about the size and colour of impalla, and went bounding and popping about in elusive and disconcerting fashion. We sneaked here and there catching an occasional glimpse. The beasts were not very wild, but it was almost impossible to get a plain sight of them. Finally got a good offhand chance at a reasonable distance—and missed! No excuse, except that owing to continued heat and hard work I had a streak of bad holding. Immediately set out in pursuit and fired four more shots without result. This was very sad.

We went on, crossing the stream on the men's backs, and working cautiously down through another strip of

cover along the side of the river.   Saw no animals, and
only a few old tracks.

The Kavirondo now began to come down from their
villages into the swamps and thickets to cut firewood
and thatch; and our guides, who seemed to know the
game thoroughly, told us we might as well quit, as now
the cob would all retire into the densest cover.   Therefore we again crossed the river pickaback and started
for camp.   On the way we ran smack onto a fine
buck cob, in plain sight, broadside on, about 200
yards away.   It was a good fair chance, but I missed
him, and also two other take-a-chance shots at long
range as he went.   Had the same sort of nervous jerks
as my other bad streak.   Hard luck to get this case of
"willies" just when we are after a rarity.   Too much
work and sun.   Overcast, with heavy showers all the
afternoon.   The weather is very oppressive.   Rain all
night.

Twelve and a half miles; morning, 65; noon, 94;
night, 68.

October 18.—Regretted still more yesterday's slump
in shooting when we hunted all morning without seeing
a hoof.   Covered the same ground as yesterday, and
now find that there is in all the country no other place
for cob!   I think we have taken the entire cob census
—three or four bucks and a dozen does.

After we had looked the field all over thoroughly, we
made some visits among the villages, and had a lot of

fun. One place seemed to have struck an umbrella craze. Everybody, who was anybody, owned one, and it was certainly very funny to see stark-naked people under opened sunshades. In each village one or more talked Swahili, and we conversed at length. Things were always swept clean, with no filth. I liked the people. One very polite person informed me, in answer to a question:

"I have two children alive, and one that has just finished dying." This was a literal translation of what he said.

Rested in the heat of the day, and out again in the same country in the afternoon. Had the good luck to see three cob, and by a most careful (probably needlessly careful) stalk got in range. Hit two of them badly before they got off; and I got one, and Cuninghame finished the other in the high grass. Dozens of Kavirondo came running from everywhere at the sound of the shots. We wanted the meat for ourselves, but they took the entrails down to the very last bit. Glad we have the beasts, as the double walk every day in this climate is killing work.

Eighteen and a half miles; morning, 58; noon, 96; night, 69.

October 19.—Went out alone with Kongoni on the chance of seeing another cob. Blundered into a bushbuck and killed it. It proved to have a whacking big head—sixteen and a half inches as opposed to about twelve inches of my others. The Kavirondo gathered, and I promised them the meat if they would stand for photos in their village. They are very shy of the camera. To this they agreed, but even as it was they dove for blankets, skins, etc., before they would pose. I do not think this indicated any sense of feeling naked, but rather a vain desire to show off their wealth. In the afternoon I again covered the little round but saw nothing. In the meantime Cuninghame had struck camp, and when I got in all was ready for the train. At 8:00 we started for Nairobi.

Seven and three quarter miles; morning, 59; noon, 97; night (?).

CHAPTER XXIV

THIS practically completed the trip into the "new" country. The rest of the journal is here included simply for what interest may inhere in it as a hunting narrative. On our return to Nairobi we resolved to go into the forests about Mount Kenia in search of elephant. There are a great many elephant there, but they dwell in such thick jungle and are so truculently inclined that Cuninghame had uttered his intention of never going after them again. However, he changed his mind in the enthusiasm of camp-fire talk. We purposed paying off a portion of our men, and sending a small safari on to Fort Hall—four days' march. There we would join them by the new Thika tramway and two days' march.

(The Journal Resumes)

October 20.—Have only to record the extreme pleasure we felt at our first gulp of the cooler air of the highlands. For some months we have been in a high, humid temperature, day and night; and we have almost forgotten what cool air feels like. At Nairobi ran into James Barnes who, with Cherry Kearton, is out here taking moving pictures of game. He says they have films of thirty-three species, none of them frightened in any way.

October 21.—Down to the store at 9:00 and found Cuninghame paying off some of the men and so chattering and wild with fever that he hardly knew what he was doing. Several of us had to exert mild force to get him away, as he was sufficiently out of his head to feel that he ought to work. Twenty men had already started for Fort Hall before this attack came on. Wired them to sit down there until they heard from us; and got Cuninghame to bed. Dined with the Newlands. The other evening Wuznam, the game ranger, was riding along near Nairobi on a motorcycle and was for some distance pursued by a lion! I wonder what sort of game the beast thought he was chasing! And isn't it a "comic supplement" picture!

October 22-28 inclusive.—In Nairobi waiting for Cuninghame to get well. We moved him up to Newland's house. Everybody was most kind to me, and I did not take a dinner at the hotel. Occupied the daytime in making maps, writing, etc. A good deal of rain at night and in showers.

October 29.—Started at 10:30 for Fort Hall in a twenty-horsepower Minerva touring car that had seen better days. It was a terribly heavy piece of ordnance for its power, but it had four speeds. The chap who drove it was firmly convinced that it could not last much longer anyhow and he might as well use it while it held together. Also the Fort Hall road is no level macadamized boulevard! We charged down hills and across the flats with a grand clatter and bang, bouncing in and out of holes with such a whack that we had hard work to stick in; and crawled slowly up hills on our lower gears. However it was a heap faster than safari; and by a little after noon we had reached Blue Post— ordinarily a two days' journey! Ate lunch there; and reached Fort Hall at 4:00. Our boys seemed glad to see us, and had camp all fixed in shape. Fort Hall is situated on one of the long tongues of land that radiate out from Kenia, with a cañon several hundred feet deep on either side. Usual officials' quarters, *askari* tents, and Indian *dukkas*. Many trees and green grass. Met the A. D. C., Lawford by name, a young and enthusiastic chap who had killed his first lion and could talk of little else. Mrs. Lawford gave us tea. Rained in the night, so we were very glad we had finished the motor-car end of the journey.

Night, 70.

October 30.—Dropped down from the tongue of land to a vigorous mountain stream, followed it a short distance, wriggled through a pass in the hills, and rested at the celebrated government bridge across the Tana. This is the Kikuyu country, and the *shambas* are everywhere. As it is now the beginning of the small rains, everybody is farming. The soil is turned up by means of a pointed stick. It would astonish one who had never seen it to observe how well the ground is prepared and over how great an extent. Both men and women work in the fields at this the rush season, though generally the woman does the labour. A banana leaf skirt is the sign of husbandry, and is only donned when farming is on. There is a good deal of system in the way old bean stalks, etc., are gathered in rows and finally disposed of by burning. In addition to the bean fields and grain fields are many large banana groves.

At the bridge we found a native spear market, and a native general market. The latter consists in bringing what you have to sell or barter and displaying it under a suitable tree. Here we procured a guide. The network of hills from here to the slopes proper of Kenia is so complicated, the cañons between them so deep, and the cultivation so shifting that even Kongoni, who had been up here several times, would not undertake to find the way. We marched until about noon, the foothills getting gradually higher; then camped in an old bean field. Rained heavily in the afternoon; but at 5:30 Kenia broke through the clouds, glittering like an opalescent jewel of a mountain far in the depths of an African evening sky. Feeling seedy.

Four hours fifty minutes; 12 miles; morning, 64; noon, 94; night, 66.

October 31.—We now began to thread our way along high rounded ridges between which were tremendous cañons and dashing streams of water. The huts clung to the side hills, or were perched atop the divides. A high growth of bracken or blackberry vines clothed all the country with a green mantle ten feet high.   The paths ran like narrow lanes through this rank growth. Although at one time forested there were now no trees, with the exception of solitary specimens perched here and there on commanding heights.   Cuninghame says these have been spared because they are considered sacred. At many of the villages the natives were making *tembo*.*

A log with many shallow holes connected by channels and a hard rounded stick as pestle was the whole apparatus.   A string of women brought up loads of the sugar cane.   Others hacked off the outer covering and shredded the pulp.   A third lot pounded out the juice. After it should have fermented to a certain point it would be drawn off in gourds.   Then the village drunk!

Our guide, becoming a trifle uncertain, called in from time to time the assistance of others.   They dropped whatever they were doing, and quite cheerfully walked an hour or so over these ungodly hills, and then said farewell.   All this without reward of any kind.   It rained heavily from time to time, and we became well soaked through.   In addition the downpour made the clay of the hills very slippery.   As a consequence it was not until about three o'clock that we burst out of this vine country to a little open space.   Here abruptly began the forest.

Near the edge of the forest stood silently a dozen

---

* Native beer.

THE COUNTRY OUTSIDE THE ELEPHANT FOREST

THE UPPER TANA RIVER NEAR FORT HALL

THE BASE CAMP IN THE ELEPHANT FOREST.   DRYING OUT DURING ONE OF THE RARE INTERVALS BETWEEN RAINS

SEE PAGE 279

naked red-brown savages with spears. They were fine, lithe creatures. The news of our coming had gone ahead of us, and they were waiting for us. Cuninghame is well known among these wild people. Following closely on their heels we plunged into the deep woods, and after a half-hour turning, twisting, and ducking about, apparently at random, we popped out into a tiny grass meadow right in the middle of the big trees. It was about 100 yards in diameter, like a shallow saucer in shape. This, Cuninghame explained, was his customary camp, known as "Tembo Circus." Even he, many times as he has been here, is unable to find it without the help of his Wanderobo friends; and many other people have tried in vain to reach it.

We made camp, and managed to get a fire going and to dry off. Everything was steaming with dampness. Occasionally low heavy clouds swept across and dumped their contents down on us. The tops of the great trees by which we were surrounded often touched the lower fringes of these clouds.

Let us now consider why I am here, anyway. Before I went to Africa the first time, I rather looked down on elephant shooting. "Anybody ought to be able to hit an elephant," said I to myself. It seemed to me a good deal like shooting at a barn. Beside which, I had a soft spot in my heart for my old circus friend.

But I had not been very long in Africa before I began to modify my ideas. In the first place, the African elephant was not my old circus friend at all, but a beast two and a half feet taller, very much longer, and possessed of a truculent disposition. Nobody has successfully domesticated the African elephant, much less taught him to work and be useful. Carthage used him in war, but even for that purpose was able to employ only the immature beasts of a northerly race now extinct. In the second place, the African elephant—unless one makes a special very long unhealthy journey —is to be found only in thick forests where one can see but a few yards in any direction. The hunter has to approach very near before he can see to shoot. Furthermore, since the law prohibits the shooting of cows and of bulls with tusks that weigh less than thirty pounds each, he must maneuver to examine his beast, and must arrange to back out again—undiscovered—if the elephant is not the right sort of an elephant. As there may be forty others scattered about, and as any of the forty, on getting his wind, will tell the others about him, and as the lot will probably then try deliberately to kill him, it will be seen that the game is not so simple as it first appears. Furthermore, an elephant can travel faster than a man; he can break any tree the ordinary man can climb; and he is exceedingly persistent. And, finally, it is not at all like shooting at a barn. There is just one spot, three inches wide by seven inches long, where a shot is instantly fatal; and only a few other small places where a shot even does any ultimate good. One must know his anatomy; and even then it is generally very difficult to make out fatal spots through the dimness and the screen of a forest. And, lastly, an elephant is a great traveller; so that a fresh trail means little unless it is instantly and rapidly followed. When I had learned these things I began to see the reason for Cuninghame's emphatic statement: that the man who got his bull elephant—in this country—had earned him.

Cuninghame is the greatest elephant man in Africa. Therefore when three years ago he told me that never again would he go among the elephants of Kenia, I believed him.

"They are getting too *kali*," said he; "it isn't good enough. They have got so that if they hear a shot or a broken twig even, or smell the faintest indication of a human being, they come for him at once."

Then I talked to a member of the Swedish Zoölogical Expedition. He had gone up to Kenia with Cuninghame to get elephant. The hunt ended by Cuninghame's going down into the herd and killing the beast. He also fired twelve shots from his heavy gun merely to keep off the herd. He himself acknowledged that twice he had nearly been caught.

"I wouldn't have gone among that screaming lot of devils for anything on earth," the Swede told me frankly. "I told Cuninghame if he was fool enough to do so, he had my permission. I sat down on a rock."

Nevertheless, here we were! It is always that way with hunters' good resolutions.

After tea we called up the Wanderobo for a *shauri*. The Wanderobo are little wild men, forest dwellers, who have no houses, no crops, no cattle; whose sole possessions are a few wire ornaments, their bows and arrows, skin robes, and a wonderful instinctive knowledge of the woods. These four knew Cuninghame of old and were willing to trust him. Very few people ever get to see them at all. They agreed that they should go scouting in different directions to-morrow, on the search for fresh tracks, while we awaited in camp for the first report.

CHAPTER XXV

THE forests of Kenia are of hardwood. They grow
on the lower slopes of the mountains, extending up to
the 8,000-9,000 mark, where they are succeeded by the
bamboos. Therefore the surface of the country they
cover is hilly, consisting of long spur-like ridges or
hogsbacks with steep sides separated by deep cañons
and short lateral ravines. The forest growth itself is
of three kinds: Imagine, first, the planting of single
great spreading trees at spaced intervals; trees in shape
like elms, maples, or beeches, but three or four times
their size. Fill in the spaces between them with a very
thick growth of smaller trees—one hundred feet high
and a foot or so through. Then below that a leafy
undergrowth, so dense as to be literally impenetrable
to either sight or locomotion. This undergrowth is of
many varieties. It puts out big leaves, small leaves;
grows on hard stems, watery soft stems; it stands a foot
high or forty—generally both. Vines of all sizes tie it
together; vines ranging in size from little tough ones as
small as a whipcord through which you think you can
push easily (you cannot!) up to big cables. Underfoot
are ferns. Along the slanting trunks of trees grow
other ferns and damp mosses. Streamers of moss de-

pend from limbs and sway in the currents of air. Orchids cling. All small dead twigs are muffled tightly in vivid moss. On the slopes of the cañons and the heads of ravines are little forests of tree ferns, feathery and beautiful. These run to thirty feet in height.

Everything is dripping wet. Indeed the strongest single impression that remains to me of that forest is that it was a varnished forest; every leaf, every branch, every smooth surface shines polished. Always in the ear is a slow and solemn dripping.

When one, with difficulty, forces himself ten feet from the track, he knows not where he can go next. Were it not for elephant tracks he could not get about at all. Old *tembo* makes nothing of what to his little enemy is an impenetrable jungle. When he wants to go anywhere, he goes; and he pushes aside trees as we push aside blades of grass. Nothing inspires more awe and respect for these animals than, first, these paths broken through the jungle; and, second, the sight of the great beasts themselves, calmly, ruthlessly, without hurry, without effort, bursting the barrier of the forest.

Another impression of the unique character of this forest for two days eluded my analysis. I felt that here was something strange and unusual, but I could not seize it. It made its impress, and yet it eluded; and in the end it haunted me, worried me, as the forgetting of a name that one has "on the tip of the tongue." Finally I got it. Here are no "dead and

ONE OF THE "DEROBO" ELEPHANT HUNTERS

SAVAGES IN THE ELEPHANT FOREST

N'JAHGI (READER'S RIGHT) AND HIS HEAD ASSISTANT

MT. KENIA. IT IS VERY DIFFICULT TO GET A PICTURE OF THIS MOUNTAIN OWING TO THE MISTS THAT ENSHROUD IT

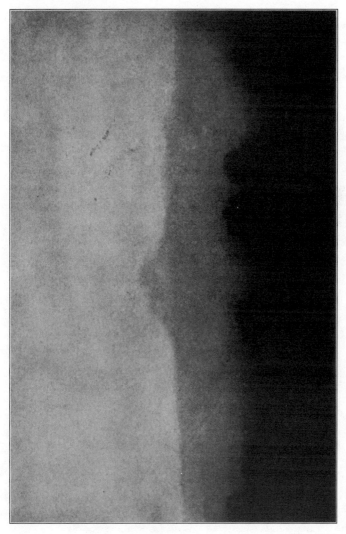

THE MISTS CLOSING DOWN ON KENIA FIVE MINUTES AFTER THE OTHER PHOTOGRAPH WAS TAKEN
(TAKEN WITH LONGER FOCUS LENS, WHICH ACCOUNTS FOR THE DIFFERENCE IN SIZE)

TYPICAL ELEPHANT FOREST. THE TREE FERNS ARE 30 AND 40 FEET HIGH

down" trees. These massive giants fall at such intervals; and they are so immediately absorbed by the forces of dampness and decay! With us a down tree may lie twenty years or more before it disintegrates. Here it is gone in two.

In daytime these forests seem almost void of life. There are few birds, few visible or audible animals, few insects. Silence holds, save for the voices of the wind or the rain. But with the fall of dusk strange creatures awaken. Leopards sigh and the tree hyraxes and the colobus raise their strange and eerie cries. There are few wilder sounds in nature than the long mournful crescendo shriek of the female hyrax. It is demoniac. The moment the night is dark they begin, near the very edge of the camp, in the blackness of the depths beyond, far off in the distance, like lost souls groping and crying for each other's guidence.

November 1.—Early in the morning the Wanderobo prepared to set forth. The pursuit of the elephant is much more than a sporting incident in their lives; it is a real and solemn end of existence. Before starting out they drew a little to one side, squatted in a circle, and made medicine. It was really impressive. An old man performed the ritual, raising his hands, palm up, to heaven; facing in turn to all points of the compass; bending humbly, his hands crossed on his breast; calling on the forest and the Powers in a loud voice. The others, their heads low, muttered choral responses, and at times beat the earth softly in unison with the palms of their hands. It was genuine "high church" for them, and when they had finished they arose and immediately disappeared in the forest.

The morning was clear. At about eleven, however, the clouds blackened with inconceivable rapidity, and in ten minutes rain was falling heavily. At about the same time in came two of the Wanderobo to tell us that they had actually seen an elephant. Immediately we called the gunbearers and plunged into the dripping woods. We followed our two Wanderobo at a great pace for two hours, crossing two deep cañons on the way. It rained steadily all the time and we were soon wet and soggy. Once N'jahgi, the elder, pointed to a hollow in a tree closed by a rude door of bark, and gave us to understand that it was one of his residences. On top of the last ridge above the second stream they showed us some red mud rubbed smooth and shiny, as though with an immense trowel, and plastered high up on the trunk of a big tree.

After staring at it a moment I realized that here an elephant had rubbed his huge flanks, and was amazed at the height of the mud above the ground. We followed that elephant's spoor until three o'clock. He wandered steadily up the slope of the hogsback toward the mountain. Sometimes his great footprints were as plain and about as large as a foot-tub; at others they could be distinguished only with the greatest difficulty, and the 'derobo had to look very carefully at the junction of two elephant trails to see whether the beast had gone on one or the other.   Going up or down hill he had made some grand slippery slides in the red clay, and we had a high old time getting up at all.   It was like climbing an icy roof.   At three o'clock we had to turn back.   It was that or spend the night in the forest.   The rain continued.   Our little Wanderobo shivered like dogs, and wrung out their little pieces of cotton cloth.   When we got to camp we gave them each a blanket.

The men had succeeded in coaxing up good fires; and had built an open-front shelter for the savages.   We got into dry clothes.   At dusk the rain ceased; and almost immediately the demons of the forest lifted up their wild shriekings again.   I feel I can hardly exaggerate the wild and uncanny effect of these voices.

November 2.—We now prepared in earnest to follow the trail of the elephant, and to stay by the spoor until we came up with him.   We took one light tent, blankets, and some cold food.

Before we started the Wanderobo again made medicine; for the pursuit of an elephant is a very solemn thing.   Each snipped a link from his ornamental steel chain; one produced an old dried piece of elephant meat; another built a tiny fire.   The elephant meat was thrown on the coals, and the links of chain laid atop it.   N'jahgi performed the ritual while the rest of us squatted in a circle below him. As yesterday, he raised his hands, palm up, to the skies; he faced in turn all parts of the compass; he bent humbly, his hands crossed on his breast, calling on the forest, the Powers, and the gods of elephants in a loud monotone. The others, once more, their heads low, muttered choral responses, and at times beat the earth softly, in unison, with the palms of their hands. Then suddenly they rose and disappeared, leaving us by the little fire. After a short interval they returned, bringing tufts of some herb. These N'jahgi dipped in the white ashes, and with them spattered each countenance, muttering some sort of a charm. The herbs were distributed. Each sat on his share, while N'jahgi intoned another invocation. Obeying a gesture we arose and started for the forest. But this was not all. At the beginning of the elephant spoor the little men all knelt down in a row, beat the earth softly with their palms, shook their herb bundles in the air, bent forward and blew three times on the trail. Then they planted the herbs beneath trees on either side of the trail. We started in good earnest.

It rained steadily. For three hours we followed the Wanderobo at a great pace, crossing two deep cañons on the way. At dark we camped where we found ourselves. The rain continued. Our little Wanderobo shivered like dogs.

It took half an hour to make a fire. These tropical

forests are almost hopelessly without the facilities our own woods offer for such a purpose. There is no dry wood, no tinder, no green wood carrying pitch. Every dead twig is sodden through; the under sides of down or slanting trees have become wet by capillary attraction. A pinch of powdered bark is a treasure to be gained only by long searching. At the end of the full half hour our united efforts gained us a sort of dull smoulder, without flame. Some one had to blow on it continually to keep it from going out. Only late in the evening did it spring into a flame that had value for drying; and even then a relaxation of vigilance would drop it back to a sullen smoking mockery. As we were soaked through, and our tent was wet, and we had only cold mutton, bread, and peanuts to eat, this was not the most comfortable camp in the world. However, we smoked our pipes.

CHAPTER XXVI

NOVEMBER 3.—This morning the spoor led us up beyond the forested belt and into the bamboos. It was like a fairyland—sometimes a rather steep and scrambly fairyland, but full of glades and little levels. The bamboo is of the giant type, thirty to fifty feet tall, and from four to six inches in diameter. The stalk is bright green. Its tendency is to grow evenly thick and impenetrable, but that tendency has been modified by the tramping of generations of elephants, so that in all directions through it are winding paths, short vistas, and tiny open glades.

Sometimes it is as dark as evening; and as mysterious. Sometimes the light strikes down brilliantly from above. Underfoot the whole surface of the ground is carpeted with tiny feather ferns only an inch or so high, indescribably soft and beautiful. Occasionally in the more open places these spring to the dimensions of bracken. And occasionally, too, we came upon single wide-spreading trees that had cleared themselves a space amid the bamboo, like rest houses beneath which to stop.

Everything is green—the bamboo stalks, the fine soft ground covering, the damp moss that seems immediately to cover the dead stalks, the shadows, the very light itself striking through the feathery tops. There is here no active animal or bird life; and therefore it is extraordinarily quiet. No sharp sound breaks the stillness; only are heard the hushed rustling of the slender bamboo leaves far above and the muffled dripping of the rain. A mysterious, cool, green, quiet place, like the bottom of the sea.

In the bamboos one can never see over ten yards, and rarely that. They offer no barrier whatever to an elephant. If one should come upon him at the wrong end, so to speak, he would have to back out and go around. These considerations made us rejoice when our elephant's spoor led us down again and into the forest.

All this, while interesting, was hard, hard work for everybody. It now came on to rain harder than ever; in fact the torrent roared down on us so copiously that we could not face it and had to get beneath the slanting trunks of trees until it had eased up a bit. Here we made shift to eat a few *potio* cakes, peanuts, and chocolate. After a bit we went on.

About one o'clock suddenly we heard him trumpet. The sound was very loud, and like a rather shrill locomotive whistle. We went on cautiously. The trail led us down the middle of a stream for some distance, so we had to wade nearly up to our waists; but we were already well soaked, so we did not much mind. The beast was wandering along aimlessly. We followed two hours without being able to catch up. Then abruptly we all saw him, about sixty yards away, down through a chance thinning in the smaller trees. At the very instant, without a sound, he seemed to evaporate into thin air. Never would I have believed so enormous a creature could have moved so quickly and so silently through that dense cover. If it had not been for his indubitable spoor, I should almost have been willing to believe him a creature of the imagination. But for the brief instant I had seen him plainly. My most vivid impression was of his *length*, for I had not realized how "long coupled" the African elephant is as compared to the Indian elephant we see in circuses. The next most vivid impression was of his bulk and the golden yellow effect of his tusks against the dimness of the forest.

We had made no noise, but an eddy had swept our wind around to him.

We sent back one of the Wanderobo to bring up the men; and again took the trail. At five o'clock, as he was still travelling, we reluctantly came to a halt. Another cold camp in the rain—a cheerless, wet, smoky camp; and we took our water supply from the natural reservoir of one of the elephant's footprints!

November 4.—This morning we followed on until eleven o'clock in generally southeast direction, wandering in the heavy forests, in the lower fringe of bamboo, and occasionally out to openings grown twenty feet high with vines and bush undergrowth, but from which we could see the sky. At last Cuninghame stopped short with an exclamation of dismay.

"We're in for it now!" he whispered.

The side hill looked as though an avalanche had swept down it. Our elephant had joined a herd!

Almost immediately afterward we heard a queer, subdued, roaring sound, exactly like distant thunder. This was the stomach rumbling that attends an elephant's digestion. I had heard of it, but I had not before realized how loud it is nor how far it carries.

Elephants were trumpeting on the hill opposite; the occasional distant thunder sound rumbled across to us; every few moments a rending crash startled us like a distant pistol shot. We gazed anxiously at the moss dependent from the higher trees, to ascertain the direction of the wind. We left all but N'jahgi and Kongoni, and moved cautiously in the general direction of the row.

We tried to keep well to leeward of the whole lot; but twice outlying elephants somewhere to our right trumpeted or rumbled, and twice we backed out and tried again, before we had given them our wind. We had first of all to get outside of every beast before we could begin to look for individuals. Thus we descended our side hill, and prepared to cross to the other. At the bottom I happened to be a little above the others and so was in a position to see plainly an elephant walking leisurely down into the same hollow from the other side. He was only about fifty yards away, and looked as big as the Flatiron building. I snapped my fingers and so got hold of Cuninghame and Kongoni, but N'jahgi was too far ahead, and wound his unconscious way steadily toward the great beast. A head-on meeting seemed inevitable; but Kongoni, on inspiration, churked a piece of earth into the high grass near N'jahgi. The savage caught the slight sound of its falling, and looked back. We motioned him to us, and the situation was saved. The elephant pushed his way slowly into the thick forest.

Now directly ahead we heard the sound of trumpeting, crashing, heavy snorting. We crept forward like snakes, our eyes straining into the dimness. Cuninghame paused to whisper back to me:

"This is highly dangerous, you know!"

I was glad to get my own impressions corroborated by an expert. The great beasts were all about us, yet we could not see twenty yards. All we could do was to listen and look and move forward by inches. Cuninghame had told me that when among elephants I should always keep clearly in my mind my line of retreat; must know exactly where I intended to dive in case of trouble. I kept picking out places and discarding them as they fell too far in the rear; though none of them looked as though they would offer an insoluble problem to a really unkind elephant.

Thus we crept for a quarter of a mile. Then we came to a tiny opening in the forest; that opening was chock full of elephants. They stood lazily, having a good time, swinging their trunks, flapping their ears, blinking their little eyes. Occasionally one of them would trumpet loudly. There were perhaps a dozen in sight, beside a lot of young ones whose backs just showed above the vegetation. To judge by the sounds, there must have been twice as many more just inside the fringe of the forest. We paused.

"What next?" I whispered.

"Go up and look at them," replied Cuninghame.

As we were at the moment within eighty yards of them, this seemed an act of supererogation. However, I followed my leader. Cuninghame turned to whisper another warning:

"For God's sake move quietly. If one discovers us, the whole lot will come after us."

We crept to within forty yards and stopped. Cuninghame examined them in detail for "shootable ivory." I examined them in detail for indications of suspicious dispositions. It seemed incredible that they did not see us, for our heads and shoulders were in plain sight. Of course we did not move. We stood there a century or two while those great creatures enjoyed themselves. Every time one trumpeted, or moved, or waved its ears, I got ready to dive for the "last safe place." That, it seemed to me, was about eight miles back.

Then, very near—about fifteen yards—and slightly to our left, the screen of leaves was pushed aside and the bow of the *Mauretania* thrust itself through.

"Run!" breathed Cuninghame.

We doubled up and ran. From the edge of the woods we looked back. The elephant had stopped and was feeling about in the air with the tip of its trunk.

"That old girl is suspicious," whispered Cuninghame, "but she didn't see us."

She said something to the others, and they all waked up. An animated discussion took place. N'jahgi quietly climbed a tree. The elephant insisted on her point. The others were skeptical, but finally seemed to acquiesce. The whole lot swung deliberately and disappeared in the forest.

"*That's* all right," said Cuninghame in relief. "Thought they might come our way."

I was glad, too. For the moment I had quite lost sight of the fact that I wanted to shoot an elephant.

"What next?" I inquired.

"Follow 'em," said Cuninghame, "and try to find a bull."

So we followed 'em. Evidently they had not put much faith in the alarmist, for they had gone only half a mile. We could hear them in all directions. Unfortunately they were now in the thickest of the thick forest; and, having been aroused from their siesta, they had scattered widely in order to feed. We sneaked here and there.

Suddenly it began to rain.

Cuninghame made a gesture of despair. When it rains, elephants cease all occupation and stand as rigidly quiet as though stuffed. One depends a good deal upon the sense of hearing. Now the trumpetings ceased, the crashes of torn branches ceased. A dead silence fell on the forest, except for the pattering and swishing of the rain.

Then with terrifying abruptness pandemonium broke loose—trumpetings, shrill angry screams, wild crashings, headlong rushes to and fro. The forest seemed overflowing with devils. A twist of the wind had discovered our presence to the herd.

They did not know where we were: only that we were somewhere. There ensued the most exciting period I have ever experienced, but whether it was ten minutes or two hours, I did not know. The elephants screamed and yelled and rushed here and there looking for us. We could see the tops of the smaller trees and bushes violently agitated, often within a few yards, as the beasts passed; but so thick was the cover that we did not again actually see them. Our ears strained for every sound, we ducked and dodged and sneaked. It was no longer a question of shooting an elephant, but of remaining undiscovered—for our lives. Cuninghame seemed to know more or less of the probable course of the brutes. When he said run uphill, I ran uphill; when he whispered run back, I did so. After what seemed a very long time the row began to recede.

"That's all right," said Cuninghame. "They've gone off."

We followed them a short distance. A clear road-way twenty feet wide had been razed clean where the herd had come together and gone off in a body. I looked at my watch and was surprised to find it half-past three already. We sent N'jahgi back for the men, and huddled under a couple of big trees.

"Bad luck," said Cuninghame.

I thought it was extraordinarily good luck.

"Want to try again?" asked Cuninghame.

"Of course," said I; "why do you ask that?"

"Well," said he, "some people simply cannot stand it when the elephants begin to scream about them. Courageous people, at that. I've had any number flatly back out and make no bones about it. It's just the way it happens to hit your nerves."

We camped on the spot, at 7,150 feet elevation. Two of the giant forest hogs made off as we came up. We were so jumpy that they scared us almost to death! A lot of Wanderobo came in with provisions. In the evening it stopped raining, and we found some cedar wood that would burn. This hard, slippery, twisting work is beginning to tell on my broken leg. It is badly swollen and has begun to turn black below the knee. Cuninghame and I talked it over and agreed to try one more day, after which we would return to "Tembo Circus" for a rest.

November 5.—The fresh Wanderobo brought us news that an unsuspected portion of the herd had apparently been feeding farther to the north. Therefore we set off to look for them. Soon struck the spoor, which led us directly up the mountain. It is astonishing what steep slopes elephants will negotiate. Their great weight gives them a footing by pushing the solid earth aside. We zigzagged up a near-perpendicular on a graded trail that the day before had not existed. The surface of said graded trail had most evidently not been metalled. An elephant's foot measures from fifty inches in circumference; and in soft ground it often sinks in ten inches to two feet. Each beast steps accurately in the steps of the one before. The result is a series of babies' bathtubs, generally half full of muddy water, and always slippery. We followed this lot up through the bamboos for two or three hours; then they got our wind and evidently started off. We heard them trumpet, but did not see them. At 8,100 feet we turned back, sliding down the slopes, falling in and out of the tracks, wading the streams, and keeping a wary eye for elephant pits. These are everywhere, and are a real danger unless you watch out. They are about six or eight feet long, perhaps three feet wide, and eight or ten feet deep. Sometimes they are planted with sharp stakes, and occasionally—but not often—these stakes are poisoned. A great many of them are disused and open, so anybody can avoid them by watching out, but those covered are invisible to all but the Wanderobo. The only way is to follow the leader; and when the savage makes a little side-step, to make a little side-step, too. Shortcuts do not pay. The idea is to get the elephant's fore legs in this narrow trench; not the whole beast. It must be an incredible labour to dig these pits with knives and sticks.

I have been much interested in one of the younger Wanderobo, a youth of eighteen or so. He is so near the animal that he is attractive. His forehead is pinched, his nose wide, his mouth and chin project actually beyond the nose. But with it all he has the wistful, soft brown eyes of the monkey; hauntingly pathetic and questing, as though of an intelligence trying to break through. He is a most skilful tracker; and in these wet forests no turned leaf or muddied twig escapes him. The Wanderobo are queer, primitive little creatures, absolutely certain and competent in the forest craft, but equally helpless at everything else. This is a terrible forest in which to keep one's bearings; for there are no landmarks, no "lay of the land," no openings. Even the compass is useless, for a straight line back to camp—could it be determined—would merely plunge one into inextricable difficulties. Yet these men will follow a twisting and doubling spoor for three days, and then strike accurately out of the forest to a distant camp. It must be an instinct. But when the day's tracking is done they squat down in their wet blankets, perfectly helpless. The white man builds the fire, he rigs the shelters, etc. When he is ready, he indicates to the Wanderobo where they are to establish themselves. Otherwise they would continue squatting in the same spot until morning!

After we had lost this herd we started back for our base camp. The three days had about exhausted our cold food; and we ourselves were pretty well tired out. The travel had been hard, wet, and long; the camps without comfort; and the occasional excitement intense. My ankle had been so twisted and abused that it was swollen and turning black so that a day's rest seemed in every way advisable.

Cuninghame and I had no idea where we might be, nor how long it would take us to get to camp. Down through the forest we started and walked until one o'clock, when we emerged from the woods into the "vine country." Then we found we had been skirting the base of Kenia toward the east; and were about half-way to Embu. It behooved us to retrace our steps. The three days' hunt, however, could be compressed, for we had not now to double and twist; we were in a lower country; and we had a native track on which to travel. On the other hand, it rained steadily and heavily; the native track was composed of sticky or slippery clay, and it had a bad habit of crossing steep cañons at right angles without the slightest attempt at easing the grades. By putting one foot in front of the other, however, we made it; though some of us did not get in until long after dark, and had to be sent for with lanterns.

CHAPTER XXVII

NOVEMBER 6.—Loafed and rested all day. By luck we had a bright sun all the morning and were able to dry out our rather bedraggled belongings. A powerful chief to the west of Kenia, Kurioki by name, sent me a present of a sheep and Cuninghame a goat. Why the invidious distinction I do not know. He also sent two of his Wanderobo to hunt with us on his side of the mountain. N'jahgi presented me with his own home-made knife, ground to razor sharpness. This present really meant something, for such a weapon is very valuable to such a man. Our Wanderobo were also very busy preparing a more powerful elephant medicine, bringing in stalks of sugar-cane from some distant *shamba* and thrusting them upright in the ground either side our tents. The other medicine had brought us elephants all right: but evidently something lacked. This was to be especially powerful.

November 7.—To-day we went outside the forest and marched by native tracks, up and down a fearful series of hills, until we came to Kurioki's Land. Here we picked up the men he had promised us, and re-entered the forest. The sugar-cane medicine was finished. Each man took a piece of the stalk in his right hand and knelt, facing the trail. N'jahgi cried out a monologue, his hands raised. At the end of each phrase the others ejaculated *whah! whah!* deeply aspirated, bowed forward, and blew on the ground. Then the sugar-cane was carefully concealed to right and left of the trail.

As we marched outside the forest the news of our presence was cried from hill to hill. The carrying power of the native voice is astonishing. They do not shout, they talk, and yet every syllable is distinct across wide spaces. The speaking voices of the women are most pleasant, soft and dusky like velvet.

After two hours we came to a group of savages who announced themselves as sent by Kurioki. Kurioki himself they excused, saying that he had hurt his leg. We made more medicine, and plunged again into the forest. Kurioki's men led us directly to the trail of yesterday's elephant. We proceeded to follow it. After three hours the nature of the forest changed somewhat. We began to come across wide openings, grown with grass, like Sierra meadows. The forest and these grass openings divided the slope between them, the forest running out in tongues, wide peninsulas, and islands.

"Great luck if we should see Mr. Tembo out here," I suggested.

"Only comes out at night," said Cuninghame.

The trail grew dim and almost impossible to follow,

owing to the fact that the short tough grass springs back so quickly. Soon we lost it entirely, and sat down atop anthills while the Wanderobo scattered out to look. A smart shower drenched us and passed on. Kenia, behind us to the east, was lost in a mist that swept the tops of the gloomy forest, but before us we could see down over the wide country near Olbolosset and Rumeruti, where we safaried three years ago. We figured out we were just about sitting on the equator!

We stayed here some time. Then from around the corner of a big forest patch the youngest Wanderobo appeared. He was running, so we went to meet him.

"He says they have seen the elephant," Kongoni translated.

We hurried on after him, descending the long grassy slope skirting the edge of the forest. At the end of a mile we came on all the rest of the Wanderobo humped down behind a single thin bush, their blankets wrapped around them and their necks outstretched like a lot of very eager mud turtles. About half a mile away, walking nonchalantly about in the short grass, was the elephant, his tusks gleaming against the dark background of the forest.

Cuninghame, Kongoni, and I darted forward. The elephant was walking steadily to the left; and we, under cover of small clumps, were hurrying toward him as fast as we could in the hope of reaching him before he reëntered the forest. In this we failed, for when we were within 200 yards he swung sharp to the right, pushed aside the screen of leaves, and disappeared.

We approached circumspectly. He might continue on directly into the forest; or, again, he might turn around and come out again. We glided silently along the fringe, peering with all our mights. Suddenly Kongoni motioned us forward. Through a little opening in the leaves we saw the top of his back, twenty-five yards away. As we looked, he swung slowly and faded into the forest.

Now we at least knew definitely which way he was going. As quickly as we could we made our way to where we had last seen him. This was no easy job, for the cover was almost impenetrable. In order to get on noiselessly, we had to lift separately each branch and twig, to push individually each clump of leaves or interlacement of switches. We had to duck and squirm and twist and push very gently. A single sharply broken stick would serve to give him the alarm, in which case he would either make off and we would not see him again, or—more likely—he would look us up, in which case we would see more of him than we wanted.

In spite of the thickness of the growth the elephant himself went silently through it. That phenomenon— the stillness of an elephant's *leisurely* progression—is hard to get accustomed to. He will brush through thickets so dense that the branches make an apparently impenetrable screen and the closest listening will hardly

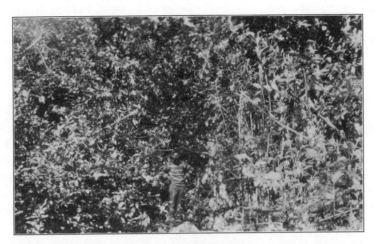

TYPICAL ELEPHANT COVER

CAMP IN THE FOREST AFTER THE ELEPHANT KILL. MEAT DRYING

"CHOPPING OUT" THE IVORY

CARRYING OUT THE IVORY

be able to determine the fact that he is there at all. His great weight and the size of his foot breaks instantaneously anything beneath them and crushes the sound; his vast bulk and length and the soft leathery quality of his skin probably push aside gently and muffle the harshness of the branches. However it is, only twice did we hear the faintest indication that the elephant was still moving; and we ourselves, as I have said, were having the greatest trouble to work our way along at all. The whiplike branches of the thicket sprang back after the beast, leaving the screen as resistant as ever. Also we could not see ten feet.

The trail led us straight ahead, then doubled back at a sharp angle, so that at one time the elephant must have been passing us a short distance to the right. We crept on for perhaps a quarter of a mile, expecting every moment we might run against his hind leg. Then through a chance opening just ahead we saw the waving of his ears. So close was he that we were looking up at him as one looks up at a skyscraper. I held for his brain and pulled trigger. Down he came with a tremendous crash. The distance was just twelve paces.

After waiting to see that he was not going to move we lifted our voices in a cheer that was immediately answered by the Wanderobo, who had been following a short distance behind. They came up, and, shortly after, our men. We got out the little flask, and, standing either side the great beast, we took a drink "across the bar." Next we measured him. He stood ten feet seven inches at the shoulder (just the height of Jumbo: the Indian elephant stands about eight feet); seventeen feet six inches "waist measure"; eighteen feet one inch long counting the trunk. His forefoot was fifty-four inches around; and his hind foot fifty-one inches. His tusks weighed fifty-six pounds and fifty-five and three fourth pounds respectively. While the men started taxidermal work I made camp. It was now 4:00 P. M. By pitch dark the headskin was off—no small job. We cooked some rice. Some cedar wood gave us a good fire. The moon filtered through the trees. The hyraxes screeched; and some leopards and hyenas, attracted by the smell of meat, snarled and uttered their cries.

Thermometer, morning, 64; night, 54.

November 8.—We sent two of the Wanderobo back to camp with instructions to bring on all the men and certain supplies. They returned with them by dark —a tremendous round trip. All day we did taxidermy. With the exception of a light shower after lunch the day was fine. Here near the edge of the forest is much more life than in the depths; and the singing of birds was a delight. All day we kept a piece of elephant trunk simmering, and at evening we had elephant trunk soup with rice. It is a very strong, nutritious brew with a marked flavour of its own, and I rather like it.

November 9.—A fine sunny day. About nine o'clock
a very ancient Wanderobo came in. He looked to be
a hundred years old, his skin wrinkled, his joints big,
his flesh all wasted away to the bones, his frame bent,
his face monkey-like and wizened, his eyes dim and
peering. I have never seen so aged a man afoot and
going. The old chief of the Wasonzi looked as old; but,
it will be remembered, he was only capable of sitting in
the sun. Nevertheless, this old boy came in quite
briskly, and without greeting or pause set to work in a
most businesslike way. He had on a hyrax-skin cap
and a skin cloak and carried a skin wallet and one
of the soft iron sword-knives. At once he attacked
that elephant, slowly and laboriously sawing off great
chunks of meat and dragging them to a pile beneath a
tree. He was entirely businesslike and paid no attention to anybody. Cuninghame watched him a
while, and then in pity lent him a sharp knife. The
old man took it, handed Cuninghame his old sword,
and by signs commanded the latter to sharpen it!
Cuninghame meekly obeyed! Hour after hour the old
boy delved away at that gigantic carcase, picking out
the choice bits—from a *shenzi* point of view. It was
cruel, hard work—for anybody—and we fully expected
to see him give out from sheer exhaustion. But
about three or four o'clock in the afternoon other
shenzis began to show up. There was enough for
everybody, but the enterprising ancient had all the

best bits! They all made camp right next the carcase. Our men constructed racks on which they laid strips of meat and beneath which they built fires. Several of the Kavirondos stripped and sat humped over the blaze while friends carefully greased them from top to toe with elephant fat.

November 10.—Our job finished, we got up very early and prepared to move. All the *shenzis* were sleeping the sleep of the stuffed—all but the very aged man. He was up bright and early, keen to capture any stray tin cans. As soon as we were packed up, he appropriated the best of our camp-sites and meat-racks. He was certainly an enterprising old person, paying attention to nothing or nobody that had not to do with the business in hand. He would probably live right there until his hoard of meat—which he would dry—would be quite gone. Poor old chap! This was undoubtedly his last raid.

We marched back out of the forest, and along the spoor by which we had come in. Many more Wander-obo were hastening in to the meat. I do not suppose a single ounce of that great carcase would be wasted! The morning was clear, and Mt. Kenia with its bold crags and glittering snows was for once visible in its entirety. It is a marvellous mountain, but we had not long to enjoy it, for soon it began to gather, a wisp at a time, the thick mantle with which it daily enshrouds itself.

Enjoyed the walk through the forest very much; for now, for the first time, we could look about us with free minds, unhampered by the necessity of searching for spoor, moving noiselessly, etc.

Near the outer edge we met a number of savages, very gorgeous savages, sent by Kurioki. They were leading two sheep, presents from his majesty. They had only one petition, namely, that we should kill one of them on the spot and return the entrails to the messengers. With some of the internal organs they would then make medicine to keep the elephants away from the crops. To this, of course, we assented; and sat down to await the completion of the ceremony. It began to rain in sheets; but we were used to it by now, and merely humped ourselves over to let the water run off. Then came two *shenzis* carrying a canvas chair and the message that Kurioki himself was coming to see us. Long pause, while the rain rained. Enter Kurioki—a tall savage beyond middle age, without much ornament, wearing a red blanket, and very lame in the right leg. He hobbled up, seated himself, smiled amiably, and gave us the "double grip" of friendship. Lacking chairs, we were seated on two porters' loads. We thanked him for the sheep. He waved his hand airily. We asked him how long he had been lame. He thought a while, said five days; then corrected it to three years. We expressed ourselves as pleased with the way his men had worked. He again waved an airy hand. We said that if he would send men with us to Fort Hall we would there buy him a present in return: and requested him to name it.

He thought a long while, then told us to send him whatever we pleased. We urged him to choose. For the first time he made a speech. Said he, in substance:

"I have been drinking much *tembo* in your honour. I cannot see you plainly, because you go like this," and he waved his hand slowly to and fro in front of his face. "I cannot now think of anything that I want, so you will have to send me whatever you please," and again he smiled amiably.

We left him there, seated under the tree, the rain streaming from his face.

The march back to camp from this point was a hard one. Our men were heavily loaded, and the hills so slippery that we could hardly stand. Indeed at one place I slid forty feet as though on ice, without the least ability to check myself. After a little over eight hours, however, we arrived at the base camp, and were able to dry off. At sundown we gave *backshish* to our faithful *shenzis*. In the moonlight they danced and sang for an hour, then filed past us and said goodbye. A lot of Kikuyu savages were in, sent by Kurioki to help us carry our goods out to railhead. We took fifteen of them, men and women, and they served us very well. One of them wanted Cuninghame to take charge of two rupees for him, and gave Cuninghame the two rupees and a potato. This potato, Cuninggame explained, must be returned with the two rupees. It was a sort of backhanded receipt, or reminder, rather.

We marched out to railhead in four rather long days. At the end of that we sent back a camp-chair, a good blanket, and twenty rupees to Kurioki. We gave Maragua, the efficient *shenzi* head man, the other camp-chair and the opera hat. He then much resembled the comic paper idea of the cannibal chief!

From November 15-19 I spent in the forests near N'joro looking for bongo. I had eight men and three Wanderobo hunters. Unfortunately five white men hunting colobus pervaded the forest. No white men had been in the district for three years. The Wanderobo said that now the bongo would depart for points unknown and would not be back for four months. That they had departed proved to be the case, so I returned. The *shenzis* gave me a hyrax robe because they said they were sorry that we had had no chance. It is a beautiful thing. On my way back to the station I fired the last shot in Africa at a colobus in the top of a tall tree, and got him very neatly through the neck.

THE END

APPENDICES

APPENDICES are meant for the seeker after special information; not for the general reader. Therefore the author makes no apology for the inclusion of the following rather specialized material:

I

HOW TO GET IN

Preliminary: In the present development of the country it is exceedingly inadvisable to make up parties of more than two—or at most three—white men. The chief difficulty is transport; and the transport becomes most unwieldy in the case of large parties. These two or three white men must reduce their supplies and equipment to a minimum. Every man saved means so much more time in the country. It is unnecessary to get a "white hunter." Such an individual knows no more of this particular country than you do. As to managing natives and the details of running a safari, it would be well for the inexperienced first to take a two or three weeks' hunt in British East Africa under professional auspices in order to get the hang of the thing.

Routes: From Marseillies or Naples take ships of either the German East African Line or the Union Castle Line to Mombasa. Thence by Uganda Railroad to Kisumu on Victoria Nyanza. Thence by steamer to either Musoma or Mwanza.   From either of these ports march inland by either one of the following routes:

(a)   To Walioba's, one day; to Missambi's, two days; up the Mara River to its junction with the Bologonja, three days; up the Bologonja to its head, four days.   You are now in the heart of the game country.   From this point you can suit yourself.

(b)   To Ikoma, about six or seven days; to Serengetti, five days.   Spend as much time as you please thereabouts; then to Olgoss; thence four days southeast to the Ssalé. Return on a circle either north or south.

On both routes (a) and (b) you get plenty of game near Walioba's.   On route (a) it might pay you to take a side trip south past Myeru's into the hills above the Ruwana River—a week, say.

Ways and Means: The only feasible scheme by which a man could stay long in the country would be this: In the first place, select a small permanent safari of about forty men.   These can, perhaps, best be recruited at Nairobi; or possibly through Hansing & Company at Mwanza. Forty men is a maximum because they will consume a load of *potio* per day.   Twenty of these should be sufficient for the white men's loads; two or three gunbearers; two or three personal camp boys.   The rest of the men can carry a day to day supply of *potio* and be ready in case of sickness and to carry trophies.   Each man is given five days' provisions before leaving the lake.   Thus in your own safari you have provisions for nineteen days.   These nineteen days are increased by the fact that for four days (or more if you stop en route to shoot) you will be in a settled country, and so able to buy as you go along. At Mwanza or Musoma engage savages to carry the rest of your *potio* supply. This can be best done through the German official; and to enlist his support you should have letters from somebody. These savages you will send forward—in charge of two of your own men—with instructions to carry the *potio* to a designated point; there to deposit it, and *immediately to return.* Somewhere up the Bologonja on route (a), and somewhere on the Serengetti on route (b). Then whenever you are in permanent camp anywhere in the game country—as you often will be—you can relay on extra supplies of *potio* from this central depot. All this takes a bit of figuring, to be sure; but it is not fatally complicated.

If you recruit at Nairobi, I should advise you to get your men through Newland Tarlton & Company. Their small recruiting fee is well worth while. If possible get them to include one of the following men: M'ganga, Memba Sasa, Kongoni, Maliyabwana, Sanguiki, Dolo, or Sulimani. They have all been through this country, and are intelligent.

Customs: Are 10 per cent. on entering a German port. The duty on a great many articles is refunded when you leave the country. You will have to bond your goods through from Mombasa in order to avoid paying British duty as well. You must enter and depart from German territory via a customs house.

Licenses: Must be procured in advance through the German consul at Mombasa. This must be arranged for by correspondence, as there are many delays. Send to the Foreign Office—or whatever they call it—at Berlin for copies of the latest regulations.

Permits to bring native servants and porters into German territory must be applied for in advance. Otherwise you will not be able to take them out again.

Maps: Besides the one in this book, send for the *Ikoma section* published in Berlin. Do not depend on it too implicitly—especially for water.*

II

OUTFIT

Riding animals are impossible in this country owing to the prevalence of the tsetse fly. Hammocks are equally impossible because of the necessity of reducing the number of your men—a hammock, counting relays, takes sixteen men. Therefore the whole journey must be done afoot. Since the *potio* must at present be arranged for as outlined in Appendix 1, it follows that a large and unwieldy safari is practically impossible. As stated, forty men is the ideal number. These can comfortably care for two white men who are willing to get down to absolute (African) essentials. Each must solve for himself the problem of what he shall take; but in our own case, the loads worked out as follows:

Two tent loads, two bed loads (includes chairs), three tin boxes, one cook box (contains both utensils and food), one ammunition box, eight chop boxes (food, repair-materials, alum, trade goods, etc.), one miscellaneous load, four boys' loads; a total of twenty-two loads. The chop boxes gradually diminished in number; the others remained

---

*The war may change the status on one side or the other of the line, but on reflection I have retained this as it was written. Conditions of subsistence will not be changed; and new regulations are easy to find out about.

constant. The rest of the men were none too many to fill in the gaps caused by sickness, to carry current supplies of *potio*, to act as guard over *caches*, and to transport the few trophies we could not do without.

We figured a long time on the tent loads, but could not, for African purposes, reduce them below fifty pounds each. This accounted for an A-tent, with fly, 7x9, made with ground cloth sewed on, and built to pitch with cross poles slipped inside a hem at either side. A certain weight of material was necessary to withstand the sun and daily handling by natives.

The bed loads consisted of light X cots, thin cork mattresses, and two blankets. One cannot sleep on the ground in Africa; and the cork mattress was lighter than another pair of blankets to go underneath one. With the bed went a skeleton frame that supported either a canvas bath or a canvas wash basin. One cannot take cold baths in the tropics without danger of a congestion; and the daily hot bath is a necessity. The folding camp-chairs were of the lightest make, but repaid their transportation as they would have done nowhere else but in the tropics.

In the tin boxes, besides our personal effects, we carried the medicine supply, the knife stones, extra parts for rifles, five volumes each of the handy "Everyman's Library," writing materials, sewing kit, our Stonebridge folding candle lanterns, and maps. My own personal outfit, outside what I wore, was as follows:

Clothes: A soft camp hat, two bandanas, one pair khaki trousers for camp, five pairs of woollen socks, one pair shoe-pac boots, one pair of moccasins, one waterproof cape, two suits of pajamas, two suits of underwear, one buckskin shirt.

Personals: Extra glasses and lenses, extra pocket knife, flask of brandy (the entire supply!), notebooks, pencils, fountain pen, ink, toilet articles, 3A Graflex camera, Goetz "Celar" lens, Cooke "Telar" lens, films, extra rubber heels, steel tape, extra gun sights, pipes, and tobacco.

By way of miscellaneous might be listed:

River rope, travelling block for same, thirty pounds of alum, sail needles and twine, one dozen trade blankets, ten pounds of beads, six coils trade wire, one pound trade snuff, five pounds trade tobacco, three hundred rupees in silver, three dozen trade knives, thermometer, three pedometers, aneroid, prismatic compass, alarm watch, tool set, boot caulks, bobbinet meat safe (necessary!), two evaporation bags, six tins boot grease ("Dubbin"), laundry soap, four *pangas* (native tools, swords), two axes, two hatchets, gun-cleaning material.

The cook box contained three kettles, two fry pans, a grid, a baker, a tea or coffee pot, a galvanized bucket (necessary to heat water in for baths), a kettle, and what food was "going."

For ammunition we had 400 rounds for the New Springfield, which we both shot; 100 for my .405 Winchester, and 50 for each of our heavy rifles.

This brings us to the food list, which was as follows:

150 lbs. flour	60 lbs. rice
4 lbs. baking powder	10 lbs. tea
50 lbs. sugar	10 lbs. salt
2 vials crystallose	20 lbs. oatmeal

10 lbs. coffee	10 tins golden syrup
1 tin pepper	20 lbs. lima beans
25 lbs. lard	curry powder
4 large tins "dehydro" fruits	12 lbs. prunes
2 large tins "dehydro" vegetables	

III

The most of our shooting was strictly for the purpose of getting food, and ingratiating ourselves with the sultans. However, we brought out a fair number of most excellent trophies. For the man technically interested in measurements, the following are quoted:

	Length of horns	Spread of horns
Bohur reedbuck . .	$12\frac{1}{2}$	
Impalla	$29\frac{1}{2}$	
Thompson's gazelle .	$16\frac{5}{8}$	
Thompson's gazelle .	$15\frac{3}{8}$	
Wildebeeste . . .		$30\frac{1}{2}$
Sing-sing	$33\frac{1}{2}$	28
Bushbuck	$15\frac{5}{8}$	
Topi	16 to 18	

Roan average rather small; lion are well maned; Roberts' gazelle (where found) rather small; impalla very large; sing-sing extra good; topi very large; wildebeeste large; eland medium; Chanler's reedbuck good; bushbuck extra good; Bohur reedbuck wonderful; Thompson's gazelle well above the old British East Africa records.

IV

By way of recapitulation, the new hunting country may be considered to extend from the escarpment above Lake Natron to within a day's march of Lake Victoria Nyanza;

and from the mountains dividing British East Africa from German East Africa south to a point yet to be determined. From the escarpment the country rises through a series of low ranges and valleys to a height of land near Oliondo, whence it gradually descends again to the shores of the lake. Twenty miles after leaving Oliondo the plateau breaks into hills, or rather low rugged mountains with many practicable passes. Here are the heights of Olgoss, Lobo, etc. These low mountains run north and south, sweeping at the extremities to the westward to embrace in their arms an immense rolling plain covered with thin thorn forest. This plain is bounded, or rather marked, to the west by the ranges of Ikorongo and Tschamlino: though a wide opening sweeps unobstructed through to Speke Gulf. These westerly mountains are rugged but traversable; generally volcanic in origin. Near the lake the character of the country changes to low hills of alluvial soil, whence emerge extraordinary rock outcrops.

In the rains this country is all well watered. That the rains are fairly heavy is proved by the size and erosion of the watercourses. On the extreme east, and close under the high mountains that divide the German from the British Protectorates, there is abundance of flowing streams: but as one progresses westward it is necessary, out of the rains, to search for springs or water "tanks." The Dorodedi, flowing past the end of Oliondo; the Bologonja, to the extreme north; and the great Mara were the only permanent and flowing streams in all this vast area. The swarms of game undoubtedly migrate, following the water and feed.

In other features of external topography: the rough rolling country to east of Oliondo is covered with spiky thorn brush in which occasional lowland stretches and openings permit small grass plots; between Oliondo and Olgoss is mixed cover, open grass, however, predominating; between Olgoss and Ikorongo is the rolling, alternate park and thinly wooded country described as visited in August and September; near the lake is a thin thorn tree alternating with open or cultivated stretches. After leaving the highest boundary mountains there is little real forest or jungle. An occasional patch near headwaters of some creek, around some spring; or along the course of flowing water is about all.

The country is sparsely inhabited by the Wasonzi—three villages to be exact—on the bench above Lake Natron. Then follows a long stretch without population until we reach the Ungruimi in the Ikorongo mountains. From there to the lake is a numerous and prosperous people of several tribes. South of the big plains dwell the Wakoma—a scanty and miserable tribe, dwelling in a dry and unproductive desert. North of the Mara sleeping sickness is prevalent and very fatal.

V

ZOÖLOGICAL

The following species of big game were actually determined by us. Undoubtedly several others could be added to the list by one who could take time—as we could not—to hunt more thoroughly, especially in out of the way places and for very localized species. To the reader desiring most complete descriptions, accounts of habits, distribution, etc., I would recommend the "Life Histories of African Animals," by Roosevelt and Heller. The notes appended to the species in the following list must be considered only as supplemental to the information to be obtained from the above volume.

1. The Lion (*felis leo*).—The lion seems not to occur or to be very unusual in the Wasonzi bench; although the Wasonzi report him as very numerous on the plains or high plateaus of Ssalé just south. From Oliondo to Walioba's country I should consider them about normally abundant; in other words, they can be heard every night, and occasionally one can be seen. The country is a difficult one in which to hunt them, owing to the continuity of the cover; but from a permanent camp a man should be fairly sure of his quarry. The male lions I saw in this country carried very fine manes. This seems to me a little remarkable, both because of the heat and the thorny nature of the bush. Theoretically, heavy manes should occur in high, cold altitudes and open country. Thorns have always been considered an important reason why the mane of a wild lion is less thick and heavy than that of menagerie specimens. Since the journal that makes the body of this book has been put into type, I have received a letter from Mr. Leslie Simpson, who went into the New Country on my advice and information. He swung down to the Serengetti, which he reports an open grass plain with many ravines and small stony hills. An abundance of game makes this an ideal habitat for lions; and in fact he reports an abundance of them there. He also remarks on

the fine quality of the manes. Roosevelt and Heller instance as a remarkable thing that once in the Lordo they
heard a lion roar after sunrise. In this New Country lions
very often roared up to ten o'clock in the morning. As a
general thing, of course, lions roar at night. But these
beasts refuse to be bound by rules. I once saw three of them
eating a decomposed waterbuck just at noon of a hot day!

It is curious that lions seem to vary little in numbers in
one part of the country or another. Of course I cannot
even guess at the probable lion population per square
mile. In an unvisited country where no lions are ever
touched, the average density seems to be no greater than
in comparatively civilized districts where a hundred or
so are killed per year. At first blush it would seem only
reasonable that in the former conditions they should fairly
overrun the whole place; but this is not so. Whether the
numbers are constantly recruited by immigration, or
whether, as at present seems to me more likely, the birth
rate varies according to conditions, it is of course impossible
to say.

2. Leopard (*felis pardus*).—Very generally distributed
in about the usual abundance. We heard them in every
part of the country.

3. Cheetah (*acinonyx jubatus*).—In the covered country
we saw none of these animals, though they may well occur.
Only west of Ikorongo did we begin to come across them
in or near the small open plains.

4. Spotted Hyena (*crocuta crocuta germinans*).—Common everywhere. Heard practically every night.

5. Wild Dog (*lycaon pictus lupinus*).—Saw one near

Olgoss; and heard packs hunting east of that mountain. Did not see signs of any to the westward.

[East African Bush Pig—*potamochoerus koiropotamus daemonis*—probably occurs.]

6. Warthog (*phacochoerus africanus aeliani*).—Not common; but everywhere to be found. Some unfavourable conditions must prevent their increase.

7. Hippopotamus (*hippotamus amphibius amphibius*).— We found the banks of the Mara River tramped with many hard, smooth trails, showing that these animals are at some times of the year very abundant in the upper reaches. At the time of our visit, however, there were none. Cuninghame saw two near Ikorongo; but the hippo population had evidently descended the river either to the Masirori swamp or to Victoria Nyanza. Abundant in the lake.

8. Masai Giraffe (*giraffa camelopardalis tippelskirchi*).— Fairly common everywhere; and in good-sized herds in the thin scrub forest south of the Bologonja. Wary in the uninhabited regions. Exceedingly tame in the Masai country, where the continued presence of native herders accustoms it to man.

9. Roan Antelope (*egoceros equinus*).—From Olgoss westward to the west slopes of Ikorongo we found this animal common. That is, common for roan. The sportsman would have no difficulty in getting trophies. They seem to prefer scant scrub cover. We saw none in the open country. The horns run rather small.

[Sable—*egoceros niger*—reported by natives as occurring directly to southward and about ten days' march. To be investigated.]

10.   Fringe-eared Oryx (*oryx beisa callotis*).—In the Lake Natron region; none after climbing the escarpment to the upper plateau.

11.   Topi (*damaliscus korrigum jimela*).—Occurs sparingly near Olgoss; in great abundance westward as far as Walioba's; then is scarce to within sight of the lake. By far the most numerous antelope in the New Country. Frequents the thin cover extensively, where, even at close range, its ordinarily advertising coloration makes it almost invisible (see later discussion). In our experience the tamest of all game, and possessed of the most curiosity. These traits, added to its abundance, make it the mainstay of the commissariat. The topi is the animal most readily "held" by a fluttering bit of white cloth. We thought we saw more twins of this species than of any other.

12.   Wildebeeste or gnu (*gorgon albojubatus mearnsi*).— Very abundant everywhere. Vary greatly in colour. I have a skin that is nearly jet black, and one that is clear brown, both from the same locality. The horns of three specimens now at hand do not curve downward below level of orbit. In spread they run rather large. In this country, contrary to Roosevelt's experience farther north, they frequented thin scrub freely, and often ventured into what might be called fairly thick cover. In fact, except at evening grazing hours, they seemed more to shun the grass openings. They are exceedingly swift, yet, as elsewhere detailed, natives run them down.

13.   Coke's Hartebeeste (*bubalis cokei*).—Both Cuninghame and myself are a little doubtful as to which of the subspecies—*nakuru* or *kongoni*—this animal should be

referred. If to *kongoni*, then possibly the other, smaller variety, will be *nakuru*, although its description and habitat do not square with the books. If *nakuru*, then the smaller variety must be undescribed. While in the country itself we always considered the larger, red tame species as the *kongoni*, and the smaller as *Neumanii;* but according to later classifications this seems impossible. For convenience I shall refer to this animal as Coke's.

It is common from Ol Sambu (above Lake Natron) to the Mara River, but not nearly as abundant as the topi, thus reversing the condition on the Loieta Plains. Gregarious, curious, tame—the typical "kongoni" of British East Africa in habit, except that here it frequents brush and shade freely, and may often be found in what might almost be described as thickets. In that respect our observations and those of the Frenchman, Vaase, stand together, and practically alone.

Roosevelt's remarkably complete and interesting account of the habits of these hartebeeste fails to mention their apparent altruism in warning other animals of danger. Of course the exact mental attitude remains to be proved, but the fact is that on several occasions I have seen hartebeeste that were not in danger themselves come deliberately into danger in order to carry off herds of zebra, wildebeeste or other hartebeeste that were in the line of a stalk. Both Cuninghame and myself observed this several times. Generally it seemed to be one or two individuals that thus took the job, and not a group.

14.———Hartebeeste (*bubalis cokei** [?]).—Beside the large red kongoni with the points of the horns slightly

* See Addenda on page 359.

diverging or parallel is a smaller species. This differs in being two thirds the size of his larger relative; in being of lighter buff colour; in lighter colour underneath, so that at a distance it has the appearance of being on stilts; in apparently a proportionately longer frontal bone from eyes to base of horns; in the fact that the points of the horns turn sharply toward each other; and especially in habit. They go in small groups of from three to not more than a dozen individuals; are always extraordinarily shy; and do not seem to care to mingle with other game. On two or three occasions we saw them with the larger hartebeeste, when they were readily distinguished at a distance. We shot one or two we thought were hybrids. The species is nowhere numerous, but always present in its habitat. It extends farther west than does the larger form. We found it on the hills above Speke Gulf.

15. East African Buffalo (*syncerus caffer radcliffei*).— Found everywhere between Olgoss and the lake, but nowhere in numbers. Widely migratory. We found indications of many more than we came into touch with—old tracks and signs. They probably follow the grass about. No large herds. Perhaps have not yet as fully recovered from the rinderpest as have the British Protectorate buffalo.

16. Bushbuck (*tragelaphus scriptus delamerei*).—Common in suitable localities. Though it is true, as Roosevelt and Heller say, that "bushbucks are solitary creatures; a buck and doe, or a doe and fawn, may be together, but generally we found them singly," nevertheless I have seen bucks together, feeding in the open, at the edge of thickets.

17. Sitatunga (*limnotragus spekei*).—In the Masirori swamp.

18. Lesser Kudu (*ammelaphus imberbis australis*).— In the region near Lake Natron.

19. Greater Kudu (*strepsiceros strepsiceros bea*).—(a) Below the escarpment northwest of Lake Natron about 15 to 20 miles; (b) in the hills between the Naróssara and the boundary; (c) near the Bologonja River.

20. Bongo (*boocercus eurycerus isaaci*).—In the forests south of the Naróssara near Seudeu's *boma*.

21. Eland (*taurotragus oryx pattersonianus*).—Common as far west as the Mara River and Ikorongo. Saw none west of that point; but may occur. No reason why not.

22. Chanler's Reedbuck (*oreodorcas fulvorufula chanlerii*). —Very common on suitable hills as far west as the Mara. I have seen groups of four to a dozen buck, apparently in company, at least they gave the appearance of a loose sort of herd. However, they may have been gathered merely because of some condition of feed.

23. Ward's Reedbuck (*redunca redunca wardi*).—Common from Oliondo west.

24. Sing-sing (*kobus defassa raineyi* [?]).—According to the books this animal should be referred to the above subspecies, nevertheless the animals we shot differ from the description in some particulars, notably in average horn lengths. "The horns of large bucks are seldom more than 25 inches in length." I should say that the *average* of adults I saw and shot would run somewhere about 28 inches. Common from Olgoss westward. The common waterbuck has been reported "as far west as

Ikoma." We saw none. These beasts decoy readily by
fluttering white flags.

25. Uganda Cob (*adenota kob thomasi*).—This animal
is reported in a small German handbook from the east
shores of the lake and the country adjoining. Perhaps on
this authority (?) Roosevelt and Heller include that country
in their distribution map. We looked into this matter
thoroughly, and are fairly certain cob are not to be found
there. The native name for both cob and impalla is
sumu, which may have caused the confusion. A small
herd is to be found in Kavirondo near Kibigori. Here,
probably due to the presence of vast numbers of natives,
the cob has abandoned his usual habits and seeks thick
cover.

26. Duiker (*sylvicapra grimmia*).—Not common; but
widely distributed. Whether subspecie *hindei* or *nyansae*
I do not know.

27. Oribi (*ourebia montana cottoni*).—Common everywhere. Roosevelt's and Heller's distribution map—
p.563—should be extended eastward to the heights above
Lake Natron.

28. Steinbuck (*raphicerus campestris neumani*).—Common in suitable cover everywhere. In seeking to hide they
often fold their ears *forward or back*, creasing them in the
middle, like a spaniel.

29. Klipspringer (*oreotragus oreotragus schillingsi*).—
Common in suitable localities. On the rolling plains,
where there are no hills within a good many miles, I found
these animals in deeply eroded creek beds filled with boulders. The boulders apparently gave them the illusion of

rocky side hills; and the little animals leaped from one rock to the other entirely satisfied.

30. Roberts' gazelle (*gazella granti robertsi*).—Quite common between Oliondo and Olgoss. Cuninghame reports it around Ikoma. None at all in the immense game herds south of the Bologonja.

31. Thomson gazelle (*gazella thomsoni*).—Nowhere abundant, and apparently very local. Many sections well adapted to "Tommies" are quite devoid of them. Nevertheless saw specimens as far west as Walioba's and as far east as the plateau above N'digadigu. It would be interesting to know why there are not more gazelles in this country. Carry very large heads. I am doubtful of the new subspecies *nasalis*. I have two heads from the region of its habitat, neither of which possess the alleged distinguishing black patch across the nose.

32. Impalla (*aepyceros melampus suara*).—Common. Carry very large heads.

33. Dik-dik (*rhynchotragus kirki cavendishi*).—We found this animal very local in its distribution.

34. Rhinoceros (*disceros bicornis bicornis*).—Common in the mountains between the two protectorates, where their trails helped us greatly; but unusually scarce in the new country. They have been much hunted there by Wanderobo, who take their horns.

35. Zebra (*equus quagga granti*).—Common everywhere; but not so common as the topi or wildebeeste. Seem in this country rather to prefer cover to the open plains. They are there practically invisible (see discussion elsewhere).

36. Elephant (*loxodonta africana capensis*).—In the

Masirori Swamp, where they stick until driven out by floods. We saw much sign of them around the edges. Inaccessible except at flood times.

To the above "game" animals may be added the following large species:

37. Crocodile.—Mara River and Victoria Nyanza.
38. Ostrich.
39. Jackal.
40. Serval.

VI

I shot again the new Springfield rifle, using the spitzer pointed bullet of 165 gr. and 172 gr. weight. Some of these had been exposed to tropical conditions for three years, but I could see no deterioration. Their performance was uniform and very deadly. The same could not be said of the 150 gr. service bullet, forty rounds of which I used as a trial. Their action was too erratic, as a certain proportion of them showed a tendency to dive outrageously. In my opinion the 172 gr. U. M. C. bullet is an ideal hunting cartridge; as was also the Winchester 165 gr. The latter, unfortunately, is no longer manufactured. An analysis of the work done by this weapon results as follows:

Shots fired 260	Animals shot at . . 161
Hits 199	Animals missed . . 26
Misses 61	Animals killed . . . 135

Of the above 135 animals killed with this rifle, 98 went down to one shot each. The longest range was 421 yards; the average *for antelope*, 196 yards. These measurements were all paced.

For a second gun I used, as before, the .405 Winchester. It is light, handy, and delivers a very hard blow at close ranges. Beyond 150 yards, however, it loses velocity too fast to make it of the first use.   It is a good brush gun, and has always done me well with lions.   Its record was:

Shots fired	33	Animals shot at . .	14
Hits	29	Animals killed . . .	14
Misses	4		

In the case of the four lions I was forced to take on at once, I used alternately the Springfield and the Winchester. One of these was a bolt action, the other a lever action arm. According to those who argue most vigorously on either side of the rather bitter controversy, this alternating of weapons should have confused me, or at least caused me to take thought.   As a matter of fact, it did nothing of the kind.   I used either with equal facility and with equal unconsciousness.   My firm belief is that neither action has the slightest advantage over the other in practical work.

My third, reserve, weapon was the Holland and Holland .465 cordite.   This was useful only on the very heaviest game.   Except for buffalo, rhinoceros, and *perhaps* elephants, I could very well get on without it.

VII

These paragraphs are intended in a suggestive rather than a controversial spirit.   The author advances nothing theoretical that he considers final.   The facts, however, are matters of careful observation.

We are all familiar with the rather bitter discussions into which have plunged the proponents and opponents of the concealing coloration theory. The Thayers elaborated this theory to its last conclusions in a thick volume and numerous pamphlets. Certain naturalists, Colonel Roosevelt the most conspicuous among them, criticised the theory and its application. The ensuing discussion reached its greatest height between my two African trips. Therefore I went on this last journey with all data freshly in mind. Both Cuninghame and myself were throughout the whole time in the field keenly alert to prove or disprove—in our own minds—the contentions of both parties. It might further be pointed out that at the start we were neither of us partisan for either side of the discussion; that we are both, in a sense, trained observers; and that we had here unrivalled opportunities for studying tens of thousands of animals in undisturbed country. In order to define my position clearly at the outset, I will state that in general I hold with Colonel Roosevelt, and unqualifiedly advise the reader to peruse his chapter on this subject in "Life Histories of African Animals." What follows is intended merely to call attention to certain phases. I believe most of these to be of optical rather than evolutionary value.

The only points which seem to me important in Mr. Thayer's contention are these:

1. The theory of counter-shading. That is to say, most animals are coloured lighter underneath than on top in order to compensate for the shadow cast by the animal's body. The net result is supposed to be a monochrome.

2. The theory of night blending. A great many beasts are conspicuously white somewhere on the upper body line. The tails of white-tailed deer or prong-horned antelope are

familiar examples. Mr. Thayer contends that this white
tends to blend with the night sky in such a way as to render
the animal invisible to an observer placed close to the
ground. This brings us to:

3. Mr. Thayer tries to show that in testing out these
theories we should take the point of view of the animal's
"natural enemies," i. e.: we should crouch down to the eye-
level of the lion or other carnivore.

4. The theory of broken coloration. Mr. Thayer maintains that stripes, blotches, and patterns are intended to
break the mass, and that against normal backgrounds such
patterns are more invisible than a uniform mass.

5. The theory of imitative patterns. That is, that
stripes of a zebra simulate reeds; patterns on the ends of
ducks' breast feathers imitate wave ripples, the blue jay's
colour is like shadows on snow, etc., etc.

There are various corollaries to these five major theories,
but I feel no injustice is done the argument by their omission,
because they must necessarily stand or fall with the major
premises.

In order to clear the decks for all parties and both sides
of the discussion, it cannot be too strongly insisted that
no possible pattern or scheme of coloration is either concealing or revealing at all times and in all circumstances.
Combinations of light will conceal the most vivid and conspicuous object in the world. Or, conversely, an exemplary
—artificial or otherwise—of all the principles of protective
coloration can be so placed—*and in normal environment*—
so that it will show as plainly as a flag in the wind. I once
tied a brilliant red bandana handkerchief to a bush for the

purpose of guiding myself and packhorse back to a sheep I had killed. It took me a quarter of an hour to find that handkerchief, simply because a queer combination of light and shade had temporarily made it absolutely invisible. And certainly if a red bandana handkerchief is concealingly coloured, then all objects in nature are so coloured. Therefore I have scant patience with the type of argument in rebuttal—on either side—that says in effect: "You say the whiffenpoof is—or is not—protectively coloured. Now the other day I was out, and I saw—or did not see—a whiffenpoof, etc." That sort of argument is barred. It means nothing. We are dealing with tendencies, not hard and fast invariabilities. If protective coloration always worked, the beasts would be always invisible. If we always saw every creature, we would come precious close to omniscience.

Let us now take up in detail the five items of theory, and see how much or how little they are borne out by our own observations.

1. Countershading. Considered as a tendency, as a fact, among others, that tends to render an animal less conspicuous than if he were a monochrome, I believe this idea has merit. A countershaded object is in most circumstances less conspicuous than an object in monochrome. A countershaded animal, afoot and in normal circumstances, is less easily picked out by the eye than an animal not so countershaded. In other words, countershading tends not so much to conceal an animal when he is aware of danger and attempting to hide* as to cause him to be over-

*A hiding animal generally squats, thus concealing his light under parts.

looked in favour of a more conspicuous creature. Every
hunter knows how instinctively he picks out for his shot the
most prominent member of a flock or herd. The lion, or
native hunter, seeking his victim in a prospect full of game
takes the line of least resistance. His eye falls on the beast
that is most conspicuous, and, other circumstances being
equal, he proceeds with his stalk. The animals, or the
species, that have not happened to catch the eye first—
even if skilled scouting might discover them—escape for the
time being. That they are overlooked may be due to a
variety of circumstances—their position, the cover they are
in, the direction of the light, their colouring, etc. Also
their luck! But undoubtedly countershading often helps,
and helps materially, in causing individual animals or
species to be overlooked in this first survey of a well-stocked
field.

Logically, given sufficient opportunity for observation,
one should find, of two species, one countershaded and the
other not, that the former should escape oftener than the
latter. This is sometimes, but not always, the case. In
some parts of our hunting field where topi* and hartebeeste†
existed in fairly equal numbers we found many more lion
kills of the former than of the latter. Yet I think nobody
with field experience could for a moment maintain that
the hartebeeste is a first-rate example of concealing coloration, or that he is hard to see. But I noted this, and I
noted it many times over: in a herd of mixed game, feeding
in the characteristic thin cover such game frequents when

---

* Not countershaded.
† Countershaded.

not disturbed, my eye caught first the topi, second the harte-beeste, and lastly the zebra. The reason for the comparative invisibility of the latter belongs under a different head.

In a letter to me Colonel Roosevelt takes the position that if such a tendency exists, "even to the extent that would represent the killing of say a hundred topi by lions for every ninety-nine hartebeeste. . . . If it exists in the locality you mention, the fact will be proved by the speedy extermination of the topi in that locality." And he calls to my attention the indisputable fact that both beasts are well known, possess equal fecundity, equal wariness, etc. I am not quite willing to admit this. The fecundity and infant mortality of different animals in different localities have not yet been studied. That breeding is affected by conditions is indisputable. Before a drought season California quail will raise one brood—or none; in seasons of plenty they may raise three broods. If this is true, it may well be that in a locality better adapted to topi than to kongoni the former may breed more freely than the latter; so freely as to more than compensate for lion killing. It seemed to me that, in this new country, I saw many more young topi than young kongoni, and more twins of the former than of the latter; but this is only an impression. Certainly if some such explanation is not adopted, it would be very difficult to account for the fact that in different localities species practically alike in habits differ so widely in their relative numbers. On the plains north of the Naróssara River the kongoni outnumber the topi by about ten to one; on the plains south of the Mara River the exact reverse is the case. On both plains there are, however, plenty of both species. I should say the lion population is about equally divided. The disparity of numbers, in my mind, is not due to lion killing, but to some as yet unexplained breeding dissimilarity due to some as yet undescribed advantage or disadvantage to one or the other species.

Of course it may be superficially argued that if this is true, it should also follow that beasts not countershaded should be fewer in numbers than the others, because more of them are killed. But this might, and probably does, depend on other factors—how prolific are their breeding habits, tendency to infant mortality from other causes, etc., etc.

In short, countershading seems to me to be a principle that on broad general lines works out. It does not always work out, and its possession would not for a moment conceal any individual from me—let alone a native or a lion—if I were looking for him. But it might cause me to pass him by for a more conspicuous animal if I were just after meat in general. That would be a chance; and of a great aggregation of chances is made the fate or the evolution of species, provided, of course, that the theory of evolution or survival is accepted.

2. The theory of night blending: This, as an explanation of white tails, and generally white upper parts, seems to me a mistake. Mr. Thayer's optical contention is undoubtedly true, as it affects human eyes. A white object, at a reasonable distance, is in many circumstances—but by no means always—less visible at night than a dark object.

But only rarely is this true at a very short distance. Further-more, the application of this optical principle to game would imply that an animal's enemies always approach and spring exactly from the rear. This is not true. As far as I can determine, the lion generally springs from a point a little to one side, in order to land on the withers of his victim. If the white tail or rump tends to conceal at the flurried moment of escape, what of the rest of the creature's outline, which is dark? I place little importance on the expla-nation that the flash of white as the beast leaps tends to confuse the would-be captor. It would have to be a very stupid or inexperienced preying animal indeed. When I was young, the flash of white in the white-tailed deers' rumps as they ran made for me almost irresistible marks to shoot at. I could hardly help taking them for my target, and in consequence shooting behind. But I got over it very soon. If I had not done so, I would not give much for my chances as a hunter. And if a lion, or leopard, or weasel, or any other rapacious animal or bird is seriously or often or re-peatedly confused by so simple and constant a mechanical device as a show of white at the moment of escape, then there is something the matter with him, and he deserves to die of starvation, as he probably will.

Another *possible* element of doubt in this theory is that we are not taking into account the fact that the eyes of a nocturnal animal differ from the human eye in their ca-pacity for light. Such a beast "sees at night." It is possible that to him the general appearance of things is much as it is to us at, say, early twilight. So the cases are not quite on all fours. A quite sufficient explanation of such markings might well be that they are warnings of danger to others. Indeed they are most prominently displayed only when the beast is in rapid motion.

Concerning the top markings of the skunk: as far as my experience goes the skunk is in no way desirous, either by day or night, of escaping observation. He and the solemn porcupine have other reliable means of defence.

3. The theory that in order adequately to test out these hypotheses we should adopt the viewpoint of the preying animal is an interesting one. Before we came to a conclusion satisfactory to ourselves we gave more attention to this than to all the other branches put together. Before I left on this last trip Mr. Thayer very kindly sent me a copy of a pamphlet wherein, by text and diagram, this was all very carefully worked out. He showed that in the majority of cases a man on all-fours or prone would see the animal against the skyline, while a man erect would see it against a solid background. He maintained that the former was the viewpoint of the beast's "natural enemies," and that from that viewpoint the "concealing coloration" had fuller effect.

Now, in the first place, I do not quite see the justice of excluding mankind from the catalogue of a beast's "natural enemies." Man has probably lived always contemporaneously with the present species of game; he has always caught them for food; his success has probably been as great as that of his rivals the lions, leopards, etc., that are generally considered as the only accepted "natural enemies." That his hunting has modified the habits of some no man can doubt; that his continued and persistent pursuit from the dawn of his race until the present time is as capable of modifying structure and colour * as the continued and persistent pursuit by lions and other carnivores, is at least a debatable possibility. Personally, I do not see, if a beast is to be concealed at all, why it is or has been of more importance to him to be concealed from the erect or the prone destroyer.

But let that pass. Let us consider the case entirely, as Mr. Thayer asks us, from the lion's point of view. Also, for the sake of the argument, let us for the moment pass over the point as to whether or not an animal against the skyline is any better concealed than an animal against a solid background. From the lion's point of view is an animal in the majority of cases seen against the sky? On the open plains, yes. In cover or in a country the least bit broken, decidedly not. This is a matter of repeated experiments in the field, on living game, and is a definite conclusion.

This is of course at a distance of from thirty yards out to any limit; but if I understand Mr. Thayer's diagram aright, he claims the action of this principle for all distances. Of extremely close range, say within the three or four yards of a lion's spring, I am unable to advance evidence from the field. It is not my purpose to offer my private opinions unless apparently supported by actual observation.

As to the point we waived a moment ago, i. e., whether or not an animal is on the average more or less visible against the sky than against the earth, my opinion is against Mr. Thayer. I came to this opinion only after repeated obser-

---

* That the habits and environment of a *large* beast do modify his structure or colour is denied by men of very good judgment.

vation, for the theory is fascinating and intrigued my interest. I have tried it out on all colours, all sizes of beasts, in all lights from early twilight to night so dark the human eye could not even make out the silhouette, and from every point of view. It must be repeated, that to the cat we must allow a greater illumination than to the man. The conclusion could not possibly be dodged. No matter what the colour or pattern of the animal, it shows up nine times in ten more plainly against the sky than against the earth. In this case I cannot even see the *tendency* toward helping the animal escape observation.

Parenthetically, this seems a good place to protest against the finality of the kind of argument that consists of placing stuffed animals, painted objects, or drawings before an observer and asking him to note the effect one way or another. Early in my own investigations I abandoned that method of observation. It is useless to place an oryx head in a treetop, as did Mr. Thayer, or a white towel in a dark night, as he challenged Mr. Roosevelt to do, and call upon the bystander to observe the invisibility of one or the visibility of the other. And for this reason: I will guarantee to place the same oryx head in the same treetop, without trickery, so it will stand out like a crow on a snowbank; and the same night and in the same field I will shift the towel to the vanishing point. The oryx head and whatever that towel represented would in nature be quite as likely to be in one place as another. The only test is the actual field test. I have seen some thousands of oryx and I do not suppose that of that number two dozen were in the slightest degree concealed from me by the face markings.

Mr. Thayer, paradoxically, was wrong though he was right. His own oryx was concealed; but that was not a legitimate argument simply because wild oryxes do not happen to do what stuffed oryxes did. Photographs are equally *ex parte*. They have relief, no colour, and the relative tones are often false. They are not evidence; for they do not reproduce.

And here seems a good place for the insertion of another parenthesis of protest against another mistaken line of argument. This merely to clear the decks.

The proponents of "concealing coloration" may bring against me an argument they have already used against others. They may say: "Yes, you may have seen some thousands of oryx; but what of those you did not see? They remained *concealed, and therefore illustrate our point!" But by a very simple method I tested this. As I moved forward, I was constantly on the lookout to determine how many beasts in the direct line of march escaped my visual attention. If an animal I had not previously seen jumped and ran from in front of us, I naturally concluded it had remained concealed. Then I tried to determine *why* it had remained concealed. And let no one imagine that African animals to any great extent "squat" while a safari of forty noisy natives howls by! We saw eventually everything in our path. I mention this merely to show that our methods foresaw such obvious objections.

4. The theory of broken coloration. Mr. Thayer advances the theory that a broken coloration is often more concealing than a uniform coloration. The theory is not original with himself, but the extent of its development is.

There is so much of value in it that it is a pity his natural enthusiasm for so pretty a hypothesis should have carried him beyond all reason. Thus he seriously maintains that the wavy marks on the ends of a duck's breast and side feathers are imitations of ripple marks on the water wherein the duck swims; and that for that reason they tend to conceal the duck from its "natural enemies." A moment's reflection, without the necessity of actual experiment, shows that such fine markings are invisible at a very short distance, and that within the distance of their visibility the duck is very plainly in sight to anything with any eyes at all.* He instances the scarlet tanager, and can, of course, easily prove that it is often invisible in thick woods. He attempts to tell us this is because of the black and red markings of that brilliant bird, forgetting that when the scarlet tanager is invisible any other bird whatsoever would be equally invisible. Or that the thin white transverse stripes of the eland tend to break up that animal's bulk, whereas, of course, as every one who has ever seen an eland knows, the stripes are quite invisible beyond forty yards. And any one who has been within forty yards of an eland and not seen it is either in completely concealing cover or should depart for the nearest oculist. Mr. Thayer's interest in working out possible applications† of this fascinating idea has led him into a mental point of view very like that of an enthusiastic lawyer toward a technical case. Each quite honestly rather loses sight of the verities.

---

*A duck in the water is a mass, always! Yes; I have looked at them from above!

† For a great number of instances, *see* his book. Most of them beg the question and imply such close proximity to the animal before the markings can be seen at all that the mass of the beast could not possibly be overlooked.

So numerous are the instances where Mr. Thayer has over-refined his argument after the manner of the examples given above, that he has ended by goading his opponents to the opposite extreme. They are, it seems to me, not nearly enough inclined to admit whatever of value there is in the theory.

Every hunter in a fairly open country knows that a varied costume is better than a uniform costume. Thus the sheep hunter who wears a gray cap, a khaki-coloured shirt, and breeches of "pepper and salt" stands a better chance of remaining unnoticed than he who dresses entirely in even the celebrated "olive drab." A wildebeeste, in or out of cover, is more visible than a zebra. The mottled horned toad is less easily seen than the lizard. All this quite irrespective of movement. Nobody will seriously deny this. Furthermore, as a general thing, in thin cover the patterned animal will remain unnoticed longer than the animal in monochrome. But in thick cover, except under exceptional circumstances, a good neutral monochrome or a broken pattern seem to be on equal footing. On the open plain no animal is concealed, unless there be high grass; when, naturally, the environment must be considered as cover.

Let us elaborate. In the new hunting field we have been describing, the game had not been disturbed by man, either savage or civilized. This was a most unusual condition; for even where the white hunter has not penetrated usually the black hunter has been active for untold generations. Therefore here the game may fairly be considered to frequent the type of country it likes best, its ideas unmodified by humankind. In this country at the time of our visit we found the zebra inhabiting the thin bush. There were plenty of open plains, and occasionally bands of zebra wandered out on them, as do impala; but by choice, and as a matter of course, they held to the thin thorn scrub, and the light growths of small thorn trees. Elsewhere the zebra is a plains-dwelling animal; and all arguments as to his gaudily striped person have been based on that fact. But elsewhere he has always been in contact with humankind. It is at least a fair assumption, in view of our observations, that he may have been driven out to the plains,* although I am not yet convinced that such is the case. At any rate, in the thin cover described he is the most invisible of animals. The stripes of white and black so confuse him with the cover that he is absolutely unseen at the most absurd ranges. Time after time not only did Cuninghame and myself fail to make them out even as close as forty and fifty yards, but Kongoni confessed himself baffled. And of the many keen-eyed savages with whom I have had to do, Kongoni can see farthest and best. A switch of the tail, or the actual movement of the head was time and again our first warning. This same cover was open enough so that we could see topi or wildebeeste up to 200 yards.

The other usual larger inhabitants of this thin cover were topi, wildebeeste, eland, hartebeeste, and impala. The smaller antelope I do not count, as they generally lurked in grass or bush. Of these the wildebeeste† is to all intents

---

* The native most often hunts by *driving* his game.

† The wildebeeste is countershaded. But mere countershading without the help of a neutral colour is ineffective. Countershading does, however, help the neutral colour.

and purposes a black bulk, and he is easily the most conspicuous of the lot.   I don't think I ever failed to see a
wildebeeste not entirely concealed by cover, unless I happened to be careless.   But wildebeeste belong on plains, prefer
plains, and are only lured into the bush occasionally by feed
or a wandering spirit.   Eland were to me the next most
conspicuous, less from their coloration than from their size.
They have occasionally proved rather hard to see, when
they stood motionless in shadow; just as is any neutral-
coloured animal in the same circumstances, but their transverse stripes never had anything to do with it.   Topi, on
the whole, are the next easiest to make out, but in certain
lights they are as invisible as zebra.   We have all of us
missed seeing them time and again, at close range, toward
evening.   An analysis of the situation disclosed these facts
concerning a normally conspicuous beast: the topi is a dark
animal, without countershading, with nearly black legs to
the knee, with buff "stockings," and dark pearl gray patches
on the rump and shoulders.   The variations in tone, with
the exception of the buff stockings and buff face markings,
are very slight.   Yet they were sufficient, *at the proper
time of day*, to break the monochrome and blend the animal
into the darker lights and shadows of its background.   The
topi, in this new country, lived on both the plains and in
cover, with a preference for the latter.   In British East
Africa he is more distinctly a plains beast, where—like the
zebra—he is visible as far as the eye can see.   Hartebeeste
and impalla are countershaded beasts, and hardly come
into this discussion.   In many circumstances their countershading helps them to be overlooked in favour of more con-

spicuous beasts, but it never *conceals* them in circumstances where any animal would not be concealed.   The zebra and topi, however, are very often actually "concealed" when in reality standing in "plain sight."

I offer these as new and interesting facts, well established by repeated observation.   Whether the zebra's stripes are developed by the necessity of concealment in thin brush or not I leave to deeper philosophers than myself.

In thick cover, however, any motionless animal is pretty well concealed, whatever his scheme of colour.   I have been within a few yards of elephants, rhinoceros, and buffalo—all large monochromatic beasts without a hint of countershading —and had difficulty in making them out.   I honestly do not think they would have been more invisible had they been spotted or striped.   On the other hand, I have without difficulty made out leopards, giraffes, and spotted hyenas in the thickest sun-and-shade surroundings.   It is my deliberate conclusion, that, in thick cover, the variety of light and shade, of mass and detail, is normally so great that it has room for any mass or any combination of dark and light.   In other words, almost any beast not advertisingly blazened is none too easy to make out visually.

On open plains concealing coloration drops almost to zero in its importance relative to other reasons for coloration.   In certain slants of light and mirage from noon heat a zebra or a herd of zebra, some of the gazelles, hartebeestes, or topi will shimmer at extreme distances into white alkali-looking streaks or queer, dancing patches; while wildebeeste will hold their solid character.   This difference of effect is undoubtedly due to difference of coloration.

But never would any experienced man—or beast—mistake the white shimmer for anything but zebra, or the queer patches of colour for anything but game. And when he had approached to within a half mile or so he could plainly see the individual animals.

We have already discussed night appearances—which *may* be day appearances to the lion. And the lion hunts by scent as well as by sight.

As a fact, by the way, which may be applied as the reader will: Mr. Thayer says the longitudinal body stripes on such beasts as the Thompson's, Grant's and Roberts' gazelle bring these animals under the working of this theory, break up the monochrome, and tend to make them more visible. This is not so. The Roberts' gazelle just east of Olgoss are of mixed characteristics. In some the body stripe has so faded as to be almost indistinguishable. In every light the latter type were less visible than the former.

This leaves the situation rather anomalous. If a beast is of a broken pattern he is less visible in certain circumstances than a monochromatic beast; if an animal is coloured in countershaded monochrome he is, in certain other circumstances, less visible than a striped or spotted or variegated beast.

The apparent contradiction can be lessened, however, by the reflection again, that no beast, of whatever colour, is always invisible; that "concealing coloration" seems, in the case of larger game animals, not so much to conceal all members of a species absolutely, as to *tend* to render the individuals likely to be overlooked in favour of the more conspicuous. It is possible that *both* the variegated and the monochro-

matic are "concealingly" coloured, in that sense of the term
—nature may use a double instead of a single barrel—
widely diverse optical laws may have the same affect—and
their differences in marking may have quite a different purpose.   Concealing coloration—again, I must repeat, in the
case of larger game animals—may prove to be a sort of by-
product of other purposes, a supplemental use thrown in by
an economical nature for good measure, an added principle
on the side of safety that may work at times and may fail
to work at others.   Just as nature creates a thousand individuals in order that one may survive, so she may invent a
dozen expedients of safety in order that one may work.
The occasions wherein coloration fails to work—which may
be the majority of cases—does not necessarily stultify the
scheme of decoration—as they would were concealment the
sole or principal reason for it.   And when it does work, why
there is so much gained.

    5.   The theory of imitative coloration.   This means
simply that the animal is so coloured as to imitate its
background.   My remarks as to the preceding hypothesis
apply almost verbatim to this.   Excellent examples are a
nighthawk on the ground, treefrogs against bark, wood-
cock on the nest, etc.   So pretty is this theory that it, too,
lends itself to over-refinement.   If a man seriously starts
to drawing analogies in the mental world, he speedily and
logically arrives at the absurdly fanciful; if a man sets out to
trace resemblances in the physical world, he arrives with
equal speed at the fantastic.   Thus because a flock of
flamingoes a-wing at a distance of several miles looks to the
poetic eye like a pink cloud of morning—as it does—

your enthusiast thinks himself able to prove that this resemblance is intended to conceal those flamingoes from
observation! Such reasoning quite loses sight of the hunting attitude of mind. It presupposes on the part of
the flamingoes' natural enemies an almost unbelievable
stupidity and indolence; so that the sight of a pink cloud in
one portion of the heavens would mean instant departure
for somewhere else. An absolutely innocent and unsophisticated bird or beast of prey on the search for flamingoes might conceivably be fooled by one or two pink
clouds. But that could not continue for long. Sooner or
later he would discover that *pink clouds may mean flamingoes*, and unless I much mistake the hunter psychology,
he would thenceforth cruise in the direction of likely looking pink clouds. That is, unless he had a flamingo flock of
his own already. For again, your true flamingo eater—
whatever that is—would not be setting forth each day re-
gardless and at random. He would have his permanent
residence not far from a private flamingo-preserve of his
own. The resemblance of flamingoes to clouds would not
interest him in the least: he would probably never get that
far away from them.

It is useless to multiply examples. The gaudy plumage
of the wood duck much resembles at times certain re-
flections of light and branch, or certain aspects of the same
against the sky. When caught just at that moment the
wood duck is only slightly visible. A coloured drawing of
the episode is most interesting. But it seems to me carrying it a bit far to claim that the wood duck's plumage imi-
tates sky and branch. The wood duck is not a common

bird at present, but my boyhood saw many of them; and for once the bird was obliterated by his background, I should say he was revealed at least fifty times. In other words the imitation, while real, is poetic. The bluejay against blue snow shadows is another case in point. The resemblance and the blending are there, but one has only to reflect that, even in winter, for once the jay is to be looked for against snow, a hundred times he is silhouetted in trees against the sky. That leaves out of account the fact that bluejays live right on through the summer. Why, in the name of common sense, if a bluejay or a wood duck were to be "concealingly coloured," should the rare fortuitous background be chosen for imitation rather than the daily environment? The battleground for opinion is here enormous. I have no intention of entering it, and cite the wood duck and the bluejay merely as examples.

Carried into the world of the larger animals the poetic resemblances, while not less numerous, become more fanciful. One of the most plausible examples is the mottling of the leopard to imitate sun spots in the forest. I am far from saying that this effect does not help in concealment. But from what little I have seen of the leopard (a) he is more likely to be found in dense shade than in spotted shadow; (b) he hunts at night when there is remarkably little sunlight; (c) he has no "natural enemies" from which he could wish to conceal himself.* If this is true of so strikingly poetic a resemblance as "spots" for light and shadow, how much more true is it of more fanciful resemblances. The larger animals move about so constantly,

---

*Prehistoric man had little use for a leopard outside a trap!

they occupy such a diversity of country, and appear in succession against such a variety of backgrounds that it is extremely unlikely that the colour pattern of any one of them can be considered as imitating any one environment. Zebra stripes do resemble reeds; they do not in the least resemble open sky, distant hills, high grass, thorn scrub, or tree trunks. I have seen thousands upon thousands of zebra against the latter backgrounds. *I have never seen one,* either at drinking holes or elsewhere, among reeds.

As a matter of personal belief I do not think that imitative patterns exist in the larger animals. I grant you may trace very interesting analogies between some of these patterns and something in nature. You can do that in thunder clouds. The nearest approach to anything of the sort is in the case of dull ripe-grass-coloured beasts. They are of a neutral tint because most of nature is in a neutral tone. To that extent they are concealingly coloured.

That covers the five points of concealing coloration theory as we studied it in the field. Let us now venture for a moment into the realm of pure speculation. There every man's right of denial or doubt is the equal of every other man's. If you do not like my ideas it is your privilege to reject them; and I assure you I shall accept their rejection good-naturedly. Only it seems to me only fair that you should not use that privilege unless you can substitute in their place something you consider better.

Nature loves at once economy and variety. She loves economy; and therefore creates an organ, a creature, or a process to fulfill some major function in the life of the world, and immediately sets to work her ingenuity to adapt it also to as many minor and incidental functions as possible. She loves variety: and therefore brings into being a dozen conifers instead of one "standardized" pine; hundred species where half a dozen would do; a thousand wild-flowers instead of a score that would adequately enough fit the changes of condition.

This being so, we can conceive that one of the important reasons why birds, beasts, insects, and flowers are striped, variegated, spotted, mottled, and otherwise decorated is that thus they respond to Nature's demand for variety. If coloration were intended solely, or even primarily, for purposes of concealment, it would be only sensible on Nature's part to fit her creatures with the very few combinations that are best adapted to the purpose in different circumstances. To a large extent I, personally, am willing to agree with Emerson that beauty may be its own excuse for being. To those who insist on a purely utilitarian reason for everything, I would call attention to the zebra. For the sake of argument only, let us assume that his stripes are for the purpose of concealing him—or attracting attention of his own kind, it does not matter which. If that were the only reason, a regular and uniform pattern of stripes would fulfill every requisite. Then why, as is the case, does every zebra differ from every other zebra in the pattern of his hide? More: why, even, is the pattern on the right side of any individual zebra different from the pattern on his left side? The permutations and combinations are as limitless as thumb points. When the strict utilitarians have given good reasons for this one astonishing fact, then we are ready to go on. In the meantime it seems to me probable that, as Nature likes zebras all different, she may like variety in other ways.

We may then name as the reasons for varied colouring, (1) Nature's love for variety; (2) concealing coloration; (3) facilitating recognition between members of the same species; (4) sex attraction; (5) revealing for the purpose of warning. These are by no means named in the order of their relative importance.

At first glance there seems to be a contradiction between some of these functions. For example, number three, four, and five are advertising, revealing; while number two is quite the reverse. This has been recognized by both sides of the controversy. "How can a thing be both concealing and advertising?" ask the opponents triumphantly. And the proponents, instead of accepting the indubitable fact and trying to find it reasonable, make the mistake of bolstering their argument by super-refinements.

As a matter of fact there is only an apparent contradiction. Those who claim that a zebra, or a topi, or our common deer or any other of the larger animals are when in motion quite the most conspicuous objects in the landscape, are right. My notion is that they are intended to be conspicuous. I have often amused myself when in an abundance of scattered game, inhabiting a broken bush-covered country, by revealing myself suddenly to some little group of animals. Off they would go, helter-skelter, as fast as they could run. Those near at hand would follow their example; those farther away would catch the flash of moving bodies—the revealing stripes of the zebras, the flicker of the gazelles, the shifting advertising lines of a number of species—would raise their heads, stare for a moment, and join the stampede. None but the first little group had seen me, but all had caught the warning of danger from the flash of stripe and colour, and all were heeding it. On one occasion, six minutes by the watch after the first beasts had departed, game was still plodding by across our front. They were plodding very slowly and mechanically and in a bored fashion, because by now the warning had been much diluted, but they were doing their duty. Now of all these beasts nine tenths were more or less unnoticeable as long as they stood still. Their coloration, or the light or the cover, or all three tended to obliterate most of them sufficiently to cause them to be overlooked by a cursory glance. But the moment any of them moved, they became instantly and plainly visible. In other words, the same pattern that fulfilled one function one moment in certain circumstances fulfilled another function the next moment in changed circumstances. To go back to our zebra, because he is easy to discuss, no creature was harder to make out in thin cover as long as he held still; no animal was easier to see the instant he moved. As long as he held still he was presumably in no danger of which he was aware, and his pattern helped him to remain unobserved; the instant he became aware of danger and ran, that instant by his very conspicuousness he served as an easily visible warning to all other beasts that something was wrong.

It is useless to discuss the point played by coloration in recognition and sex attraction. The uniform of a particular species is as definite as the uniform of a regiment, and perhaps fulfills much the same function. Of course the influence of plumage and pelage on sex attraction is well known. The point to remember is that all these functions —of variety, sex attraction, concealment, warning, recognition—are definite functions; that one in no sense excludes another; that any one may at any time act the leading part and at another be relegated to the subordinate part. Such being the case, it is ill-advised to lay so much stress on any one function that all others are warped and bent to fit it. Whether Nature so patterned her creatures that they might be distinguished one from the other, and then incidentally arranged that those patterns should help conceal or reveal at need: or whether she intended concealment as the major requisite, and handily fitted in the other functions; or whether, quite simply, she was working out the mysterious world-need for beauty and infinite variety, it is each man's privilege to decide for himself. But I think it should be remembered that most often she works by *tendency* rather than by hard fact.

ADDENDA

Mr. Edmund Heller, of the Smithsonian Institution, identifies the smaller, light-coloured hartebeeste as *bubalis cokei kongoni*. The inference then is that the rufous, larger form is *bubalis cokei cokei*. But in the technical descriptions of these animals (*vide* Roosevelt & Heller, *The Life Histories of African Animals*) *kongoni* is described as larger than *cokei*. Unfortunately our very small expedition was unable to bring out adequate specimens, so at present a final determination is impossible; but I wish here to venture the prediction that in this region a new type of hartebeeste will eventually be determined. Either the rufous type (the larger) is new and bigger than any other hartebeeste save Jacksons; or—what is more likely —the buff type (smaller), while in general agreeing with *kongoni* of the Loieta Plains—with which I am familiar— will be found to be a distinct variety.

Stewart Edward White
1873-1946

White was born in Grand Rapid
Michigan, of Thomas Stewart and Ma
White. His father was a milliona
lumberman and Stewart was educated
tutors. He did not attend public school
early life. His interest in firearms a
hunting was prompted by an outdoorsm
father, interests to which Stewart pa
homage all his life.

Thomas White bought a ranch in Cali
nia and in 1884 the family moved there,
maining for four years before returning
Michigan. Here, White acquired the m
tar which bonded the bricks of his car
in writing and his love for hunting a
shooting.

His prolific writing career spanned ab
64 years and totaled almost a book a ye
In his interesting writing style, he wr
24 nonfiction titles and 34 fiction, some
an autobiographical nature. His th
African safaris, 1910, 1913 and 1925, ga
him a large reservoir of hunting
periences to draw from. His 1913 h
lasted 22 months.

"Nothing can equal the intense interes
the most ordinary walk in Africa," he sa
"It is the only country I know where a m
is thoroughly and continuously alive

Stewart Edward White was a succes
man and a noted American rifleman of
time. He was more than a riflem
however, and more than a hunter, fo
assessed the environment around him
froze time with his words, verbally
lustrating historical notes for all to r
into the future.